D1738835

A SURGEON WITH
STONEWALL JACKSON

Dr. Harvey Black, 1827-1888

A SURGEON WITH STONEWALL JACKSON

The Civil War Letters

of

Dr. Harvey Black

Edited by
Glenn L. McMullen

Baltimore
BUTTERNUT AND BLUE
1995

First Edition

ISBN 0-935523-45-6

Printed on acid-free paper

Published in 1995
as the third volume of the
Army of Northern Virginia Series

by

BUTTERNUT AND BLUE
3411 Northwind Road
Baltimore, Maryland 21234

To the memory of my father

Contents

Illustrations

Acknowledgements

I began research on this project in 1989 in Blacksburg, Virginia, the home town of Dr. Harvey Black, and finished it in 1994, a thousand miles away in Ames, Iowa. Over the course of five years many librarians, archivists, historians, and descendants of Harvey Black have assisted me in my research. I owe a special debt to Dorothy H. Bodell of the Special Collections Department of the Virginia Polytechnic Institute and State University Libraries, who generously shared her knowledge of Blacksburg history and families and who tracked down many an obscure fact for me after I had left Virginia. Robert K. Krick of the Fredericksburg and Spotsylvania National Military Park was likewise generous with his knowledge of the Army of Northern Virginia and with his ability to help identify elusive Confederate soldiers from the most meager of evidence.

I also want to thank Michael Musick and Michael Meier of the Military Reference Branch of the National Archives; James I. Robertson, Jr., and Peter Wallenstein of the Virginia Tech History Department; Laura Katz Smith, Eric Ackermann, and Stephen J. Zietz of the Virginia Tech Libraries Special Collections Department; Cathy Carlson Reynolds, formerly of the Virginia Tech Libraries; Esther Bishop of the U. S. Department of Justice Civil Library; Rebecca A. Ebert of the Handley Library in Winchester, Virginia; John T. Kneebone, Brent Tarter, and Edward D. C. Campbell, Jr., of the Library of Virginia; Jodi Koste of the Tomkins-McCaw Library at the Medical College of Virginia; Joan Echtenkamp Klein of the University of Virginia Health Sciences Library; E. Lee Shepard of the Virginia Historical Society; Richard Shrader of the Southern Historical Collection; Guy R. Swanson of the Museum of the Confederacy; Ray Brown of the Manassas National Battlefield Park;

James H. Cook of West Virginia University; Mary Freymiller of the Karmann Library at the University of Wisconsin-Platteville; John Hennessy of the Harper's Ferry National Historical Park; Twyla Kepler of the Brewer Library in Richland Center, Wisconsin; Lisa McCown of the Washington and Lee University Library; Ann L. Miller, formerly of the Orange County, Virginia, Historical Society; Peter B. Hirtle, formerly of the National Library of Medicine; Peter W. Houck of Lynchburg, Virginia; Ruth Fowell of Richland Center, Wisconsin; Jim L. Price, Harry D. Temple, and Virginia Hummel, all of Blacksburg, Virginia; Ben Ritter of Winchester, Virginia; Barbara Rennie of Richmond, Virginia; Elizabeth McDonald of Austin, Texas; E. E. Billings of Washington, D. C.; and the late Dorothy F. McCombs. To Greer and Mary Kent Elliott of Blacksburg, Virginia, I owe a special debt of gratitude. Their encouragement, and that of other Black family descendants, has meant a lot.

Harvey Black's letters appropriately reside in the library of the university he was instrumental in founding, Virginia Polytechnic Institute and State University, and I thank that library's Special Collections Department for allowing me to publish them. My colleagues in the Iowa State University Library and before that in the Virginia Tech Libraries have been supportive of my research. The Travel and Research Committee of the Iowa State University Library helped fund two research trips to other archives and libraries. To the staff of the ISU Library's Interlibrary Loan Office I owe a special thanks for their prompt, informed, and cheerful assistance in supplying research materials.

My wife Judy, son Patrick, and daughter Emily all helped with the research, poring hours over scratched and faded National Archives microfilm searching for obscure individuals mentioned in the letters of Harvey and Mollie Black. Their willingness to indulge me in turning vacation trips into research trips allowed me to finish the project, even when it seemed that it might never be finished. Judy's talents and labors as a copy editor, Emily's attentiveness to detail, and Patrick's skills as a researcher and his day-long visits to the National Archives at several critical junctures made a difference in how this book turned out. My parents, brother, and in-laws gave me encouragement and moral support. My father, though he did not live to see this book finished, nonetheless provided inspiration in writing it. He exemplified the maxim that all education is self-education; his interest in the Civil War was but one of the many intellectual passions in which he found sustenance. I know that he would have enjoyed reading this book, and I dedicate it to his memory.

O n the morning of May 10, 1863, Dr. Harvey Black wrote his wife Mollie from Guiney Station, Virginia, having recently arrived there from the scene of the conflict. "I had a very pleasant time in the practice of my profession in the late battle," he boasted. "I have the Corps well organized, and all worked well and efficiently."[1] Black's confident tone that Sunday morning contrasted with the dark letters he had written home in 1862 after Second Manassas and Fredericksburg, recounting the hardships he had faced in these battles. By 1863, he had become almost upbeat when writing to his wife, no doubt to shield her from much of the suffering he witnessed daily. To judge from these remarks alone, however, one might not conclude that Black's profession was medicine, that his occupation was Confederate surgeon, or that the "late battle" to which he referred was Chancellorsville, one of the bloodiest engagements of the Civil War.

The Corps was the Second Corps Field Hospital, Army of Northern Virginia, of which Black was surgeon in charge. A week earlier, the hospital had received its most famous patient. Lieutenant General Thomas J. "Stonewall" Jackson was brought to Black's field hospital after he had been wounded at Chancellorsville at dusk on May 2. Frank E. Vandiver described the scene:

> Not until sometime after 11 P.M. did the ambulance roll up to the field hospital at Wilderness Old Tavern. Quickly Jackson's litter was carried inside a tent already warmed for him by Dr. Harvey Black, the surgeon in charge. More whisky and water were given the general; he dozed and gradually began to revive. After two quiet hours had passed, Dr. McGuire, seconded by Surgeons Black, Walls, and R. T. Coleman, told him that chloroform would be administered preparatory to a careful examination of his wounds. From all indications, said McGuire, the left arm

must be amputated; if that proved necessary, should the operation proceed at once? "Yes, certainly; Dr. McGuire, do for me whatever you think best." [2]

Early in the morning of May 3, Dr. Hunter McGuire, Jackson's personal physician, amputated Jackson's arm, with Black and two other surgeons assisting. Years later, John S. Apperson, one of the hospital stewards at the Second Corps Field Hospital, recalled how he learned of the events that transpired that evening. After Jackson was wounded, he wrote,

> he was brought to our hospital at the old Wilderness Tavern. For some time after he was brought in his being wounded was kept from the soldiers as much as possible. I noticed Drs. Black and McGuire were in close conversation and the subject was of serious import I could well see. Sometime during the night Dr. Black told us that Gen. Jackson had been wounded. How seriously he did not say. [3]

Jackson would die of pneumonia on the afternoon of May 10, the day Black's letter was written. Anticipating his death, Black wrote in the same letter, "you can scarcely conceive the affection which his men have for him. He has outlived every prejudice and is regarded [as] a great Military Chieftain and a faithful Christian." Whether Black ever wrote about the amputation of Jackson's arm cannot be determined. None of his extant letters mention the operation. Had he written about it at all, however, Black's self-effacing nature probably would have kept him from commenting at length on the event.

Harvey Black's presence as one of four surgeons participating in the amputation of Jackson's arm has raised him from historical anonymity, though barely. [4] Biographers of Jackson have remarked on Black's role in this incident and have noted in passing the existence of the Second Corps Field Hospital, but Black has not received the attention he deserves. [5]

For Harvey Black was a significant figure in the Civil War and in postwar Virginia medicine and education. During the first twenty months of the Civil War, he served as regimental surgeon of the Fourth Virginia Infantry, part of the celebrated Stonewall Brigade. After the Battle of Fredericksburg in December 1862, he was appointed surgeon in charge of the Second Corps Field Hospital, the first field hospital at the corps level on either side during the war. After 1865, Black played a key role in founding the college now known as Virginia Polytechnic Institute and State University. During the last two decades of his life he served as the administrator of public mental institutions in Williamsburg and Marion, Virginia, where his leadership was a progressive force in the treatment of mental illness.

....

Harvey (sometimes spelled "Harvy") Black was born in the southwest Virginia village of Blacksburg in Montgomery County on August 27, 1827.[6] He was the second of twelve children of Alexander and Elizabeth McDonald Black. The Black family was well known in Blacksburg; Harvey Black's granduncle, William Black, and his grandfather, John Black, had founded the town in 1798.[7] Receiving his early education in the common schools of Blacksburg, Harvey Black might have become a farmer, a teacher, or a lawyer. Instead, he chose medicine as a career, and in 1845, at the age of 18, he began the study of medicine under two local doctors.

In November 1846 he enlisted as a private in the First Virginia Volunteer Regiment and set out to fight in the Mexican War. Although he saw no action in the war, he was made a regimental hospital steward, further advancing his career in what had become his chosen profession.[8] Following his discharge from the army in July 1848, he entered medical school at the University of Virginia, graduating in 1849.[9]

After graduation, Harvey Black journeyed to the northwestern United States, hoping to find a suitable location in which to set up his practice. He scouted potential homesites during a four-month trip that took him to Ohio, Michigan, Illinois, Wisconsin, and Iowa. In October 1849, Black purchased a piece of property in Richland County, Wisconsin; he used a land warrant from his Mexican War service and paid an additional $150 in cash for the homestead.[10] Instead of settling in Wisconsin, however, Black came back to Virginia and began his medical practice in Blacksburg.

His motives for returning to Virginia were probably mixed. He may have felt some uneasiness at Northern ways, as comments in a diary he kept during his trip suggest. In his diary entry for November 1, 1849, for example, Black remarked on the first African Americans he had seen in Wisconsin. He wrote with some amazement that a "Negro man went to bed in the same room with the rest of the travelers and slept in as good a bed as any of us." On the same day, he recounted conversations with several Wisconsin abolitionists, whose arguments he found flawed. He wrote, "They usually express themselves warmly in favor of the slaves but usually in general terms and when questioned as to . . . whether they are willing to admit them to their family and all other social privileges, they show a want of consistency." [11]

But Harvey Black had another, more personal, reason for returning to Virginia. As he recalled in a letter to his wife in November 1863, "I traveled in the west and expected to find a home in some western state, but not finding a place to suit me, together with the persuasions of that fair face, induced me to return." That "fair face" belonged to Mary Irby Kent. Black met her sometime after 1844, courted her for several years, and married her on September 15, 1852. Harvey Black always called her Mollie.

Coincidentally, Mollie had come from Illinois, not far from the Wisconsin territory in which Harvey Black had contemplated settling. She was born in the frontier settlement of Rockford in 1836, though her family moved to Blacksburg, her mother's home, eight years later. [12] Mollie's father, Germanicus Kent, was something of a pioneer. Born in Connecticut, he attended Yale College, then moved to Huntsville, Alabama. In 1827 he married Arabella Amiss of Blacksburg. They moved to Illinois seven years later, where Kent is generally regarded as one of the founders of the city of Rockford. Though Mollie's immediate family left Rockford in 1844, other Kent relatives remained behind in Illinois, Wisconsin, and Missouri.

Harvey and Mollie Black had four children, three boys and a girl. All were born before the war, two years apart. The oldest, Kent ("Kentie" in the letters), was born in 1853. Elizabeth Arabella ("Lizzie") was born in 1855; Alexander ("Alex") was born in 1857; and Charles White ("Charly") was born in 1859. [13] Black's frequent remarks about his children in his letters reveal his feelings for them. "I feel mighty proud of them," he wrote in April 1862. "I dont think I would be half so good a soldier if I did not have so many little fellows to fight for."

Harvey Black established his medical practice in Blacksburg during the 1850s, entering, as he wrote in his November 1863 letter, "actively into the pursuit of [his] profession with the determination to make at least a fair reputation" for himself. By 1860, he was one of three physicians in the small town of 406, a population that included three free blacks and 52 slaves. One of those slaves, a domestic servant named Adeline, belonged to the Black family. [14]

An analysis of the Blacksburg census for 1860 shows that nearly thirty people in the town — almost one-tenth of the free population — were related in some way to either Harvey or Mollie Black. [15] But not all the Kent and Black relatives lived nearby. Like his wife, Harvey Black had relatives in the North. Black's granduncle William Black had moved his family years earlier to Clark County, Ohio. [16] In 1854, Harvey Black's father, mother, brothers, and sister had moved to Richland County, Wisconsin, settling on the property that Black had purchased during his trip to the Northwest in 1849. [17] The fact that both Harvey and Mollie Black had close relatives in the North had important consequences for them during the Civil War years. Ardent Southern patriots who were convinced of the justice of their cause, they were nonetheless concerned about their relatives who lived in the North, some of whom fought on the other side.

When civil war broke out in April 1861, Black enlisted as the regimental surgeon of the Fourth Virginia Infantry. The regiment was raised from the counties of Rockbridge, Montgomery, Smyth, Grayson, Pulaski, and Wythe, all on the western side of the Blue Ridge Mountains. The Fourth Virginia became part of the First Brigade of Virginia, initially commanded by former Virginia Military Institute professor Thomas Jonathan Jackson. [18] On July 21, 1861, at the Battle of First Manassas, the brigade would become immortalized as the Stonewall Brigade. Always one of the most stalwart regiments in the brigade, the Fourth Virginia fought hard. In many battles its casualties were the brigade's highest. [19]

In the early months of the war, Black met John Samuel Apperson, who had enlisted as a private in the Smyth County Blues, Company D of the Fourth Virginia Infantry. Born in Orange

County in 1837 and thus a decade younger than Black, Apperson moved to the Southwest Virginia county of Smyth in 1859 and apprenticed for a local physician before the war. Like Black before him, Apperson was headed toward a career in medicine when he joined the army. [20] Apperson must have impressed Black with his medical abilities, as Black had him detailed as a regimental hospital steward on June 2, 1861. This proved to be a fateful day for both men. As Black advanced from regimental surgeon to surgeon in charge of the Second Corps Field Hospital, Apperson stayed with him. They were together at First Manassas and they would be together almost until Appomattox. [21]

Black became a mentor to the younger man and guided his medical education throughout the war. In 1867, Apperson would earn a medical degree from Black's alma mater, the University of Virginia. Toward the end of Black's life, the two men would work together again as superintendent and assistant physician in the Southwestern Lunatic Asylum in Marion, Virginia. Ironically, their relationship widened after Black died in 1888. Apperson's first wife died in 1887, and he married Black's daughter Lizzie two years later, one year after Black's own death. Apperson later reflected on the importance of his appointment as Black's hospital steward to his medical career. He wrote, "[I] can look back to the day when I went into the medical department of the regiment, under Dr. Harvey Black, as the longest stride I ever made towards the realization of my hopes and desires for the future work in medicine." [22]

If Harvey Black played an important part in advancing John Apperson's career, Apperson repaid the favor by helping to document Black's Civil War activities. Apperson began keeping a diary in 1859 and continued to do so, with some gaps, throughout the Civil War. Altogether, six diaries have survived. The entries in them provide an important source of information about Black's activities, even his words. In addition, Apperson wrote an autobiography late in his life. Never published, the work exists only in manuscript form. Like the diaries, the autobiography contains nuggets of information about Black and his activities during the war.

Apperson viewed Black as thoughtful, even-handed, and optimistic, if occasionally somewhat stern. It is clear that he admired

Black, associating his presence with a spirit of regularity and efficiency in the medical corps. Apperson commented in his diary in 1862 on Black's return after being on leave: "This morning Dr. Black came in. I was glad to see him. Things will soon assume some regularity in the Medical Department, I presume." [23]

Though his diaries contain no description of the elder man, Apperson later recalled Black's physical features when they first met in 1861: "I was impressed, but cannot describe clearly in what way, with the appearance of Dr. Black. He was a tall spare made man, quiet and thoughtful in manner, [with] very black whiskers with a forward inclination of head and shoulders when he was walking." [24] Apperson added that "Dr. Black was quiet and seldom said much except in the line of duty." [25]

Apperson's diary recounts an event from April 1863 that illustrates two central aspects of Black's character—his optimism and his faith in education, even in desolate times. In the weeks before Chancellorsville, Black was asked to speak to a group of hospital stewards who had formed a study group to learn more about medicine. Apperson wrote:

> Dr. Black was present and was invited to make some sort of address which he did in plain, candid style. He said he was heartily glad that we had formed ourselves into a class for the purpose of doing something for our advancement. . . . He asked the hearty cooperation of everyone in making the sick and wounded comfortable, and pointed out the advantages that must inevitably acrue from a firm desire to study. [26]

Throughout the war, Apperson reported to Black while Black, in turn, reported to Dr. Hunter McGuire. [27] As medical director of the Stonewall Brigade, the Valley Army, and the Second Corps of the Army of Northern Virginia, McGuire served under Stonewall Jackson until the latter's death. Known for his innovations as a medical administrator, McGuire created an ambulance corps, established field hospitals at the corps level, and promoted the principle that medical officers should not be made prisoners of war when captured. Black's references to McGuire in his letters are frequent and warm, and the admiration must have been mutual. After Black's death, McGuire recalled how he and Black "during the four years of civil war . . . were daily together, and many a night slept with the stars above them, under the same blanket." [28]

In May 1862, Black played a part with McGuire in promoting the humane treatment of captured medical officers. At that time, surgeons were treated as prisoners of war when captured, subject to incarceration like other officers. When Jackson's Valley Army took the city of Winchester on May 25, 1862, however, a series of events helped establish the principle that medical officers were non-combatants, not to be taken as prisoners.

The exact nature of Harvey Black's role in these events is uncertain. It is known that Black was Acting Medical Director of the Valley Army when the events began to unfold, in place of McGuire who was on leave. Neither Apperson nor Black commented on the events, and official records are skimpy, particularly from the Confederate side. What has survived comes from Dr. J. Burd Peale, a Union surgeon in charge of the sick and wounded at the Union Hotel hospital in Winchester at the time.

On May 25, the Confederates took possession of the town, placing a guard around the hospital. On that afternoon, Peale wrote, "Dr. Black, acting medical director for the rebels, called on me to say that I should continue to give necessary attention to the sick unmolested." Black let him take in wounded men and directed him to take charge of the hospital as surgeon-in-chief. After the number of patients had grown to 330, Black permitted him to have "64 attendants from the prisoners, necessary for carrying on the hospital, and their commissary issued provisions" on Peale's requisition. [29]

The climactic step came on May 31, when Peale and Hunter McGuire signed a document in which the Union surgeons were paroled as prisoners of war. The Union surgeons in turn pledged to work for the release of an equal number of Confederate medical officers held in Union prisons. Thus began the practice of viewing surgeons as non-combatants, a practice that some have seen as contributing to the origin of the International Red Cross. [30]

In December 1862, McGuire named Black surgeon in charge of the newly-formed Field Hospital of the Second Corps, a position he held until the end of the war. John Apperson was charged with maintaining the hospital's records. This field hospital was larger and better equipped than regimental hospitals, but unlike general hospitals, it was mobile. It followed the Second Corps during campaigns; between engagements, it served as a receiving hospital to care for soldiers sent by the regimental surgeons. The only published description of the hospital comes from the pen of John Apperson:

> So great was General Jackson's concern for the sick and wounded of his army and the efficiency of his medical corps he encouraged the organization of a travelling hospital or field infirmary. . . . It was a distinct organization, reporting directly to headquarters. It had its [own] commissary and quartermaster, ambulances, transportation wagons, hospital tents, medical supplies, stewards, detailed nurses and matron in addition to a sufficient number of commissioned medical officers. . . . [T]here were also, as part of this outfit, some ten or twelve milch cows, a part of which accompanied the army through the Pennsylvania campaign and back to Virginia. Surgeon H. Black was put in charge of this department at the time of its organization, and remained in charge of it until the war closed. [31]

Chancellorsville was the first significant engagement of the Second Corps of the Army of Northern Virginia after the hospital's founding. At the time, four or five surgeons and an equal number of stewards were attached to the hospital. According to Black's testimony, the Second Corps Hospital "worked well and efficiently" in caring for the wounded at Chancellorsville. The hospital would be in place for Gettysburg and for the Wilderness, and through Jubal Early's Shenandoah Valley Campaign in 1864, with varying numbers of medical staff attached to it.

After the surrender at Appomattox, Harvey Black returned to his family and his medical practice in Blacksburg. He was not broken by the defeat, but concentrated on quietly working to rebuild the society he had been absent from for four long years. In 1872, two events called him from the quiet vocation of country doctor into the wider world. Black was elected president of the state medical society and he was instrumental in founding a land-grant college in his home town.

Black was one of six vice-presidents of the Medical Society of Virginia during 1871, and at the third annual meeting of the society held in Staunton in 1872, he was elected its president. [32] Presiding over the 1873 annual meeting at Norfolk, he delivered an address on "The Duties of the Society and the State Regarding Irregular Practitioners and Adulterated Medicines." [33] At the same meeting Black was elected an Honorary Fellow of the society. [34]

Black was also active in 1872 in the political negotiations that led to the founding of the Virginia Agricultural and Mechanical College (VAMC), now Virginia Polytechnic Institute and State University. He and the Reverend Peter Henry Whisner, president of the struggling Preston and Olin Institute in Blacksburg, suggested to state senator John E. Penn that the property of the Institute could be given to the state in return for the town being chosen as the location of a land-grant college. Black was instrumental in securing a bond issue by the citizens of Montgomery County that resulted in a $20,000 grant to the state to further assist the college. On March 19, 1872, Governor Gilbert C. Walker signed the bill that established the new college in Blacksburg. Black was chosen to serve on the VAMC Board of Visitors, and he was named the first rector of the board at its initial meeting in Richmond. [35]

In November 1875, Black's medical career took an unexpected turn when he was nominated as the superintendent of the Eastern Lunatic Asylum (now Eastern State Hospital) in Williamsburg. [36] Though he had no training in psychology and the nomination took him by surprise, he accepted the position and served six years as superintendent, beginning in January 1876. Under his leadership, the asylum pioneered in allowing some recuperating patients periods of reentry in the outside world as a means of preparing them for living apart from the institution. [37]

Black returned home in 1882 to resume his private practice as a physician, but he was called into the public sphere once again only three years later. In 1885 he was encouraged to run as a Democrat for Montgomery County's seat in the Virginia House of Delegates. Winning the election in November of that year, he served in the two sessions that ran from December 1885 to March 1886 and from March to May 1887. [38]

One of the causes for which Black fought in the House of Delegates was a newly-authorized mental hospital to be built in the southwestern part of the state. In March 1884 an act of the General Assembly had approved a board of commissioners who would select the site for the new asylum; Harvey Black was placed on that board. After the board chose Marion, in Smyth County, a building committee was authorized, with Black as its chair. On March 1, 1887, the Board of Directors of the new Southwestern Lunatic Asylum (later renamed the Southwestern Virginia Mental Health Institute) unanimously chose Black as its first superintendent.[39] Black, in turn, named John Apperson as his assistant physician.

Black did not serve long in his new position. For several years prior to this he had suffered from disabling symptoms of prostatic enlargement and vesical calculus. In October 1887, Dr. Hunter McGuire, Black's Civil War superior, performed an operation to relieve his pain. McGuire performed a second operation in October 1888.[40] Black grew progressively weaker after the second operation and died in St. Luke's Home in Richmond on October 19, 1888, at the age of 61.[41] He is buried in Westview Cemetery in Blacksburg along with other members of the Black family.

....

Twenty-seven of Harvey Black's Civil War letters to his wife, dating from April 4, 1862, to December 3, 1864, have survived. In addition, three letters written from Blacksburg by Mollie Black between November 29 and December 22, 1863, are extant. We know that Black must have written letters before April 1862 and after December 1864, and can only surmise that these were never kept, or were later discarded or lost. In addition, internal evidence from the surviving letters demonstrates that other letters were written by both Harvey and Mollie Black between 1862 and 1864.

Those letters that we have are valuable and make us wish that more had survived. Harvey Black's letters are both literate and perceptive. His observations on events and people surrounding him, including generals Stonewall Jackson, Robert E. Lee, and Jubal Early, are acute. Seldom emotional, Black was reserved in his manner. His wit was droll, his optimism inextinguishable. Mollie Black, somewhat less literate than her husband, was certainly more expressive of her emotions; her letters exhibit a poignance that her husband's letters seldom attain. Unlike Harvey Black, Mollie always seems to have spoken her mind.

The thirty letters have been grouped into seven chapters. Those in Chapters One and Seven were written by Harvey Black from the Shenandoah Valley, during the Valley Campaigns of 1862 and 1864. Those written in 1862 express Black's certainty that the war would soon be over and Southern independence secured; those from 1864 are far less certain. Chapters Two and Three cover the period from Second Manassas through Gettysburg. The letters in Chapter Two are dark and somber; those in Chapter Three are less so. But all are alike in recounting the hardships that Black and other surgeons faced in caring for the sick and wounded during a trying period.

Mollie Black and the town of Blacksburg take center stage in Chapter Five. Her three letters were written in November and December 1863, a period in which Blacksburg citizens anxiously awaited a Yankee invasion of their town that never came. Mollie graphically expressed her fears and privations in the letters. The absence of her husband prompted expressions of loneliness, but that feeling must have been tempered by frequent visits from townspeople to pass the time. Indeed, the townspeople of Blacksburg play a central role in her letters, and they are often in the background in her husband's. To give the reader greater insight into Blacksburg's populace, an Appendix transcribes, collocates, and briefly analyzes the 1860 free and slave census schedules for the town.

Finally, Harvey Black wrote the letters in Chapters Four and Six from Orange Court House during the fall and winter of 1863-64, while the Confederate and Union armies camped in central Virginia waiting for the spring campaigning season to begin. Apart from Confederate embarrassments like the engagements at Kelly's Ford and Rappahannock Bridge in November 1863, Black had little military action to report in these letters. His thoughts were focussed not on war but on the pleasures and memories of life at home, as well as on social engagements at Orange.

The Civil War presented Harvey and Mollie Black with complex and wrenching moral questions. Each had close relatives in both North and South. As owners of one slave, they had no real stake in the institution of slavery, though other Black and Kent relatives in Blacksburg owned larger numbers of slaves. [42] The Blacks said little about slavery in their letters. They loudly professed the justice of the Southern cause for independence, however, condemning the dastardly Yankees who were invading Southern homes.

Still, their support of the war must have been tinged by the knowledge that they had relatives fighting for the North and among the very invaders they cursed. Harvey Black expressed wonder that none of his brothers in Wisconsin had taken up arms against the South, though "scores" of his relatives in Ohio had done so. Mollie Black's brother Lewis Amiss Kent had attended college in Wisconsin and had become convinced of the evils of slavery. He fought with a Wisconsin regiment in the Iron Brigade, facing the Stonewall Brigade in battle after battle. The Blacks seemed uncertain which side another of Mollie's brothers, John Edwin Kent, was fighting on, and were happy to learn that he was in a Missouri Confederate regiment. Mollie's sister Cecelia White lived in West Virginia, where her husband was an official in state government. With relatives on both sides, Harvey and Mollie Black must have felt profoundly ambiguous about the war, no matter how strongly they affirmed their Southern patriotism.

Even in Virginia, the war did not provide clear answers as to who was friend and who was enemy. Harvey Black's letters contain cryptic references to Unionist activity in the Montgomery County area. In 1862, he spoke of apprehensions in regard to the Price family in the Brush Mountain area of the county. Later, he decried those who would not lend a helping hand in the South's time of need, like "D. H." — presumably Daniel Hoge, who was associated with the Unionist Heroes of America. In asking about another neighbor who was a possible reconstructionist, Black advised Mollie to "enquire cautiously." Black found evidence of Unionist sentiment in parts of the state that would become West Virginia as well. When the Fourth Virginia went through Martinsburg in 1862, he reported that a young girl came up to him and called the Confederates "devils" who caused "nothing but trouble," while praising the Union soldiers who had been there before them.

Though Harvey Black's letters comment on everything from military affairs to family matters, they offer special insights into

Confederate medical practice. Confederate medicine — its administrative structure and personnel more so than its operations and medical procedures — serves as a backdrop to the letters. Black wrote often of other surgeons and hospitals. He also wrote about the patients he cared for — the wounded, the sick, and those who had died. Details on operations and other medical practices are absent from his letters, however, and the reason is not hard to understand. Black's sanguine personality, coupled with a desire to protect his wife from the grim details of much of his day-to-day existence, explain his reserve. Among Confederate surgeons writing to their wives, such reticence apparently was not unusual. [43]

Still, the limitations under which he constantly worked occasionally came to the surface in his letters. "I have under my charge the wounded of the division — have but one assistant and about 225 men to take care of," he wrote shortly after Second Manassas in August 1862. "This is more than we can attend to, to do them justice." He noted how local residents were offering to take the wounded to their homes, an indication that medical officers alone could not care for them. Indeed, he sent Mollie Black's cousins Ed and Bob Peck, both wounded at Second Manassas, to a private home. He admitted that they would be better off there than under his responsibility.

Medical practice in the Confederacy was, as Black's comments suggest, a study in limitations. [44] Not only insufficient numbers of medical personnel, but shortages of medicine and poor facilities all combined to make the surgeon's plight a difficult one. In the South more so than in the North, surgeons worked with makeshift medicines and insufficient medical instruments; often what supplies Confederate surgeons had were captured from Union forces. It is well known that only one-third to one-fourth of the 250,000 Confederate soldier deaths occurred in or from battle. Disease, much of it attributable to practices that would seem archaic only decades later, was the greatest killer of Confederate soldiers.

The Confederate Medical Corps was a complex and evolving organism. Though records are incomplete, perhaps some 3,000 surgeons served the Confederacy. The main distinction among these surgeons was between those who served in general hospitals and those who, like Black, served in the field. There were 39 general hospitals in Virginia alone, most of them in larger cities. These hospitals held patients in need of long-term care. They received the sick and wounded when their condition allowed them to be released from the field hospitals—or when the field hospitals, facing a new wave of wounded soldiers, had to make a place for them.

It is fair to say that the medical officers in the field, who marched and camped with the soldiers for whom they cared, were often both contemptuous and envious of the so-called "hospital doctors" who seemed to have an easier situation. John Apperson probably spoke for many in the field when he confided his opinions of "hospital doctors" to his diary in 1862. Briefly serving at York Hospital in Winchester in November of that year, he had occasion to witness the doctors there:

> I have been struck by the ordinary appearance of a majority of the medical officers connected with the hospitals at this place. They are small in stature and don't seem to portray the vivacious energetic character men ought who are entrusted with the health of an army. They seem too careless, almost to look foppish! The whole dread now is that [they] are afraid they will be sent to the field. [45]

Whether or not Apperson's remarks were entirely just, it is true that medical staff in the field faced trials unknown to their hospital counterparts, especially in times of battle. As Horace H. Cunningham wrote in his study of the Confederate Medical Corps, the medical officer in the field "endured the long marches with the troops and shared their peril on the field of battle. His hospital frequently fell into the line of fire, and, during the din of battle, and after, he was called upon to perform hour after hour the most serious operations." [46]

The regimental surgeon, the assistant surgeon, and the hospital steward all had different roles and duties. Regimental surgeons like Black had overall responsibility for the health and sanitation of the regiment, as well as for keeping and reporting information on those under their care. During battles, the surgeon's role was to establish a field hospital in a sheltered spot one-half to one mile behind the line of battle. Often these hospitals were in gullies or valleys. Just as often, however, churches, hotels, warehouses, shops, barns, and private homes could be pressed into service as temporary hospitals.

Below the surgeon in the regimental hierarchy was the assistant surgeon. He assisted and relieved the surgeon in camp and on the march. During action the assistant surgeon followed the regiment into battle. He gave immediate first aid attention to the wounded and directed their transportation to the field hospitals in the rear.

Such transportation was, especially at the beginning of the war, primitive in the extreme. No organized ambulance corps existed until 1862; before this time members of the regimental band and those whose battle-worthiness was suspect were charged with moving the wounded from the field of battle. Because these men often fled in the face of danger and because other soldiers were forbidden from dropping out to help fallen comrades, the wounded were often left on their own. If they were able to walk at all, they had to make their own way to help. If not, they may have been left on the battlefield until the action had subsided.

The hospital steward, near the bottom of the hierarchy, nevertheless played a key role in the Confederate Medical Corps. Stewards in the field were selected by the regimental surgeons. They were generally skilled in pharmacy, and like John Apperson, many had some medical education. Some stewards held medical degrees but served in lesser roles because they could not get appointments as surgeons. Stewards were responsible for the cleanliness of the wards and kitchens and had charge of medical and surgical supplies. They might supervise the cooks and nurses, assist in keeping medical records, or act as medical dispensers and apothecaries. During and after battles, they would assist the regimental surgeons at the operating table.

Many surgeons and hospital stewards were evasive in their letters home or in their diary entries about the operations they performed following battles. Apperson, for example, often merely recorded in a perfunctory manner that the days following battles were spent in operations. Black wrote of "quite a number of interesting operations" performed in his hospital at Chancellorsville. We know, of course, that almost all of these operations were amputations of arms or legs or hands or feet, with a few resections of limbs or ligatures of arteries also taking place.

Although some Confederate surgeons were accused of sawing off limbs in a nonchalant fashion, there is little doubt that most of the amputations were necessary, given the limitations in which the surgeons worked. Most wounds were to the extremities, and the large caliber and low muzzle velocity of Civil War rifles caused horrible and jagged wounds to arms and legs. Bullets usually stayed in the limbs, making amputations the most common treatment to stop gangrene or other infections.

There was general agreement that operations should be performed as soon as possible after the wound was received, and for that reason most amputations took place in field hospitals. Often they were performed in the most makeshift manner, with doors from buildings and tails of wagons sometimes serving as operating tables. Sterilization of instruments and dressings was simply not practiced.

Though Harvey Black's letters begin in April 1862, he had received his baptism of fire as a surgeon nine months earlier at First Manassas. The Fourth Virginia suffered 131 casualties in the battle—31 dead and 100 wounded—and its losses were the highest in the First Brigade. Black must have been overwhelmed by the carnage. John Apperson later recalled that even though Dr. Black had been in the Mexican War, "this was the first time he had ever been under fire, and knew as little perhaps of what he had to do . . . as the rest of us." [47]

Apperson's diary gives a vivid account of events at First Manassas. As the battle began, Black and Apperson were about a mile behind the front, preparing as best they could to take the wounded. Around noon the wounded began to arrive. Apperson wrote in his diary:

> The first man wounded in our regiment was T. A. Oury of Co. D, 'Smyth Blues.' He was struck in the mouth by a fragment of a bomb. He came out and we commenced dressing the wound, but before we had done anything others were brought out, and being desperately hurt we left him to attend to them. From this time on numbers were brought out. The fight in the meantime grew hotter and hotter. We found it very unsafe for us to remain there, so we fell back some distance in the rear. [48]

Apperson saw his first amputation at the battle; it must have been performed by Black. His diary entry indicates that he thought in advance of what he might see. He wrote, "we had the wounded conveyed to a creek nearby and did all that we could for men in their fix. I witnessed an amputation, and my ideas were not very far from right." [49]

Manassas was the first engagement in which Harvey Black would transmute his skills as a country physician into those of a field surgeon. It would not be the last. The conditions described by Apperson must have been present throughout the war, though advances in medical administration and facilities like the Second Corps Hospital would make medical officers more efficient. Horace Cunningham quotes an unidentifed Confederate surgeon who modestly summed up his medical experiences at the end of four years of war. "We did not do the best we would," the surgeon wrote, "but [we did] the best we could." [50] Though Harvey Black was not the author of these words, he would have shared the sentiment. To his credit, Black played a part in the process of turning an always grisly business into something more acceptable and humane. Perhaps his ingrained optimism made the difference, as did his commitment to the simple goal he articulated to the group of medical stewards just before Chancellorsville to "make the sick and wounded more comfortable."

....

The editorial practices I followed in transcribing, editing, and annotating the letters of Harvey and Mollie Black are standard ones. The transcriptions remain true to the text—there are no silent emendations of any kind, either modernizations or corrections. Because both Harvey and Mollie Black were literate and wrote well, their letters present few problems in comprehension to modern readers. Apart from occasional misspellings and idiosyncratic practices such as leaving an apostrophe out of words like "can't" or "don't," there was little in any case to correct.

I have, however, introduced three kinds of editorial changes. First, I placed text in brackets to supply words that were left out, or to fill in abbreviations intentionally used—for example, "Bob F[rancisco]." Second, in three instances I omitted short and incoherent sections in Harvey Black's letters to preserve the flow of the letters. In one such section, for example, he wrote about an apparent mistake in his bank account, doing the arithmetic in the letter. Where text has been omitted, this is indicated in the endnotes. Third, I introduced paragraphing throughout the letters. Civil War correspondents often wrote letters in long blocks of text to make the best use of precious paper. In a different situation, they might have been more generous with white space. To transcribe the letters without additional paragraphing would mean presenting modern readers with solid and almost unreadable text. To prevent this, I inserted paragraph breaks where they logically seemed to fit.

In annotating the letters, my goal was to elucidate references to obscure people and events mentioned by Harvey or Mollie Black. For those whose military records are not common knowledge, I referred to their Compiled Service Records. I included census information for a variety of individuals: residents of Montgomery County, Virginia; relatives of Harvey and Mollie Black; civilians with whom Black had contact; soldiers in the Fourth Virginia Infantry Regiment; and surgeons and hospital stewards. Civil War armies were made up of all kinds of ordinary citizens; shoemakers, farmers, lawyers, and doctors suddenly became privates, officers, and surgeons. Providing both military and census information on those who served tells something of their background and adds an important dimension to their identification.

going up the hill. He saw Dr. B's insignia of officer, a star on his coat and says to him "Major rally your men here," [then] pointed [to] a space along a fence over which his horse had just passed . . . he then recognized Dr. Black and says "Excuse me doctor, I thought it was one of the other officers." [1]

On April 2, Jackson established his headquarters at Rude's Hill, on the Shenandoah River. There his forces stayed until April 17, when they moved to Conrad's Store (now Elkton) at the foot of Swift Run Gap in the Blue Ridge Mountains. This began a period of hard marches and diversionary tactics. By June 9, Jackson's 16,000 men would march 350 miles and defeat three separate Union armies in five battles: McDowell (May 8), Front Royal (May 23), Winchester (May 25), Cross Keys (June 8), and Port Republic (June 9).

During the spring of 1862, sickness invaded the Stonewall Brigade. New recruits who came in when the Conscription Bill was enacted on April 16 were especially susceptible to childhood diseases like measles and mumps. And the lengthy marches of the Valley Campaign in the cold and rain made all soldiers potential candidates for illness. By April 23, Black could write to Mollie that he had been "beseiged all day with applicants" for medical discharges, "some entitled and a good many not."

Black was also concerned over men who were gaining exemptions from military service. "It's shocking that every fellow that can find salt peter enough to put on a ham should be excused from the service," he wrote on April 4, alluding to the home production of nitre, used for gunpowder as well as for curing meat. Such exemptions went against his patriotism, which seemed unshakeable. "The war has nearly reached a point that we must lay waste our own fair land that the enemy may not enjoy it," Black wrote on April 28. "It must be done no matter how great the sacrifice."

Recent Confederate defeats at Shiloh and Pea Ridge, coupled with the fall of New Orleans and the Union advance on Richmond, certainly were reason enough to think that the Confederacy was in danger of being defeated. But Black's letters during this period reflect an optimism that the war would end soon and with a Confederate victory. "There never was a war but this that ended at some time, and this will do so too," he wrote on April 23. While admitting in early May that he was "no prophet," he ventured a prophecy: "I dont hesitate to say that whip them we can and whip them we will."

....

Camp near Mt Jackson
April 4 1862 [2]

My dear Wife—

As Mr. Gardner starts home in the morning, I write you a few lines. [3] I wrote you 3 or 4 days ago by Capt. John Wade who has gotten a clerkship in Richmond. I sent by him $300 to send you in the form of a Certificate of deposit. My letter to you will explain how to dispose of it. [4]

On the 1st we marched down from Camp Buchanan to near Edinburg to skirmish with the enemy, but they did not advance. [5] Ashby burned a bridge which stopped them. It is said that he killed about fifty of them at two shots by shooting through a column in Edinburg. [6]

In all probability you will see a notice in a few days of Ashby firing on our own town's women and children as observed in regards to Newtown. They say [what] they have been doing is to plant their cannon in the streets and fire on our men thinking they will not return the fire on account of the town, but Ashby managed this time to get the exact range of the street and probably has taught them a lesson that they will profit by, and so far as we know without damage to the town. [7]

Late in the evening we came to near Mt. Jackson and encamped. On Wednesday we came to this camp which is nearly 4 miles above Mt. Jackson. On yesterday morning we left about 3 o'clock in the morning and went back to within about 1 1/2 miles of Edinburg. We were placed in position and remained until about 4 o'clock. The enemy making no advance we returned to camp, and today we are lying about on the leaves in the sun.

Some of Col. Fulkerson's brigade went down this morning, and I suppose we will have to go back on Sunday if they do not advance sooner. [8] The enemy comes on very cautiously. Ashby fired a few shots at them yesterday, but they did not return the fire.

which carried him off the field and died in 2 or 3 hours afterwards. [22]

It rained tremendously yesterday. I have had one of my old attacks of diarrhea but am getting better again. Indeed I feel as well as usual this morning.

I rcd your letter by Mr. Ridley. [23] He came through in 2 days.

When I get time I will write you a letter. I am kept busy on account of the reorganization of the rgt. [24] The boys do not get to go home. Ours have to remain in the same Company they were in before. There will be an election in the Highlanders today. [25]

My best love to you and the children. Direct your next letter to Valley District. I dont know where we will be.

Yours affectionately   H Black

....

Camp Swift Run
April 23 1862

My dear Wife—

As John Black will probably leave in the morning, I will try and write you a few lines. [26] We have not moved since I wrote to you by mail day before yesterday. [27]

Yesterday was spent in the reorganization of the regiment. Lt. Col. Ronald was elected Colonel. [28] Capt. D. Gardner, Lt. Colonel [29] & Capt. Terry, Major. [30] In the Blacksburg Company, Bennett was elected Captain. [31] John Howe 1st Lt., [32] Green Wall 2d Lt., [33] & Joseph Barton 3d Lt. [34]

Capt. Newlee was elected Captain again but declined to accept. [35] Jack Keister was elected 2d Lt. [36] & W. H. Thomas (not Col's son) 3d Lt. [37]

I have examined a good many men today for discharge—and have given certificates to about 15 men. In our Company, John Jernell, [38] George Richardson, [39] John Galloway, [40] John Black, [41] Geo. McDonald, [42] Ed Caldwell, [43] and 1 man I forget now who. [44]

I have been besieged all day by applicants. All day—some entitled and a good many not. And of course there will be the usual complaining with the disappointed.

We are in a very lonesome place — dont hear or see too much besides our own army. The enemy took possession of Harrisonburg yesterday. [45]

I cant do much writing — about a dozen are sitting around talking. The Col. has just been discussing what a boy Alex is, and some of them are trying to plague me about having so many children and so fast. And in turn we have been jeering the Col. and & Lt. Col. about being so unfortunate as not to have any. I feel mighty proud of them. I dont think I would be half so good a soldier if I did not have so many little fellows to fight for.

Ridley has been appointed Adjutant and I suppose will make a very good one. [46] Bob Francisco went to Staunton 4 or 5 days ago with the extra baggage, and I learn today that he has gone on to Gordonsville. [47]

The Hospitals have all been removed to Charlottesville — and all the movements indicate that if we move from here shortly we will go across the Blue Ridge in the direction of Richmond — though of course we cannot anticipate any movement Genl. Jackson may make.

Bob Peck is very well, and he told me today that he had been appointed Commissary for the Company, which relieves him from general duty. Major Pendleton started home this morning. He did not get but 4 votes for re-election. His great consolation was that he was going to see his sweetheart. [48] Of our old mess nobody is left but Crockett and myself. [49]

I am glad Capt. Newlee is going home. He will be a good man in the neighborhood in case of any difficulty. Though we hate to lose him from the regiment for I think he was the best Captain in it.

I have just read your letter sent by Mr. Ridley over again. How heartily do I cherish and reciprocate the warm expression of love contained therein. As you say, bread and water would be as a feast to us if this despicable war were over and we could be together again.

It is getting cold in our tent & I must stop and go to bed to keep warm. You ought to have seen me last night shovelling away the rocks to get a smooth place to put down my bed. Dont you think I will appreciate the comforts of our humble home when I get there.

We will all probably have to make up our minds before this war terminates to be willing to surrender whatever we may have for the sake of the great cause in which we are engaged. Now is the time for the Southern people to show their devotion & patriotism by burning everything that the enemy can appropriate. The war has nearly reached a point that we must lay waste our own fair land that the enemy may not enjoy it. It must be done no matter how great the sacrifice. Personally, we have but little to lose, but if necessary, I would apply the torch to it as readily as I would a brush pile.

From all that we can see, the struggle for the next 3 months must be a desperate one, but Providence in his wisdom will guide the storm and will in his good time cause the bright rays of peace again to shine upon us.

Yesterday was Sunday and a long day to me. We were expecting orders all the time to march, but they did not come until nearly night, and I had nothing much to do, to read, or to eat. Dr. Dabney preached in an adjoining brigade, and I went to hear him — and a most excellent sermon it was, too. From the text that "no man knowest what a day may bring forth." He has been recently appointed Genl. Jackson's Adjutant General and was one of the professors at Hampden Sydney. [57]

We are all getting along very well under our new organization. Everything so far going on pleasantly, and I hope may continue.

Tell Aunt Liz that Bob seems to [be] very well satisfied. [58] He is a boy of fine courage, and while he is very anxious to see his friends, he sees that importance of everyone remaining and fighting bravely until our liberties are achieved.

We had a terrible week of rain and snow last week, but it has cleared off again and is now pleasant.

I dont think it is yet decided whether Whitescarver will be continued as quartermaster or not. [59] If he is not, I think Bob Francisco will get it, though the Col. has said nothing to me about it. I think it is the general desire of the regiment that he should have it. [60]

I hope to get a letter from you tomorrow. We send to Stanardsville for our mail, 14 miles, but very rarely get any. Direct your letters to 4th Rgt., Va. Vols., Army Valley District, without naming place, for we have no abiding place now.

Remember me kindly to the relations and to Mrs. Mary Preston. [61]

Tell Mr. Spickard to make me another circingle and send to me. [62] Somebody stole the one he made. A man has to be on the lookout here, or he will lose everything he has. My canteen had been out about two weeks, but I found it yesterday across a fellow's shoulder.

Accept my warmest love for yourself and the children. Kiss them for me and tell them I think of them every day & night and will come home to see them and stay with them just as soon as we whip the Yankees.

Your ever devoted husband   H Black

....

Near Port Republic
May 2d 1862 [63]

My dear Wife —

I rec'd about an hour ago three letters from you bearing date 17th, 21st, 22 April. I am truly sorry to hear that our precious little boy has been so ill again but was gratified to hear that he had again been enabled to swallow. I hope he may yet recover and that an operation may be performed that may relieve him. It would indeed be hard to give up so interesting and dear [a] child. While with you, I feel that if it would be the will of Providence, I could do so believing that he would be a little angel in a better land. [64]

Knowing that you will have everything done for him that the kindest of mothers and friends can do, I know nothing to suggest more than your own knowledge of what would be right. As he has got to swallowing again, he may continue to improve, and until an operation can be performed, I think the least done the better — except what you can do for temporary relief, which in his case can be but little.

In regard to the house, Squire Peck has had the renting of it heretofore, and he and Capt. Newlee who is interested, can act as they think best. [65] I have no objections.

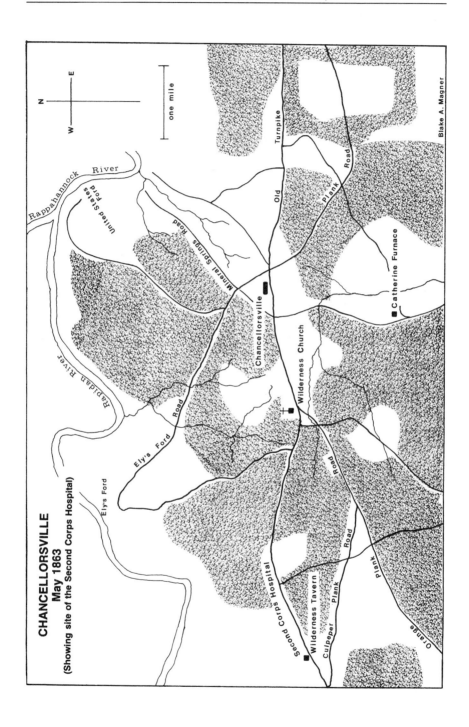

CHANCELLORSVILLE
May 1863
(Showing site of the Second Corps Hospital)

Blake A. Magner

Two

"Their Loss is Much Greater than Ours in Numbers
But Not Equal to Ours in Worth"

August 31-December 15, 1862

T he three letters in this chapter are darker in tone than those from the Valley Campaign. Their themes are loss and hardship. Two were written shortly after major engagements—Second Manassas and Fredericksburg—and the third was written nine days after the Battle of Antietam. Black was Brigade Surgeon for the Stonewall Brigade during Groveton and Second Manassas, at a time when its "brave men" were being "mowed down," to use his words. His letters from this period recite the casualties in the brigade and the Fourth Virginia Regiment, especially those from its Blacksburg companies. The same young men whose childhood diseases Black had treated several years earlier now came to him mangled and dying. "I will try and write you a short letter," he began on August 31, but he could not. Instead, he reported at length and with pathos on the Blacksburg dead and wounded. Exhausted, he finally ended the letter at midnight with a plea that "this bloody struggle" might soon cease.

This must have been an especially difficult period for the medical staff, who were always overburdened in the days and nights after a major battle. Black expressed his concern over the lack of personnel available to help him treat the wounded. At Second Manassas, he had charge of a divisional hospital of 225 wounded, with only one assistant. The situation hardly improved three months later at Fredericksburg, when it took him over a day to write a one-page letter during respites from treating the wounded.

order to move the wounded to Aldie & Middleburg. This made it necessary that they should be moved.

John English came to me just afterwards and insisted that I would permit him to take them to his house — a distance of about 8 miles. [16] He had his carriage, and I consented for them to go where they will be under the immediate charge of Dr. Powell, a man of reputation, and I will go to see them as often as I can. [17] English lives in Middleburg. And tomorrow I will move the Hospital to Aldie where I will be 6 miles off. [18]

I have under my charge the wounded of the Division — have but one assistant and about 225 men to take care of. [19] This is more than we can attend to, to do them justice, and which was one of the reasons that induced me to let Bob & Ed go from under my immediate care.

I have been this particular in writing about them that your Aunt Liz & their father might know their condition. I have stated their condition as plainly as I well can & without reserve. I think Aunt Liz ought to come and see them if she can — both for her gratification and theirs. While I believe they will have every attention that can be given them — for the people of this county have been coming to me constantly today and asking me to let them take the wounded soldiers to their houses.

Our wounded are a good deal scattered. One Hospital we had to abandon but recovered it yesterday. Being Brigade Surgeon, I was not required to cast lots to remain with the few wounded men that were left. Otherwise, I might have been a prisoner. [20]

Tell Mr. Robinson that Tob has a flesh wound of the leg and is doing well. Capt. Bennett has a flesh wound in both legs. [21]

The loss in our Rgt is about 100. Capts. White [22] and Gibson [23] was killed. So was Cols. Baylor [24] and Neff. [25]

It makes my heart sad to think how this Brigade has struggled to maintain its fair reputation — how its brave men have been mowed down and that today it paraded under but one flag instead of 5. The 27th Rgt may be regarded as broken up. [26]

And the 4th has not more than one good Company present. Major Terry [27] & Capt. Fulton [28] are both wounded. Also Lt. B. Fulton. [29]

We took 24 pieces of cannon & 1500 prisoners yesterday and some today. Our forces have advanced as far as Centreville. The great battle was fought in part on the old battlefield of Manassas. Much of it near Sudly's Mill.

Genl. Ewell had his leg amputated and is expected to die. Will be a great loss. [30]

I cant give you now an account of trying and exciting scenes through which we have passed. The fighting has continued with more or less severity for 11 days and is said to exceed that before Richmond. [31]

The loss will be counted by thousands on both sides. Bro. Tebbs told me tonight that he passed over part of the field today, and the ground the Yankees occupied before where our division fought he could almost step from one dead body to another. His remark was that they looked as if they were souls. [32]

Their loss is much greater than ours in numbers but not equal to ours in worth. I cant write more tonight. It is now about 12 o'clock, and I must try and get some sleep which I need very much. God grant that this bloody struggle may soon cease, though I hope it may never cease if it has to end in subjection to the northern vandals we fight. I will write to you again in a few days. My love to the children.

Your affectionate husband   H Black

Send my clothes by the first chance. I have not yet seen Bob F[rancisco]. He is back with the army. I cant read this over tonight. I believe that I omitted to state that Ed Peck has a slight flesh wound of the left arm.

....

Martinsburg
Septemb. 26, 1862 [33]

My dear Wife —

We arrived at this place yesterday morning and we are encamped a short distance from town. I have had the pleasure of receiving I think five letters from you in the last 4 or 5 days. I suppose all the old ones have come to hand for they run from the 2nd of June to the 16th of Sept.

I was sorry to learn that Middleburg and Aldie had fallen into the hands of the Yankees. This however can not detain Bob & Ed long from home as they will probably be exchanged as soon as they are able to travel. I did not get away much too soon or I would have been also captured.

I rcd your letter by Mr. [illegible].[46]

Ask Sheaf if he will make me a pair of cavalry boots. [47] He has my measure. If he can have them done by the 1st of December without fail, I can wait until then. Tell him to let me know. I want a substantial pair and the legs not made too small at the ankle. I want the legs a little larger than the pair I have which he saw. Otherwise my feet will swell so that I cant wear them.

If we go into Md. again, I will try and get you the calico. My sojourn was too short, and the Yankees rather troublesome to attend to it before.

I have not had the pleasure of meeting Major Palmer, although we can not be far from each other. [48] You have no idea how difficult it is to find a friend in the army. You sometimes see men hunting 3 or 4 days for their regiment before they can find it. If we remain here 2 or 3 days longer, I think I will try and find him. I am happy to hear that he has escaped in the severe battles through which he has passed. Indeed, the way our men fight it is remarkable that anyone escapes for the bomb shells and minnie balls fly almost everywhere.

Tell Kentie I am always glad to hear of him standing head in his class. [49] Tell Lizzie if she wants to be considered a good girl and one that everybody will like, she must learn to talk right. [50] I was sorry to hear that she had to be punished for ugly talk. Surely she thinks more of her Pa & Ma than to be guilty of this again. Everybody likes sweet, modest little girls, but not bad ones.

I am sure Alex will try to learn. [51] The weather is getting cool now, and he can probably manage to sit up long enough to learn his lessons. Tell Charlie that if Ma whips him too much that I will have it attended to when I come home, but that I reckon he has to have a letter every few days to make a good boy of him. Poor little fellow, how I would like to see him.

As we may fall back towards Winchester, I think I will write a letter to Ceal and leave it in the hands of someone to mail. [52] This however is such a den of unionism that I dont know who to entrust a letter to, unless I can find Miss Bell Boyd, of whom I have not heard since our arrival here. [53]

I think at least one half of the citizens have gone into Md. A little girl remarked yesterday as we passed along the street that "when the Yankees were here we could lie down in peace, but now [that] *you devils* have come there is nothing but trouble." This is the only place in Va. that I know of that our cause has not gained ground by the presence of the Federal Army. It is due to the fact many of the mechanics of the Baltimore and Ohio Railroad live here. I hope before the war is over that we will have torn up the last rail and blown up the last terminal belonging to it. [54]

It is nearly dark, and as we scarcely know the luxury of candles, I must stop. My love to all. Let me hear the latest news from Bob & Ed Peck. I feel much interest in their case.

Your devoted husband   H Black [55]

....

Hospital near Fredericksburg
Dec. 15th, 1862 [56]

My dear Wife—

I take time to write you a few lines. The papers will give you an account of the fighting so far. Gen. Hill did most of the fighting on the 13th—lost about 900 to 1,000 men. [57] Whole loss of our Corps about 1,500 killed & wounded. Our Brigade has been under fire but not engaged. [58]   4 men from Pulaski wounded slightly. Lt. Col. Gardner had his jaw fractured but was doing well when I saw him last night. [59]

The enemy was handsomely repulsed at every point. Longstreet lost about 300 men. [60] The enemy sent in a flag of truce yesterday evening to bury the dead. Loss of the enemy much heavier than ours.

I commenced writing this morning but was interrupted, and it is now after dark. We have been expecting the enemy to renew the attack for 2 days, but as yet they have not done so. There is occasionally some firing of the skirmishers at Batteries. Our position is

Corps Field Hospital included four or five surgeons, four stewards, eight cooks, thirty-one nurses, four washers, two druggists, one agent, and one ward master.[2] When it was in winter quarters, it had its own hospital matron, Keziah Shepherd of Fredericksburg.[3]

Harvey Black may have remarked about the hospital functioning efficiently and pleasantly at Chancellorsville, but it had its quota of misery. Apperson kept the records for the hospital and also recorded its statistics in his diaries during its opening months. He noted that during February, for example, 493 patients were received; 57 died during the month, 31 of smallpox.[4] Another of the hospital's stewards, Charles W. Sydnor, seems to have found it an unagreeable assignment, at least at this time. "We are still at this place of misery and distress dragging through the days and nights like so many convicts," he wrote from the hospital when it was at Guiney Station on February 1, 1863.[5]

The Second Corps Hospital would follow the Army of Northern Virginia in both of its campaigns during this period. At Chancellorsville (May 1-3) Lee and Jackson collaborated on their most daring and successful initiative, defeating the Army of the Potomac, twice the size of Lee's army. Jackson, however, was wounded by his own pickets on the evening of May 2 and would die eight days later. Lee reorganized his army into three corps after Jackson's death; Richard Ewell commanded the Second Corps. Early in June, the Army of Northern Virginia invaded the North once again and met the Army of the Potomac at Gettysburg (July 1-3). In a climactic engagement, Lee was sent in retreat across the Potomac, sustaining over 25,000 casualties. Black's letters contain post-battle commentary on both Chancellorsville and Gettysburg, reporting, as always, on local soldiers who had been wounded or killed in action.

Besides his duties administering the Second Corps Hospital, Harvey Black had something else on his mind during these months—his relatives who lived behind Union lines, some of whom were in the Union army. While the Blacks might have hoped that none of their "near relations" would fight for the Union, they knew otherwise. Lewis Amiss Kent, Mollie's younger brother, had joined the Iron Brigade, the Union counterpart to the Stonewall Brigade. Harvey Black found himself looking for Kent whenever he was in hospitals containing wounded Union soldiers. Trying to comfort Mollie, he promised that for her sake and "common humanity" he would give Kent all the attention he could if he found him wounded or a prisoner. Black seemed saddened to admit that "scores" of his Ohio relatives were fighting on the Union side. While this was probably an exaggeration, some did, and several of them died fighting for the Union.[6]

None of Black's brothers in Wisconsin appear to have fought in the war. Still, he felt uncomfortable remaining in contact with them, his sister Retta, or his parents, as he apparently had done earlier in the war. When he was in Pennsylvania during the Gettysburg campaign, Black had the opportunity to send a letter to his family in Wisconsin, but he did not take it. "I dont feel much like corresponding until the war is over," he wrote. "I can only write under great restraint which is but little pleasure to me and but little comfort to them."

....

Hospital 2 ANV Corps
Guiney Station
April 1, 1863 [7]
My dear Wife

I rcd your letter of the 27th on yesterday, and if my letters cheer you up when you are sick, I am willing to write you any day. I hope that when you are up again you will feel better than you have for some time, as you have had your system pretty well cleansed from what you say of the quantity of medicines you have taken. [8]

I am glad your cousin Lizzie has helped to nurse you for she is usually so cheerful that she will help you to keep in the same mood. I am sorry that she is not relieved of her anxiety yet. I hope she will soon be either one way or the other and I think it would be charitable to wish that it might be as usual in the hope of a male heir apparent. [9]

I have no news to write you. No fighting nor change of any sort. I have nearly everything ready now to move and expect to follow closely the Army wherever it may go.

for us. [24] They are beautiful silver perch and with you and the children to help eat them, how much we could enjoy the feast.

General Jackson is staying at Mr. Chandler's, about [a] half mile distant. [25] I have not been to see him since my return, but learn that he is very ill. He got along well until Friday when he was attacked with pneumonia and his recovery is rendered thereby especially doubtful. He has been something of an invalid for many years and has a great partiality for the use of cold water. On Thursday he bathed his chest freely with it, and it is supposed this caused the attack. He is delirious most of the time — talking about his troops, issuing orders, directing those around him to sing and pray.

How we would all mourn his loss — and how great it would be to the Country. You can scarcely conceive the strong affection which his men have for him. He has outlived every prejudice and is regarded [as] a great Military Chieftain and a faithful Christian. [26]

The remarks of Gen. Lee which you see published in the papers that he would have rather borne the wounds in his own person and that the late victory is due to him was written the day after the battle. [27] Dr. McGuire told me of it the day that the letter was received. This shows the high appreciation that Lee had of him — and further shows how magnanimous Lee is. With two such men to lead us, victory will continue to be ours.

I have just had a letter handed me which I see is from you, so I will stop and read.

I have rcd your letter and Retta's. [28] I had hoped that none of our near relations would engage in the war on the Yankee side, but with young men it was hardly to be expected that they could be kept aloof from the struggle, and it has been a cause of great pleasure and almost of surprise to me that my brothers have not engaged in it. [29]

In regard to Lewis, his active temperament together with the fact that his uncle (no doubt conscientiously) has aided to impress his mind with the wrongfulness of slavery has made him feel free to enlist. [30] We could hardly expect it otherwise.

Of my relations in Ohio, I have no doubt but scores of them are in the field. [31] These things I expected and felt reluctant to engage in the war — but it can not be avoided. Were all my brothers in the field, it would not alter my course to continue in this war until our independence is achieved. Our future happiness and prosperity as a nation and as individuals depends upon our success. And while it grieves us to find them invading our homes, we are consoled by the thought that our children will reap the rewards of our sacrifices.

Lewis may be with Burnside whose Corps was withdrawn from Army of Potomac and finally transferred to Kentucky. [32]

I was in several of the Hospitals where the wounded Yankees were and had about 28 under my care. I saw no one that I recognized. [33] Should I meet with Lewis as a prisoner or wounded, I will for your sake and common humanity give him all the attention that I can.

But do not allow yourself to be much disturbed by the news that he is in the Federal Army — for of the large number engaged but comparatively few are killed and wounded. Hooker is supposed to have had engaged about 125,000. There were about 7,000 prisoners here, but they were started to Richmond yesterday before I came.

I dont know how my friends could have heard that I was wounded for thanks to a kind Providence so far I have not incurred a scratch. I thought it not improbable last Thursday that I with all our wounded would be captured, but good luck attended us. Genl. Lee marched nearly his whole Army back to Fredericksburg, leaving only 2 Brigades at Chancellorsville, about 5 miles from us. As Stoneman was returning, part of his forces came in about 3 miles [from] us, but fortunately for us turned off and crossed the river. [34] Situated as I was, duty would have compelled me to remain much as I would have regretted it.

I have not seen Ed Peck, though he may have gone on to the regt before my return.

Genl. Longstreet has arrived with his staff, & it is said his army is on its way. [35] Some think that Hooker will try to again advance soon, but if so, he will find Lee with his gallant army in his path — determined never to be conquered.

I had a very pleasant time in the practice of my profession in the late battle. I have the Corps well organized, and all worked well and efficiently. We had quite a number of interesting operations, all of which cases were doing well when we left. Two young men were attached to the Corps who were introduced to me by Edmund Hurt [36] who are very clever young men indeed. Dr. Ellsbury [37] and Mr. Drain, [38] the latter a student.

I did not get to see Major Palmer — indeed, did not hear that he was injured until Friday when I had read a note from Dr. Powell in answer to one from me making the inquiry. [39] He stated that he had his horse killed and in the fall had his shoulder broken and would not be fit for duty for weeks. I hope he is now with his wife and that she is well again. [40]

My love to all. Kiss our dear little children for me. It is just 2 years today since I left home. I hope a few months more will enable me to return to enjoy the fond wish of my heart to be with those I love best & so dearly.

Most devotedly   H Black

....

Sunday night May 31 63
Guinea Station

My dear Wife —

I believe I have not written you since last Sunday, a longer time than usual between letters. [41] Yours of the 25th was rcd Friday and which I will now answer. I cannot get coffee without getting it from Richmond. If you want some, you had best send there or to Lynchburg and get it. Also the rice. I may however be able to get you some of the latter.

I am sorry to hear that Aunt Cook is again complaining of her eyes. [42] With so many attacks and of this duration, will it [cause] a return of the old disease without regard to this cause. I hope not the latter. If I were to try, I could fix up a tent very nicely for you and Aunt Cook, but I think you would be in rather close proximity to a melee of bugs, and if a windy night were to come, such as we sometimes have here, you might find your self more suddenly enlarged to a disagreeable capacity.

So if you visit me I shall not hazard this experiment but will get the best boarding house I can. I would ask you to come down with Henry Earhart the next time he comes, if I felt better assured that we would remain for some time at this place, but at present I am afraid to make the arrangements. [43]

What will you do with the children or would you rather Kentie would come along with you. I would like for him to come while I would be somewhat afraid of the dangers of disease to him from travelling. Though I believe he has had measles and scarlet fever, and there is not much risk of anything else. You can do as you like about bringing him.

I was in hopes that we would be put up in the Orange & Alexandria R.R. where you could get here easier, but with Henry you could get along without much trouble, and he could go back with you. I will write to you again about it after the Vicksburg fight is ended, and from the news we rcd today, if true, it is probably over and a great victory to us. [44]

In regard to Adeline, I think it is probable that the blood comes from the stomach and that it has caused derangement in her monthly changes. See Dr. Evans and ask him to prescribe for her. [45] I think it will be best not to give her blue mass or calamel when she has these attacks unless it can not be avoided. While it gives her temporary relief, it may gradually undermine her system. Tell the doctor to question her closely and find out all he can about her condition and prescribe for her. I think it may become necessary to put her upon a course of Iodine. I dont like however to prescribe for her unless I can see her.

I used to sell the Ring pessary at $1.50. [46] Mary H. can have one at that price, or if it will benefit her, make her a present of it. [47]

I am glad that you have got the money from Smith. I thought my letter would bring it. Credit the money on the Acct. I made as Executor of your Pa's Estate. [48]

I have not yet seen Ed Peck. I think I will probably see him this week as I have some business at Genl. Ewell's Hd. Qrs. and will call by if I have time.

Ewell came up a few days ago, and it is understood that he will take command of 3 divisions of Jackson's Corps—and that Genl. A. P. Hill will have a Corps composed of his division and one of Longstreet's. This will throw me in Ewell's Corps—also in the Stonewall Brigade and the old division. I think the arrangement will give general satisfaction to both the advocates of Ewell & Hill. The former retains Jackson's old staff, if they are willing to stay and which I think they are. [49]

Tell Bettie & Lizzie I did not get any spoils in this last battle— that if I have a chance, I will get them one apiece. [50]

Who keeps the tanyard since Chs. Miller left. [51]

I went to church today about 5 miles distant and heard a good sermon from Mr. Coleman. [52] He gave me a cordial invitation to go home with him to dinner, and I was foolish not to accept it.

Dr. Moore [53] preaches his noted funeral discourse of Genl. Jackson at the same place tomorrow, & Dr. Duncan [54] on Wednesday. I think I will go and hear them if I can. [55]

I put calico in this letter. [56]

....

Camp near Darksville
Sunday July 19, 1863 [57]

My dear Wife—

I have just had a good camp dinner: poles & snaps, mutton, fried chicken, & Blackberry pie & milk—and as I have not had such an abundant variety for some time and ate heartily, I fear that I will not be able to write you a very interesting letter, if I be able to complete it without a nap. I have a respite from work at present, and no one but a soldier knows how lazy a soldier can become who has no duties to perform.

I came back from Jordan's Springs Thursday and went into camp with command of my own time. [58] Friday and Saturday I employed in working at my papers, and it will take 4 or 5 days more to get my reports made and my papers all arranged.

This morning I went over to the Stonewall Brigade for the first time since the fight to see the remnant of the 4th Regt. [59] When I contrast it with the Regt that it was when it first came into service, it almost makes me sad. The whole regt now is but about 1/3 larger than was Col. Ronald's Company when it marched out of Blacksburg. [60] But those that are left are cheerful and determined as ever and as gallant a little group as ever engaged in war.

Major Terry being absent on special duty, Capt. Evans is in command of the regt. [61] I asked him where I would find his Company. He told me, and one of his men remarked they could nearly all get under one oil cloth. So with Capt. Bennett's Co. [62] The former has 12, the latter 13 present.

I found Ed Peck, Bob Harris, [63] George Barger, [64] & Green Wall sitting around a large stump writing letters, and the rest lounging around, talking & laughing. They stopped, and after remarking that the stump was their office, went on to give me the particulars of the fight. All had some interesting incidents either about themselves or some others to relate.

Ed says he was close to Andrew Hoge when he was killed and that he had one of his legs cut off near his body by a shell. [65] Bob Calvert was standing behind a tree when an awful enfilade fire was made upon them and [was] shot in the breast, sat down, then lay down and in a few minutes was dead. [66] Poor Kent Ewing was not dead when last seen but supposed to be mortally wounded. [67]

Capt. Wade is the only officer with his company and is quite well. [68] I left him reading a letter which he had just rcd from home by Sam Snider who came this morning and says he saw you in Christiansburg. [69]

The boys were laughing about a joke they have on Major Terry which occurred while they were expecting an attack at Hagerstown. The Regt was out on picket. A Company or two was on post, the balance sleeping. About 2 o'clock in the morning the major roused them up, selected a position, and set them to work to throw up breast works of stone rails and whatever they could get that would turn a ball, telling them that the enemy was advancing, that he heard the artillery. After they had completed the work they found that the sound of artillery moving still continued, and on a more minute investigation they found that it was a waterfall in a creek not far distant. They named the *fort, Fort Terry.* [70]

McGuire has just sent for me to go to his camp, so I must stop till I ascertain his commands. I hope not to take charge at Jordans Springs.

Well, the Dr. only wanted me to have some medical stores turned over.

There is a move on foot—most of the men think we are going back into Maryland. I cant tell. If we had about two weeks to recruit our army and get the men all well clothed, I should think it more probable. If we can go and remain for some months, I shall be pleased. I want to make the North support both armies and I have so little hope of Maryland that I am willing to see her bear a heavy portion of the burden. But I suppose you are tired of so much written about the war.

I went to hear Mr. Lacy preach today.[71] He preached the same sermon that he preached in Blacksburg several years ago on the first Saturday night of protracted meetings he held, the main proposition of which was that what a man most wanted and labored for, he obtained.[72] I was forcibly impressed with it then and was equally pleased with the second discourse, for it is aptly suited to both temporal and spiritual things. I used often to think of it in regard to the education of our children—that if we would make that one of the main objects of our life, we would be successful in having it thoroughly done.

The first thing I think for which we should labour is to secure the salvation of our souls. And as far as our influence and means will permit, that of others. Next the education and moral and religious training of our children, and next to provide such property as will enable us to live comfortably. With all our energies employed to the accomplishments of these objects—and which do not conflict in the least with each other—I think we will prove in our case the proposition of Mr. Lacy to be true & render us, or rather continue us, a happy family.

When at Jordans Sprgs, H. Earhart gave me the Bible (which I hope to preserve) and the socks. I looked for a letter in the leg of the socks, but he said you had given them to him just after he got home. I hope you have gotten the little trunk. I want them (the pants) reduced in size. At least I think they need it for I never tried them on. You need not be in a hurry about it, however. I will try and get another pair to do me until next February when I hope you will have an opportunity to see how they fit. Seven months — may it fly like lightning.

The last letter I recd from you was dated the 2nd. I know there are some on the way. A batch came up today for my men from Guinea, and mine will all come, I suppose, after a while. Direct to 2 Corps Hospital, and they will come to Genl. Ewell's Hd Qrs. All my mail comes through this channel.

McGuire wanted to know the other day how many times I write to my wife. He thinks it is very often.

Dr. Coleman told me today that he got a most disturbing letter from his wife — that she seems to think the Confederacy gone. I hope no such gloomy forebodings have taken possession of you. If so, you do not partake of the feelings of your husband. While I regret the reverses, yet I regard ultimate success as sure. The enclosed scrap expresses my views. [73]

Ed Peck says he saw Bob White several times. [74] I dont know whether I would know him if I should see him. I saw him but once last summer and then but a very short time and afterwards saw a man that I took for him and was mistaken. I will tell Ed if he sees him again to tell him to come and speak to me. I see so many men and come into contact with so many faces that I do not recollect them as I used to.

He told Ed that Lewis was in the 5th Wisconsin Regt of Infantry. This regiment was engaged in this battle. [75]

I did not write to my father's family while in Pa. as I intended. Somehow I dont feel much like corresponding until the war is over. I can only write under great restraint which is but little pleasure to me and but little comfort to them.

Did any of the boys leave an old horse and Rockaway with you? [76] If so, take care of them. They are a present from a "Dare Devil."

I hope you are enjoying a pleasant evening. I imagine you sitting out on the porch or at Grandma's with the children around you, thinking of the rumors you may have heard today & thinking of me and wishing for the day of peace to return. [77] How pleasant to think of requited love—of a home so dear, of affections so constant, of love so precious. May you be ever happy is the constant prayer of your ever devoted husband.

Most affectionately   H Black

Four

"Very Unexpectedly I Find Myself Back at Orange"

September 22-November 25, 1863

A fter Gettysburg, the Army of Northern Virginia returned to central Virginia and the Army of the Potomac followed it, with Lee and George Meade facing each other on the Rappahannock and Rapidan Rivers. Lee sent Longstreet's First Corps to Tennessee and Georgia in September. Ewell's Second Corps and A. P. Hill's Third Corps remained in Virginia. The two months from late September through late November contained no major battles; instead, this was a period of cavalry skirmishes and minor engagements before the end of the active campaigning season in December.

Several of these engagements demonstrated that the Army of Northern Virginia had lost much of its former seeming invincibility. As the letters in this chapter open, skirmishes between J. E. B. Stuart's cavalry and Union cavalry around Liberty Mills and Orange Court House were underway. Reflecting on Confederate cavalry losses, Black wrote on September 23 that the Union cavalry seemed to "get the advantage of our cavalry most of the time." An engagement at Bristoe Station on October 14 led to 1,300 Confederate casualties in A. P. Hill's corps, compared to 548 Union casualties.

The capture of a Confederate bridgehead at Rappahannock Station on November 7 proved to be an unequivocal disaster for Lee's army, sending it back across the Rapidan River. On November 9, Black wrote Mollie, explaining how the military disaster had uprooted him from Lee's headquarters at Brandy Station and brought him and his hospital "unexpectedly" back to Orange Court

House. In the same letter, Black commented extensively on the affair, noting that it was "the result of bad management somewhere."

With the news from the front so unencouraging, it is no wonder that Black's letters turned to other matters. These letters include reports on a cavalry review by Robert E. Lee and the arrival of officers' wives at camp in an attempt to "keep house" during the winter season. Before he was brought back to Orange, Black found time to read a novel and even to complain about boredom. "This is a lonesome place, especially on Sunday," he wrote from Brandy Station on November 1. "No preaching. No ladies. Nothing but soldiers."

Perhaps his boredom that Sunday gave Black the time to pen the most remarkable letter in this chapter — a long love letter in which he affectionately recounted his courtship of Mollie and provided a good deal of information on his own background as well. In language much different from that which he used to describe battles and the wounded, Black recalled the past and looked forward wistfully to continued happiness with Mollie once the war finally was over.

By November 25, his mind was on more pressing concerns, among them the hardships Mollie was facing at home. She must have written him about them, to judge both from Black's comments and from the few letters by Mollie that have survived, letters that date from this period. He wondered if she had enough money, if she was able to get boots for Alex, and if she was still on half rations. "I dont like your being deprived of flour," Black wrote. "Such things have become not only incident to the war, but a part and parcel of it," he philosophized, expressing his frustration that he could do little to make his family's life easier.

Orange C. H.
Sept. 22 1863
My dear Wife—

I recd your letter of the 16th and intended to answer it last night but was prevented. I was delighted to hear from you. I fear this letter may not reach you for 4 or 5 days as it is probable from the indications this evening that the Yankees will reach the Central RR between Gordonsville & Charlottesville. The cavalry and part of the infantry (Yankee) have been fighting most of the day—and as far as heard from Stuart is giving back. They came today near the ford about a mile distant from where we turned back the enemy.

We rode past Genl. Hill's Hd. Qrs. this evening. They are fighting at Liberty Mills, about 3 miles from where we went. The enemy rode out in the direction of Johnson's Division. They seem to get the advantage of our cavalry most of the time. Genl. Lee has sent out Wilcox Division, but the difficulty is that they will not be able to intercept them, and there is a strong probability that they will reach Charlottesville. Our infantry so far has not been fighting further than to skirmish a little, and it is said have entrenchments thrown up at all the fords. There is still a strong probability of a general engagement. We are sanguine of success. [1]

We have rcd the intelligence of the victory of Bragg. How anxious we do feel that it may not turn out as has the good intelligence on former occasions. The victory is saddened by the probable death of Genl Hood. He has been a faithful and brave officer. [2]

I have not much news to write to you. Most of the ladies are gone, and since Ewell's Corps moved to Racoon ford, the town looks lonesome. Tell King that Bob staid all night with me Sunday night. [3] He was getting along very well. Went in to the regiment Monday.

I saw old Mr. Lipscomb today. [4] He was enquiring about you. I think he had on a little tea. He invited me very kindly to come and see him.

I have become acquainted with the family of Mrs. Williamson. [5] She is the mother in law of Dr. Newton, whom you saw. [6] I have been waiting on a sick son and find them very pleasant.

Poor D. H., he seems to be never right—always getting whipped or abused.[7] I dont know whether he is true or not. Maybe he just dont want to fight, but I tell you that the day of retribution is swiftly coming upon those that will not give a helping hand in this our time of need, and they ought to be crushed and ground into powder.

I have just heard from the battlefield. Tis said that we have captured about 150 prisoners, have probably lost some, not many killed. Part of the Yankee force has gone on to Charlottesville, and our force after them. We have just excitement enough here to give a lively turn to conversation, and excite the ladies a little. You know we dont expect the cavalry to suffer much.[8]

Give my love to all the children. I may hear some news by morning and will leave a little space. We expect to be most of the night attending to the wounded that are coming in.

Wednesday morning. No news this morning. No further indications of a general fight. Oh my, how cold my toes got last night—frost this morning. I am reading "No Name," good novel.[9]

My best love to you. How much I do love to think of you and love you, and I long to be with you. Continue to write frequently. Kiss the children for me. Tell them I think of them every day and want to see them very much.

Ever your devoted husband   H Black

....

Brandy Station,
Sunday night, Nov. 1 [1863][10]

My dear Mollie

I rcd a letter today from a very handsome lady to play cupid. Although not accompanied by her likeness yet her image was so indelibly impressed upon my mind that the likeness itself could not recall the features more vividly than they are impressed. I first met her in a village in Western Va when I was about 17 years old and she 8. I afterwards saw her frequently and occasionally was in her company, and nonwithstanding the disparity in our ages, I became so favorably impressed with her fair face and gentle manners that I frequently said to myself that I wished she was older or I younger.

In 3 or 4 years she had grown so much that the disparity in age seemed to grow less. Never did a lady witness the budding of a flower with more requisite pleasure than did I the budding of that pretty little girl into womanhood. She made much of my thoughts while in Mexico and more upon my return home. While at the University of Va., I not infrequently found my thoughts wandering from the dry textbook to contemplate by the aid of memory the features and form of this little girl.

After I completed my studies, I traveled in the west and expected to find a home in some western state, but not finding a place to suit me, together with the persuasions of that fair face, induced me to return.

I entered, as you know, actively into the pursuit of my profession with the determination to make at least a fair reputation and tried to withdraw my thoughts from everything else, but I found this little fairy constantly and pleasantly intruding into all my plans, whether of pleasure or interest. At this period she met me politely and respectfully but seemed to grow more distant, coy & reserved, so that I frequently thought that even the ordinary attentions of common politeness & courtesy were no special source of pleasure to her.

In a few instances when she had arrived at about the age of 15 this shyness and reserve seemed to be forgotten, and I would pass an hour or two in the enjoyment of her company with great pleasure to myself and I imagined with at least satisfaction, if not enjoyment, to her. I began to think that my happiness was identified with hers. I began to pay her special visits or at least seek opportunities by which I might be in her company. I sought her society on pleasure rides and thought it not a hardship to ride 65 miles in 24 hours if part of the time might be spent with her. She always exhibited or observed the decorum of modest reserve which might be construed into neither encouragement nor discouragement.

After the deliberation & reflection which I thought due to a matter which involved my happiness for life, I felt that her destiny and mine were probably intended to be united, and that all the adverse counsel which I could give myself could bring no objections. I felt that I ought both as a matter of duty and happiness give my whole life to her, who for 9 years had had my attention and devotion, though concealed love.

After a few little billets and interviews, and with a full declaration of the love I desired to bestow, I received a measured and loving response and was made most happy in the anticipation of the celebration of the nuptials fixed at some 6 months hence. This time glided nicely & happily, though not too rapidly, away from me. The hours of leisure were spent with her and my visits were always welcomed with that cordial welcome, that maiden modesty, so much to be admired. Tis true that on one occasion she did rest her elbow upon my knee and look with confidential pleasure in my face and made me realize that indeed I had her whole heart.

Suffice it to say, the happy day of our marriage arrived and since then, hours, days, and years of time, confidence & happiness passed rapidly away, and only to make us feel that happy as were the hours of youthful days, they compare not with those of later years and perhaps even these may be not equal to that which is in reserve for us.

I dont know how much pleasure it affords you to go over these days of the past, but to me they will ever be remembered as days of felicity. And how happy the thought that years increase the affection & esteem we have for each other to love & be loved. May it ever be so, and may I ever be a husband worthy of your warmest affections. May I make you happy and in so doing be made happy in return. A sweet kiss and embrace to your greeting.

But maybe you will say it looks ridiculous to see a man getting grayhaired to be writing love letters, so I will use the remnant of my paper otherwise.

I was surprised to hear you say that Crockett McDonald was handsome, for he was one of the ugliest boys that I knew when he was about 10 years old. It is not surprising that we look alike, for he is my double cousin. [11]

I am very glad you have had an opportunity to hear through him from our friends in Wisconsin. I would be delighted to hear of James trading off his farm and going to Missouri. I hope to see the day when I will know that not one of our relatives is in Yankeeland, and I hope Retta may find a more congenial clime. [12]

This is a lonesome place, especially on Sunday. No preaching. No ladies. Nothing but soldiers. I have spent this day in and about the Hospital; however, this morning I went over to Major Harrison's to send him to Staunton (sick) and had a nice plate of oysters. [13] He gave me yesterday a piece of white pudding. I brought it home and gave it to the man we have cooking for us. [14] He looked at and finally cut into it to see what it was made of. He says, "Why, it is stuffed with corn meal." So you may know our cook is not a man of much experience, though we do very well. There is a surgeon on duty with me now who has a servant who is no cook but does our other work.

Dont send Jim Price. [15] He is too much of a rascal. He would soon leave us and steal more than he is worth.

The cavalry moved today, and it it supposed to be on a raid. I will probably add a line in the morning.

Monday morning. Nothing new. The cook spoiled the white pudding. He took it out of the skin & fried & fried. I forgot to tell him how to cook it. Write more frequently. My best love to all.

Yours affectionately   H Black

....

Hospital 2 Corps,
Brandy Station
Nov. 6 [1863]

My dear Wife

I rcd your letter by Tob Robinson this morning. Also rcd one written two or three days before it on the 1st. I was glad to hear from you & glad that Tob brought it, as it relieves Nan. [16] Tell her to inform the Conscript Office of all that are home unnecessarily that they may be sent back.

This is a windy, blustery day. The wind came near baptizing, I mean capsizing, our tent. It blew over Dr. Heagy's bed and [it] is now covered all over with leaves and dust. [17] It is but the foreshadowing of what we will have if we stay here in our tents this winter—which looks now improbable from the winter quarters being built.

I was at a review yesterday of the cavalry by Genl. Lee, the first of this kind that I have witnessed during the war. It passed off pleasantly & handsomely except that 4 men were thrown in a charge and one of them seriously hurt. The force is not as large as I expected to see. A few ladies were out. [18]

Officers are beginning to look out places for their wives. Genl. Ewell brings his own down tomorrow. [19] Mjr. Ballard [20] & Dr. Coleman talk of keeping house. Mrs. Ballard was at the review yesterday. I think they will have a hard time of it.

I was very much pleased at the way in which you answered my love letter, though you do me injustice in regard to the likeness — for I left it not that it was a burden to me to carry it, but for fear that I might lose it — and being the only likeness which we have of our dear little Charly whose life seems so precious [I] would have regretted its loss very much. So you see, you put exactly the wrong construction before it — that is if you are not joking, to which opinion I incline.

I rcd two more letters from Miss Josie T., but I believe I replied to but one — the first one — as you thought it was not necessary to answer the others, as her brother could do so. [21]

I am glad to hear that Dr. Stone has come back — would like if he could be assigned to this army for duty. [22]

Is Dr. Wade at home on furlough, or is he stationed at Christiansburg, examining conscripts. [23] Someone so informed me.

It turns out that the Rev. Mr. Neal who is with me is a distant relation — through the Alexander branch of the family. [24] It was at his father's that Retta staid as she came from the west, and he came with her to Peterstown. [25] He seems to be a good and faithful young man. Mr. Miller came up and took dinner with him today. I think he will make a good chaplain, though not the dictionary that Mr. Lewis was. [26]

I am glad to hear that Alex is getting such a large amount of property on hand. As Kent claims Billy, I suppose he will have to claim the colt, but I think he better not ride the colt till his cousin John works him or uses [him] awhile. [27]

I am sorry to hear that you and your Cousin Lizzy have exhausted all your resources to get cured. Your cases are truly deplorable. You are truly unapproachable and can say "touch me if you dare." [28]

Well, the Major is more fortunate than I, for he has so lately been at home that he ought not to go again for twice 4 1/2 months, but as my time is hardly 1/3 so long, I must, I think, make you less independent and help you. [29]

I have been watching with *unusual* interest the treatment of a case in my tent which, much to my relief, seems to be cured. The case is that of Dr. Eliason, a great big fellow, weighing about two hundred and who, of course, can carry as much itch as almost any body else. [30] The remedy which I think cut it short with him was Fowler's solution, though he used the sulphur ointment for about one week. [31]

If you can not get rid of it by extreme applications, I would commence with five drops on a bread crumb, taken just after eating — and three times a day — increasing one drop a day until you get up to 8 drops, and continue at that for about two weeks unless you find it making you sick at the stomach and causing your eyes & head to pain you when you should reduce the dose to one that you can bear.

This is becoming a a favorite remedy in the army, and I would advise you to use it if you can not get rid of it otherwise. Another suggestion [is] in regard to washing your clothes. It is said the little animal upon which the disease depends can [incomplete]

....

Hospital 2 Corps A. N. Va.

Orange C. H.

Nov. 9, 1863

My dear Wife

Very unexpectedly I find myself back at Orange. On Saturday evening the enemy made an attack on Hays & Hokes Brigades who were in breastworks on the north side of the Rappahannock at the railroad crossing and at Kelly ford on Rodes Division — driving the latter back with the loss of about 60 killed & wounded and 30 or 40 prisoners — and capturing about 1200 of the former, including the wounded (except about 40) & killed, which was probably consider-able as they fought very bravely before surrendering. [32]

This loss has given rise to a good deal of criticism in the army as to where the blame of the misfortune should rest. I understand the

Enquirer has a very severe article condemning in strong terms the Brigadier Generals. This is very unjust, for they are brave men and were merely obeying orders. [33]

So with General Early in whose division these brigades are. I was riding on General Ewell's staff yesterday and heard a good deal of talk among the various officers, and the conclusion I came to was that it rests between the engineer who planned the works and Genl. Lee. Genl. Early and many others say the former.

The fault was that the enemy could have an enfilade fire upon our troops and could not be seen until within fifty yards of the works. Others say that they can not see any reason why our troops were on that side of the river at all. Be all this as it may, it was quite an unfortunate affair for us and the result of bad management somewhere.

The whole army was ordered to fall back, which they did Saturday night to within two miles of Culpeper C.H. where a line of battle was formed Sunday morning. The men threw up a long line [of] breastworks, and it is surprising how soon and how well this work was done. Our men have fought so much & so often that they seem to be very familiar with their duties. Besides, they have learned to do that which will preserve their lives.

The throwing up of these breastworks was only a ruse on the part of Genl. Lee to give him time to get all the sick, wounded & stores to the rear. About 2 o'clock the enemy came in sight and halted, except some cavalry who came unexpectedly upon the infantry on the extreme left and were well punished. About sundown large fires were built up along the whole line, and the retreat resumed, the troops nearly all crossing the Rapidan before daylight.

All are now occupying the same positions they did before we commenced the campaign just one month ago. The general impression now is that we are stationed for the winter unless the Yankees advance, and if they do this that we will fight them hard in this favorable position.

I have gotten a very comfortable room in the upstairs of the frame house attached to the hospital. Dr. Heagy and Mr. Neal are my roommates. Drs. Magruder, [34] Eliason & Wilkerson [35] in an adjoining room—the latter now at home on furlough. There was a great rush here today for rooms, and I believe I succeeded better than most any one else.

Henry came back this evening and asked me to take him again, which I did—and glad to get him, for there is a vast difference between a bad cook & a good one. [36]

I saw Mr. Lipscomb in the street, and he enquired as usual about the Madam.

If I had a good place to put a tent, I believe I would rather be in it, for I feel that I am already taking cold, though it may be from the exposure of the last two nights, and by lying in a cold room at Genl. Early's Hd Qrs last night on the floor with any bedding but my overcoat & saddle blanket. Between short rations, loss of sleep & [missing word] I was in fine plight for a good sleep tonight.

I was with Major Palmer most of the day yesterday, and he is very well. My love to all.

Ever yours,   H Black

....

Orange C. H.
Nov. 25, 1863

My dear Wife

I rcd your letter written on Sunday this evening, and as a week had not intervened since the last I presume you have gotten over your attack of the Blues and concluded to go on in the "same good old way."

I never was an advocate for this periodical letter writing; it looks too much like a business transaction instead of a pleasure. And the letters are too much like those that commence with "I take my pen in hand to inform you that I am well, hoping these few lines may find &c." There is more head than heart about these. Is it not so? & cant you write best when you feel like talking to me and not from a mere sense of duty. I feel that the spirit moves me every 3 or 4 days, and like the Quakers I then have to write regardless of the remark that we write more letters to each other than any other couple.

I dont like your being deprived of flour. I had hoped that during my absence those who had supplies would furnish my family with what they could eat at the market price. I ask it for nothing less. And as the General's memory serves him so badly, I would not renew the application for this or other articles. [37] At the same time, I would not manifest the slightest concern on the subject towards him. Such things have become not only incident to the war, but a part and parcel of it.

If you have difficulty in getting the flour closer [to] home, write a note to Major Kent and say to him that I asked you to request him to furnish what you might need. [38] And if he has it, I am sure he will let you have it.

How much money have you? If you have not enough, ask your Uncle Ed for what you need, and I will replace it when I go home or sooner if I have an opportunity to send it. Did you get the boots for Alex.

That pitiful legislature which we had might have saved our people much trouble and suffering, but they were afraid of *the Mighty people*. They were a body of men unequal to the emergency, and I expect but little from them when they meet again but to devise some means by which they can commute their pay by disparaging Confederate money. [39]

We are again under orders to be ready to move at a moment's notice. The enemy has been making some demonstrations at Ely's ford, and it is said some have crossed the river. This ford is near Chancellorsville, and it may be that another battle may take place in that Wilderness Country. It is thought by many that Meade will be compelled to fight to satisfy his government. Our men are in good spirits, and if we fight we expect a victory. [40]

Dr. Wilkerson returned last night. I look for Dr. Heagy tomorrow, and then our mess will be full again.

Your dream, if realized, would be a great pleasure to me, and my part of it I hope to enjoy ere the winter passes off.

I went round to see Mrs. Lipscomb this evening, but she was not at home. I have not called on her yet but must do so.

I hope Charly will be well when I go home this time that I may hear him talk and sing.

Mr. Neal preached a good sermon tonight. If he will study, he will make a good preacher.

Give my love to all the children. I want to see them very much. I hope they are growing up to be good & affectionate children, loving and obeying their Ma, and learning to read and write.

Hoping that you are no longer on half rations and may continue to get along well, and that you will save me a mess of sausage and no worst, I remain your ever devoted husband.

Many sweet kisses to you.   H.B.

Monday morning. No news from the front this morning.

Mary Kent Black

Five

"I Tell You I am Tired of Such Work"

The Home Front,
November 29-December 22, 1863

W ith this group of letters, the scene shifts to the home front. Although the community of Blacksburg is often in the background in Harvey Black's letters, Blacksburg and its citizens take center stage in these three letters of Mollie Black. For Mollie and her four children — Kent, Lizzie, Alex, and Charly — the four years of Civil War were years of privation and hardship. Like thousands of other women in the Civil War, North and South, Mollie suddenly had to fend for herself, raising a family and running a household on her own. Harvey Black wrote that he wanted to make Mollie "less independent" and help her, but there was little he could do to supply foodstuffs and clothing for his family in an economy marked by rampant inflation and shortages of necessities.

The three letters Mollie Black wrote between November 29 and December 22 speak in a rough eloquence all their own about the strains this independence caused her. Not polished like her husband's letters, Mollie's letters often seem more heartfelt. Where Harvey Black would later write in a droll manner of his desire to keep his family "clothed and fed at least according to Confederate fashion," Mollie wrote movingly of her attempts to get coffee, meat, and shoes for her children. In a letter written shortly before Christmas 1863, Mollie complained about the burdens the war was causing her. "I tell you I am tired of such work," she wrote on December 22. "I wish the war was over, & then I will pay more attention to such matters & be ready for the next war." She also wrote about her desire for peace. "When will it end?" she asked on November 29. "I think something must be done before spring to bring peace."

Mollie Black's letters reflect a sadness that must have been nearly chronic. Her husband commented from time to time on his desire to cheer her up, and on November 25, 1863 (just before Mollie's letters begin) he wrote that he hoped she had gotten over her "attack of the Blues." Apparently she had not; for on November 29, Mollie began a letter to her husband saying: "This has been a long, lonesome day to me. I have not even been to the front door." Later in the same letter, she wrote that all the children except Charly, her youngest, had gone to church, leaving her alone and lonely. Still, Mollie had visitors — townspeople who would come chat with her for an hour or two about the course of the war, passing along news of Blacksburg soldiers and rumors of battles and troop movements. And because her husband had been surgeon of the Fourth Virginia and still retained close ties to the regiment, she too must have been a source of news on local soldiers. In his letters to his wife, Black often gave her reports about soldiers from home, welcome news about those that were doing well and sad news of the wounded or dead.

During the month in which these letters were written, the community of Blacksburg was especially attuned to news of the war, because the war had arrived at its doorstep. Union cavalry leader William Averell, based in West Virginia, had recently made two attempts to destroy the facilities of the Virginia and Tennessee Railroad in Southwest Virginia. The most recent of these attempts had taken him to Salem, some 30 miles from Blacksburg. Though Averell did not invade Blacksburg, its citizens feared he would. On December 18, Mollie noted that she and the children had slept in their clothes the night before, "expecting the Yankees in every moment."

These are the only letters we have from Mollie Black, and their very existence may stem from the threat of Northern invasion. Mollie mentioned several times that normal mail service had been interrupted, and she indicated that one of her letters had been returned to her. It may be that none of these three letters ever reached her husband — that they all were returned to her. If that is so, she may have kept them along with the letters that Harvey Black wrote her. Whatever the reason for their survival, the letters provide testimony that for many women who were left behind the home front had its hardships no less harsh than those faced by the men in the field.

....

Blacksburg
November 29, 1863
My dear Husband,

This has been a long, lonesome day to me. I have not even been to the front door. I have read a good deal & took a nap after dinner. I was waked by someone asking if I was at home. I jumped up & found it was old brother Spickard, so we chatted for an hour & a half about things in general. [1]

Uncle Joe [2] came in & read me a letter from Pollie Gilmore giving a description of how the Yankees had treated them. They took everything she had. He is going to send for her & her children. They took about $7,000 worth from the old lady & Oscar. [3]

Aunt Mary made me a present yesterday of 8 1/2 lbs. of tallow. [4] I was very much surprised, but I tell you it came in good place for I was about out.

Bill Payne called to see me last night. [5] He told us that Gen. Ewell was dead. I hope it is not so as there has been nothing of it in the papers. He said he heard a Col. say he died on Wednesday. [6]

E. Anderson preached here today. [7] All that heard him say it was a fine sermon. He bore down on the extortioners.

All the children but Charly have gone to church, so I feel lonely. He talked to me as long as he could. This is the first time Alex has gone out at night. I think I will venture out tomorrow night as I do not itch & I have stopped rubbing with sulphur. The f.t. does not give me any uneasiness in my stomach. [8] My head feels full sometimes & my face is swollen, so I have reduced the dose to five drops.

This is a cold night. I have a fire in both rooms, & it is not too warm now; how you do in tents I cant imagine.

Payne said you were moving towards Fredericksburg, that all the stores were sent to Gordonsville, so we may expect to hear of some fighting soon. [9]

Dec. 1st

Tuesday night. I have just returned from church & as Mr. Lybrook & Cull Spickard start after the remains of Capt. Evans I thought I would add a few lines to the letter I began on Sunday. [10] I feel anxious to get a letter from you since the fight. I received one yesterday written on your departure from Orange. [11] We heard Capt. Wade was wounded & we feel anxious to hear from Ed & the other boys. [12]

I hope we may still continue to whip the Yankees there for they gain ground at every other point. It is reported here that Gen. Echols is retreating again & Col. McCauslin has left the Narrows & gone towards Lewisburg to reinforce him. [13]

When will it end? I think something must be done before spring to bring peace. Mr. Earheart was here about two hours today talking about the war. [14] He says he is about on half rations. If such farmers as he begin to complain, what will become of the poor & widows.

Our meeting is growing in interest. There have been 8 or 10 converts among the whites & as many blacks. [15] Nan T., [16] Ida A., [17] Phone Surface, [18] & a Miss Bodelle from New Market [19] are seekers.

I got me a splendid pair of shoes yesterday. Mr. Shief made them for Lizzie Palmer & they were too small, so I furnished calf skin for her a pair & took them. [20]

Alex has not got his boots yet, but Mr. Carden says he will try to get them next week for him. [21] He wears a pair of Kent's old last winter shoes that just keep his feet off the ground.

I have about $300 on hand that will last me some time.

Uncle Will Peck is trying to buy Charles Taylor's farm in Craig. Uncle Ed has been talking of buying Daniel Hoge's if he sells & Peck was to take his. [22] I think it is only mind work with all of them.

The Misses Peterman left the city today to spend the winter with Daniel. [23]

I saw Luster at church. He missed the fight. [24]

Oh my, it is so cold. I almost froze last night between Nan & Alex [and] I hope to rest better tonight. [25]

Goodnight my dearest. Ever your devoted & affectionate wife.

Wednesday — All are well & send much love to you.

Ever yours, Mollie

....

Blacksburg
Dec. 18th, 1863

My dear Husband,

I suppose you have heard of the raid into Salem. There has [been] the greatest excitement here for two days. Last night we all slept in our clothes, expecting the Yankees in every moment. I think the hard rain Providence sent kept them back as the creek was so much swollen they could not cross. The last news is they have crossed Craig's Creek. [26]

I hope Imboden may bag them, or Gen. Echols. He is at Sweet Springs. Col. McCauslin is at Fort Harris on the Gap Mountain; the latter might have caught them if he had gone up Sinking Creek last night, but he had been on the march for two days & his men were broken down. [27] I have a poor opinion of all this Western army.

We hear various estimates of the damage done in Salem, but all exaggerated very much. I expect it will be a month or more before the cars run. [28]

I hope we will get a mail soon. The time seems so long. I got all your papers & silver & packed them. Arch said he would take them with him. Uncle Will & Tom Evans left with the hack last night about 11 o'clock. [29] If the cowardly Yankees get away safely, we may expect them back any time. The children were very much frightened.

I am so sleepy I can scarcely write, but as it will take so long now for letters to pass, I thought I must write. I am anxious to get your reply in regard to selling the house. I think we better let it go. [30]

I hope we may have a mail tomorrow. I heard that Lac Miller had a letter from his son [31] stating that I. Hess Hymen, [32] E. Peck [33]

& himself were all prisoners & well. Did not learn where they were.

Old Mr. Davis is very low. [34] Also Henry Dobbin. He has brain fever. The Drs. think he must die. [35]

Brother Spickard called to see me tonight. He is a good deal excited. I will write again in a few days.

Saturday — All well, but it is dreadful cold. Good bye.   Mollie

Major Kent sent me eight bushels of wheat, said he had taken it from his own supply. [36] John Keister [37] let me have five & says [if] I can get his note from Giles Henderson from Mitchels [38] papers he will spare me some more.

How much I would like to see you tonight. I have your likeness in my packet. I thought the Yanks should not get it. Accept my best love.

Ever your devoted wife.

....

Blacksburg
Dec. 22, 1863

My dear Husband,

I wrote you on last Saturday & sent the letter to Christiansburg & the boy lost it. Mr. Robinson found it & gave it to me. [39] We have not had a mail for a week, so you can imagine how anxious we are for letters & papers. I am afraid Arch will not go in the morning. He is so vexed because he cant get hay & corn. I feel sorry for him.

I spent the day with Mrs. Green King. [40] Aunt Judy & Nannie were there. [41] We had a pleasant time.

Tonight I have been preparing the raisins for my mince pies. I get my beef tomorrow. I told Uncle Ed this morning I was glad I did not have it when we were expecting the Yankees. Tis reported they got away without a fight. About 800 were captured.

Jim Henderson went out after them & he was tight & was taken prisoner. [42] He was riding one of Uncle Ed's horses & had a fine pistol of Mr. Alexander's that Aunt Mary loaned him. [43] His mother is in great distress, but she ought not to say a word for he got the liquor from her.

It was reported that Giles Thomas was a prisoner, but he has come in.[44]

Col. Linkous got some coffee & sugar.[45] I do wish I had been close to the coffee; I would have taken a paper for I am tired of substitutes.

Arch says he dont want me to sell the garden — that he will give $200 for it. That is not enough. I think if I can get $2,500 for the house, we better take it & keep the garden. We can rent it to them, & you & Arch can fix it when you come home.

Jim Linkous made Lizzie Bell a pair of shoes, & he is going to make Alex a pair tomorrow.[46] He will get them for Christmas. I am thankful to Jimmy for I could not get any one else even to promise them till after New year. Jim is a young hand. He has only made three pair, but he makes them very nice.

Uncle Will got back last night with the bank.[47] Bird Linkous was after me this evening for a list of accounts & hands.[48] I shall get John Black to help me fix them up. I tell you I am tired of such work. I wish the war was over, & then I will pay more attention to such matters & be ready for the next war.

The wind is rising tho the moon is shining beautifully. We have a prospect of another cold night. I thought I would freeze Saturday & Sunday night. Tis going on eleven, & I must soon close.

Miss Nannie Preston asked after you this evening & sends her respects.[49] I wish you a pleasant Christmas & plenty of good things to eat. Kent is very sorry the railroad is out of fix. He was full of taking a trip home.

Wade was here Tuesday. He had been over to New Castle after the Yankees. His arm is quite sore, but he says he could not stay at home.[50]

I thought we were all rid of the scratch, but the children were complaining again.

That was a false report about Miller getting a letter from his son.

Oh, how much I wish you were here tonight. The little ones send much love & say Christmas to Pa. Give my respects to inquiring friends. Accept much love for yourself from your ever devoted Wife. Do write soon.

Wednesday. Well, everything has been excited again today. This morning before day we got word that the Yankees had burnt Tom Jones' house & were coming on, burning everything. [51]

Uncle Will in a hurry. Word was sent to Christiansburg. Col. Wade came over with his men & staid about two hours & went home. [52] Bob Peck went to Roanoke & heard from Jim Brown [53] that six Yankees had been at Mrs. Jones'. Tom was not at home. They took all her flour, meat, blankets & some beans & Capt. Evans' uniform. They told her they would not harm her this time but would make another visit.

I think if the 150 men had gone down through the mountains, they might catch them. [54] Wolf has been hollered so often, they cant believe what they hear. Seven were left at Uncle Ed's to carry dispatches if any news came.

Grandma as usual started down to see Aunt Cook before day & fell down near where she broke her leg & had hurt her arm. She contends it is broken in the elbow. She has suffered very much today & has been in bed all day.

Charly is mad today. He says if he ever was a man, he would kill all the Yankees, soldiers & the Government too, so his Pa could come home.

Arch started for a mail today but heard there was none & come back. My eyes hurt me so I must close. Good bye. I opened this after I sealed it.

Ever yours, Mollie

Six

"This War With All its Troubles
Will Leave Some Pleasant Reminiscences"

January 29-May 3, 1864

T he Army of Northern Virginia spent the winter of 1863-64 on the south side of the Rapidan River. Opposite it on the river's north side, only a few miles away, was the Army of the Potomac. The winter was an exceptionally cold one and food shortages in Lee's army became chronic. Black contended that spirits remained high, writing that the soldiers "do not mourn & will endure anything for the cause."

The Second Corps Field Hospital, functioning as a receiving hospital accepting patients from the regiments, spent the winter at Orange Court House. Camp life must have been both monotonous and grueling. John Apperson complained of the tedium on January 25: "We are now having a life similar to that of the frozen reptiles — no variations."[1] Four days later he noted that he had made out the weekly statements on patients that day. Ninety-six men had been received and seventeen had died during the previous week. "The mortality is very heavy," he observed.[2]

Apart from infrequent skirmishes, the two armies had no engagements against each other during these months. Behind the seeming quiet, however, was preparation for the spring campaigning season that would begin with the Battle of the Wilderness in early May. Lincoln put Ulysses S. Grant in control of all Federal armies in March, and Grant chose to make his headquarters with the Army of the Potomac in Virginia. Lee brought Longstreet back from East Tennessee and Georgia to rejoin the Army of Northern

Virginia. With only 64,000 troops matched against 115,000 Union soldiers, Lee was fighting against strong odds. Still, he remained a bulwark of hope. "If any man felt despondent," Harvey Black wrote in early May, "he would be revived by [Lee's] very manner and expression of countenance as he promenades in front of his tent."

During these winter months, Harvey Black found time to socialize with the citizens of Orange, to think back about the pleasantries of the past, and to have his son Kent, then 10 years old, visit him at camp. As always, Black remained upbeat, thinking more about the past and future than the grim present. The education of his children remained a priority for him. He praised Mollie for teaching the children at home and drilled Kent on mathematics and grammar during his visit. Thinking of the times he had been with his wife and children, he wrote that "these are green spots in this desert of war—joys past but joys recalled." The war "with all its troubles" would eventually end, he reasoned, leaving some "pleasant reminiscences" behind it.

The time for quiet recollection, however, would not last. On April 1, Black noted that the men were "beginning to look anxiously for the campaign to open & indications look towards the great struggle being in Virginia." As Black's May 3 letter indicates, both armies were actively preparing for a battle that looked like it might take place in the thickly-wooded region called the Wilderness. "It is mean country to fight in," Black wrote, "but not worse for us than them."

....

Orange C. H.
January 29, 1864
My dear Wife

I received your letter written on Sunday & Monday in due time and was pleased to hear that you had regained your spirits and [were] getting along so well, and I hope such will be your good fortune until the year rolls round for us to be together again. I have been so busy since I came back that I have my thoughts mostly engaged about my work. But when the day's work is over, there is nothing so pleasant to me as to turn my thoughts homeward and think of the happy enjoyment I have had with my dear wife and children.

We are all in good spirits & as you will see by the papers, all the forebodings of our men leaving the army in the spring was nothing but in the fancy of the desponding creatures that are always ready to have us subjugated.

Another campaign to Pa. in the summer is frequently spoken of and although the men have really wanted for a full supply of food, yet since that beautiful order of Genl. Lee's they do not mourn & will endure anything for the cause. [3]

No one complains of my stay over the proper time, though my QrMaster did not come off so well, as his case is now under investigation for the same offense. [4] I told McGuire I had numerous excuses to offer if necessary, but he did not require them. Drs. Heagy & Magruder did not care. The former started yesterday.

Tell Mrs. Camper that if I can get the articles for her, I will do so, but I think it is likely that I will be unable to do so. [5] She had better send by someone to Lynchburg or Richmond. I have been trying for months to get red [illegible] but cannot.

I think we are both good at running a blockade. You have conjured through and escaped the torment of your life, and I have escaped what would be the plague of my life while it lasted, the itch. I really congratulate you. Indeed, I do.

So you will come and see me next summer. Are we not favored.

I am sorry to hear Arch is fretted about the garden, but let him alone; he will come out right at last. He will make the deed when he reflects over it. The weather is like summer. What a nice time it would have been for you to move. [6] I would tell Joe that you would prefer to move in March, if the weather will permit. Unless you hurry him a little he may not move until after Aunt Mary is sick, and then it might be later in the Spring. [7]

I went to see Mrs. L[ipscomb] a few days ago. She made numerous enquiries about you. It is the only place I have been since I came back except once to Mr. Chapman to see a sick daughter. [8]

I must go to see Mrs. Newton soon as the Dr. insists on it. [9] I have not seen King since Sunday. I will ride out in two or three days if I have time.

I wrote to Mr. Amiss today on business. When you have chance, ask your Uncle Will Wade if your Uncle Peck has just asked him to write in regard to ship[ping] stock to Osborne at Petersburg and if he has done so.[10]

Give my love to the children and tell them candy is scarce. Tell your Aunt Cook that I hope that she is up again. I have been about half sick all evening from trying to help eat a greasy goose for dinner. I thought I could eat anything, but I cant go for old goose.

My best love to you. May time fly away that I may be with you again.

Your devoted   H Black

....

Orange C. H., Va.
Sunday Feby 7, 1864

My dear Mollie

This is rather a dull Sunday to me as there is no preaching. And I feel like talking to you a while, both to pass off the time and to answer your letter of the 3d which I rcd Friday.

We had a little excitement this morning from an unexpected advance of a Cavalry force to the Rapidan, 3 or 4 miles from town and some cannonading & infantry firing which commenced about 7 o'clock this morning and continued about two hours, and we hear now at a great distance an occasional shot. It is said to be Kilpatrick's division, but we do not think it will amount to much.[11]

On yesterday evening the enemy crossed some force at Morton's ford, but I have learned went back this morning. The Stonewall Brigade was on picket at that place, but as no wounded have yet been brought to the Hospital, it is presumed that there was little fighting. Our forces are so distributed along the line of the Rapidan that it will be very difficult for the enemy to cross at any point that Genl. Lee does not elect.

I was sorry your mails are so irregular for I know the annoyance of not receiving a daily paper and letters when they are expected. As neither your Uncle Ed nor Joe have been here, I suppose they have returned home. I would have been glad to have seen them.

I am glad to hear that you have resumed the teaching of the children, for it is the only thing that I feel anxious about at home for

I think in every other respect you all get along remarkably well, and I feel perfectly satisfied for you to be their teacher so long as you can give your time and attention to it, and there is nothing that will repay you so well for the care and labor in the end.

I must stop for dinner.

Dinner over—and a good one. We had roast beef, potatoes (Irish), barbecued partridges, sweet potatoes, butter, molasses, & sweet potato pie. A good "Bill of Fare" aint it.

It would do you good to see Lacy eat when we are having something good. Genl. Early says that when he has a good dinner before him and says Grace, his language is, "Lord, we thank thee for thy many blessings. Fill our hearts with gratitude, etc." When he has bread, meat & water, he says, "Lord bless us & save us. Amen." [12] Be that as it may, he evidently enjoys a good dinner, and on such occasions is loquacious & interesting.

I am glad to hear Bob has gotten a contract. [13]

If you see Mrs. Noah Kipps, say to her that I will try to ascertain what has become of John, though it probably will require several weeks to get an answer. [14] I think I can ascertain through the Commissioner of Exchange.

I received yesterday evening from Mrs. Williamson a presen[t] of a very nice pair of woolen gloves—garmitts. [15] She is an old lady that I like very much for her intelligence, good sense & goodness. I called to see the family a few evenings since and spent a very pleasant hour; & by the bye, she has a daughter who did me the honor to say that when she needed an escort to church she would invite me to accompany her. We were talking about the preaching of Mr. Lacy and she said she was sorry that she had been able to hear him but once for the want of company. I was deprecating the lack of gallantry of the gentlemen and told her Dr. Clagget was certainly not aware of it, or he would have tendered his services. [16] (He is a married man & great gallant.)

She said she had thought of writing a note to Dr. B. but did not know that it would meet his favor. Of course I told her that it would afford me great pleasure. Her sister, Mrs. Newton, laughed at her for being so bold in her requests, but she replied to her that she would not ask a young gentleman for any favor but that she had a perfect right to call upon a married gentleman for favors and certainly to escort her to church. She is not very young nor very handsome but sprightly and said to be admired by Genl. Johnson.

I called the same evening to see Mrs. Payne & her sister, Miss [blank]—I forgot her name.[17] I likewise spent an hour at the Epsicopal parsonage, Mr. Hansborough's, though this was a professional call.[18]

One of the most dashing ladies that I have seen is the wife of Dr. Higgenbotham who has charge of A. P. Hill's Corps Hospital. The Dr. is sick, and I have made him several friendly calls.[19] She was a Miss Haxall, of Richmond.[20] She talks well but has an obliquity of one of her eyes which is said by the observing to be a pretty sure index of some moral or mental obliquity, and I think the rule will hold good in this case.[21]

This morning she was a good deal disturbed that her husband was wearing a colored shirt. She said she did dislike them so much. I told the Dr. that almost the only time that I wore white shirts was when I was with my wife—that she, like Mrs. H., was not fond of seeing colored shirts; but, I presume you never thought of objecting to their use for the reasons she gave. She said, "it looked so much like a mechanic." Her manner in connection with the remark revealed very fully the supreme contempt she entertained for an honest labouring man and made me feel for that sentiment as much contempt as her words and manner expressed.

I wonder if the day will ever come when a man will be appreciated for his real worth rather than for the circle of life in which he happens to be born. It is to be hoped that the time will come when moral worth & mental attainments will govern the positions which men may hold in society rather than the accidents of birth, and while I would not build up one part of society at the expense of another, yet I should regret to see that state of refinement in society when I or any other man would be lowered in the estimation of his friends by appearing in the garb of a mechanic. They are not the men who as a class have hired substitutes and been speculators in this war.[22]

But dont think that this woman threw me into a passion by her aristocratic remark. But I only speak of these things as to the importance of properly teaching our children what constitutes a real gentleman.

Well, I see one wounded man has come in from the Stonewall Brigade, and I must go and see about him. The man wounded is a Mr. Webster, of 33 Va. Infy. [23] He says he does not think any other man in the Brigade was wounded and that they killed several Yankees and drove them back.

A. P. Hill's troops that went to the river this morning are returning as the affair is considered over.

We have heard that Major General Breckinridge has been assigned to the command of the department of S. Western Va. & Col. Jones relieved. [24] I hope it is true. I have confidence in Breckinridge and think he would produce a favorable reaction.

I will leave a space to add a line in the morning—no, I had better not for I might not get it in the mail in time. I have not seen King since I wrote to you last. I may go to see him again during this week.

Tell Kent not to become impatient for it is nearly 6 months until August, and then we have to take the chances of the army being quiet—and which I hope it will be. For I will be delighted to spend some time with you again as pleasantly as when you were here last summer.

This war with all its troubles will leave some pleasant reminiscences, and this will be over to us; but all our reminiscences whether during the war or before are pleasant, when we have had the opportunity to be together and so I think it always will be. I want to see you all the time, but I will wait patiently your cheerful coming—even to deprive myself of the pleasure in future of going to meet you.

My best love to all the children, and accept for yourself the most tender affection of one who loves you most fondly and devotedly.   H Black

Monday morning. Just as I was finishing this letter yesterday evening, Dr. Newton sent for me to come and see his child baptized. I went, afterwards, took Miss Sally Williamson to church and proposed to go with her whenever she needed an escort. [25]

Write soon.

Tell Mrs. Carden that I cannot get the articles here that she wants. [26]

···

Orange C. H.
Mch. 24, 1864

My dear Wife

I write you a few lines this morning to let you know of the safe arrival of Kent & Bob. [27] They reached here about dark last night, being detained by the heavy fall of snow, which is about 15 inches deep here. The money is all right, and I will return the bond by Bob. Kent was very sleepy last night. He went to bed early and slept until I aroused him this morning sometime after sunrise.

He has been washing & combing & dressing as if he was going to visit ladies. I will try and give him a ride on Billy today and make his stay as pleasant as possible. I was surprised indeed to see him but am glad that he has come. I will answer your letter in two or three days as I only have time this morning to write you this note.

My love to all the children at home, and accept for yourself my most devoted affection.   H Black

···

Orange C. H.
April 1, 1864

My dear Wife —

I received your letter of the 30th this evening and will write you a short letter in reply, though I believe I am without a single incident of note to relate. Kentie is busy all the time nearly engaged in riding or running about. He went to camp yesterday and brought up Bob who has been before the Board & is awaiting the action upon his papers. He says they have recommended him for detail at some post. He may be able to get a contract for tanning, though I do not think his papers are arranged in the best way for that purpose.

Col. Gardner staid with me last night on his way to the army. I suppose he will be placed on the retired list. [28]

I rode out today to hear Gov. Vance speak, but it rained so that he postponed it until tomorrow. He has been speaking to large audiences of soldiers for several days. [29]

Had I have known your Uncle Ed had as much as $1200 to turn over, I would have made another disposition of it, but it does not matter very materially. I suppose we are brought now to the necessity of living off my salary as we are so nearly out of money, but dont be uneasy. I will keep you clothed and fed at least according to Confederate fashion. I will send by Bob or Kent $50 or more in small notes which I have gotten.

Kent went today to witness the execution of a deserter. I will leave him to tell you about it.

I am anxious to hear about John whether he was a prisoner in our lines or the Yankees. [30] Did Ed write to my father's people? [31]

It continues to rain, and the water courses very high. We are beginning to look anxiously for the campaign to open & indications look towards the great struggle being in Virginia. Rumors are rife of Longstreet's return to our army. If so, we will be stronger than ever before, and I think can defy Grant. [32]

I am very sorry to hear you have such a cold. I am nearly well again—only cough occasionally. Give my compliments to Giles H[enderson], and tell him he better turn his horse over to the Artillery—that he dont suit for cavalry. I cant help but laugh to imagine how he who was always so fond of a fine horse looks on a shaved mane and tail. [33]

We are going to be reduced to the smallest amount of transportation, and I may have to send some things home. Dont send me anything in the way of clothes.

How has Ed Black gotten. [34] Dont take any $5 notes if you can help it for they will depreciate rapidly in the next month.

As you can see I am writing at random. Dont know what to write unless I change this into a love letter, which would be in bad taste with such a preface.

Henry Earhart is getting better. Has been sitting up some to-day. I am almost glad he has had this attack, for he had been well so long and looked so stout that I was getting uneasy for fear he would be taken from me, but I think he is safe now for 12 months longer at least. I dont [know] how I would supply his place.

Continue to write me frequently for it affords me so much pleasure to hear from you. If it is only a few lines, it makes me better contented. I will finish in the morning. All are asleep.

Saturday morning. Snowing and cold.

Monday. No news this morning. Kentie well and eating taffy. He says kiss Charly for him, that he is well and dont know when he will be at home. My love to all.

Yours devotedly   H.B.

....

Orange C. H.
April 6, 1864
My dear Wife

I received your letter of the 3d this evening and will take pleasure in answering it, for I was wishing for it to come.

The spirit of dancing seems indeed rife in Blacksburg and vicinity, and I suppose W. Bell feels that he is quite a hero. But I can excuse a little vanity for he will feel an additional obligation to fight gallantly in the coming struggle, and I doubt not he will acquit himself like a man. [35]

Where was Dr. Rice from? I would rather you would send Lizzie to Miss Norvell if she will take her on anything like reasonable terms. [36]

Kentie has been reading some to me and reads better than I expected. Indeed, I think you are successful in your teaching, and I can already see the benefit derived in the lessons he has taken in mental arithmetic. Mr. Bell has been asking him some catch questions, and he did very well in his answers. [37]

I have been trying to correct him in some of his expressions— such as "them horses," "they is," and jist so & so. He caught at the corrections very quickly.

He is very obedient and is not rude considering how much he is teased. The boys tease him about Minnie Humphrey. [38] He borrowed money yesterday & bought a bridle bit and head stall. He rides all the horses to water. Dr. Heagy fell down with him on a bridge, but he did not get hurt.

He went with Bob to the Regt today and is now fast asleep in my bed. He slept with Bob several nights and I think thought a little hard that I did not take him in my bed, which I avoided until I got my sheets washed.

At last he wanted to know why I did not put the two beds together. I told him I had a narrow bed because I did not like for people to sleep with me. He thought I was alluding to him and said if he had known that he would not have come to see me. I told him I meant strangers & that he could sleep with me that night, and he has been sleeping with me since and says he likes to sleep with me better than with Bob.

He told me to tell you that he would probably be at home the last of next week, and if not, then he did not know when. I dont know why he fixed that time.

If you see Mather Aiken again, tell him that I would be glad to meet him and to hear that he had settled in our town. [39] He is, or at least used to be, an excellent man and would be an acquisition to the place, and if they came, I would like for you to visit them.

I am glad to hear that your brother John is on our side. If released, why can you not hear from him? To what command is he attached? [40]

I cannot say that I was very much pleased with the widow — further than to pass off half an hour while visiting her son. Her son's boy said she was pleased that I have been so kind to her son and that she said she would send me some cloth when the son returns from furlough. This would please me "very much." [41]

It is Henry Earhart that is sick. He is getting better, now able to walk about the room, and I think will soon be out again. He still suffers a little with his joints.

I would that your dream could be a reality. I would promise to tease you at least as much as you imagined. I was also in the dream land last night and saw bright visions and had sweet kisses. Fly, time, that this "cruel war" may end. Return my love to your Grandma.

Everything indicates preparation for active service about the 1st of May. Genl. Grant's wings have to be clipped, and I think Genl. Lee can do him that honor.

What do you think of the "Miscegenation" going on in the north? [42] The indications from the north are good, but it will require a little time longer for the bitter fruits of fanaticism and abolitionism to ripen. If we even hold our own this summer and be patient, the game is sure. The skies are brighter for us than ever before during the war. May God continue to give us his favor. How joyful to anticipate that 12 months more may close the war. This is probable, though not sure. Whip Grant we must and most probably will.

Bob Peck's papers came back to the regiment today, and he will probably claim them tomorrow. He has been detailed and ordered to report to the Provost Marshal at Liberty. I dont think he intends starting for a few days. He does not know to what duty he will be assigned. [43]

Give my love to the children, and tell them that I want to see them very much. How much I would like to be with you tonight to talk with you. There are so many things I could say to you. I hope you are well of your cough. Mine has nearly left me. And I feel ready for the campaign.

The long, continuous rains and snow have ceased and the evening feels like spring, and most gladly is the spring welcomed, for with it passes away the real and imaginery hardship that have fueled the destitute thing, the winter.

My dear darling, accept the affectionate devotion of your attacked husband. [44] May you have nothing to worry or disturb you more than the anxious solicitude which I know well for those that are absent and dear to you.

Yours in love   H Black

Wednesday morning. Beautiful morning, and all's well. Write soon.

Orange C. H.
May 3, 1864
My dear Wife

I mailed a letter to you Sunday morning, but as your welcome letter of the 29th reached me yesterday, I will write again—it always being a comfort to me to write to you & more to receive yours. And I know how anxiously you are looking for tidings at this time from the army.

In this respect, I know nothing to relate further than that both armies seem to be making some slight movements towards the front and getting everything ready for the mighty conflict which to all human reason seems to be the one to decide the future progress of the war. All the important preparations on our part have been made, and so far as I can learn the minutest details have been observed. A reliance upon the God of battles, a confident and firm determination, together with a feeling that amounts almost to a decision that the fight may commence seems to animate almost every bosom, and with our just cause we feel that the victory is sure.

Burnside's force has joined Grant's, supposed to be about 25,000—and a rumor prevails this evening, which may not be true, that they are concentrating their troops near the river opposite Chancellorsville. The general expectation is that the battle will be fought near that place. It is mean country to fight in, but not worse for us than them. [45]

Genl. Lee is said to express the utmost confidence in our success, and Major Bridgford remarked this evening that if any man felt despondent he ought to visit the Old Chief, and he would be revived by his very manner and expression of countenance as he promenades in front of his tent. [46]

The papers recently have been filled with success, and today again we have good news from Price & N Ca, and we hope to hear soon of the surrender of Newbern. [47]

But I did not intend to write much about the war tonight, and you must excuse me for it is what we talk and think about most of the time.

If I have an opportunity, I will call on your cousin, Will Mastin, though your letter is the first intimation we have had of Buckner's troops coming to join us. [48]

I was of the impression all the time that the case of Dr. Woodville was a remarkable one—if he placed himself in a position to allow such grave charges to be proved upon him. It is easy to make declarations but hard to prove them. [49]

We had a very severe storm here yesterday evening, though I cannot claim that it did much damage further than to blow over 3 or 4 cars on the railroad and to take one of my ambulances about 30 yds and blow the covers off the wagons. It also blew down our cook's tent.

I wrote a letter to Geo. B. and sent it by way of truce. [50] I think it doubtful, however, about my letter going through.

I am glad to hear you are getting along so well with Mrs. Henderson, for although she may have faults, she is a very kind neighbor to those she likes. [51] Give her my regards.

Major P[almer] told me at church that he had some good things for me, and I am only consoled, as I did not get them, by the thought that some poor fellow, perhaps more in want than myself, enjoyed the feast. My kind regards to Lizzie for her instructions to have me participate in the delicacies sent.

I am always glad to hear where you have your garden made as it is the hardest job of spring work. I wish I was with you to prevent the quiet hours from becoming lonesome. I can very well enter into and appreciate your feelings, for I get so sometimes myself—and felt a little of it coming over me tonight, and this is one reason why I am now writing to you. A sure remedy for it is to do something—read, write, talk, work—anything laudable to engage our mental & physical powers.

Though sometimes one of the most agreeable pastimes I have is to get to myself and think of home and its endearments, and I often call to mind some hour or occasion we have enjoyed together which has long since been forgotten as unimportant but which I recall as an incident of peculiar pleasure, and none do I recall with so much gladness as the fleeting days which flew as moments that we have been together since the war began. [52]

In this way may I pass a quiet hour and perhaps not unprofitable, for these are green spots in this desert of war—joys past, but joys recalled. And to me these things—each a useful lesson—that the joys of wedlock pass not away with the "honey moon," but daily give increasing and more refined happiness as time glides on. And if we continue to cultivate these feelings, as I am sure love and esteem will prompt us to do in the future as in the past, so will we be rewarded by days of gladness.

But it is 11 o'clock, the fire out and my room cold, so I must stop my writing, if not thinking, of you and our precious, little children. My dear, dont I sometimes like your writing almost a whole letter about such things as make up this last page? Sometimes I think so, and yet when I judge your feelings by my own, how tenderly I love you, how much I value your love above all things else, and the pleasure it gives me to hear you say that I have it.

I think this is the more welcome than talk about tents & armies & other people. These things I can write to any one, but only to my dear wife can I reveal my thoughts, my feelings, joys, sorrows. A sweet kiss to you & love to the children.

HB (I sent $20 in new issue in my last letter).

Seven

"Good Fortune Attends Me All the Time, and I See No Reason Why it Will Not Continue"

October 8-December 3, 1864

H arvey Black's Civil War letters end where they had begun, in the Shenandoah Valley. Two and one-half years separate the two groups of letters, the first from Jackson's Valley Campaign of 1862 and the second from Jubal Early's Valley Campaign of 1864. The differences between the letters are significant. Black's 1862 letters reflected an optimism that the war would end soon, and with a Southern victory. Over two years later, the war had still not ended, and victory seemed more remote than ever. The war had also changed dramatically in nature. No longer a struggle that simply matched army against army, it had become a total war in which the devastation of the land and the demoralization of the civilian population had become primary goals of both sides. As the letters in this chapter open, Union cavalry were laying waste to much of the lower Shenandoah Valley, burning everything as they retreated northward.

Black now served under Jubal Early, who commanded the newly-named Army of the Valley, containing what was left of the Second Corps. Philip Sheridan commanded Union forces in the Valley. Sheridan and Early had engaged in battle on September 19, at Third Winchester, and Early's forces were driven from the battlefield in defeat. Three days later, at Fisher's Hill, Early was defeated again. Sheridan occupied Harrisonburg before withdrawing northward, burning the countryside in his wake. Early advanced as Sheridan withdrew, reaching Harrisonburg shortly before Black's October 8 letter.

Black's 1864 Shenandoah Valley letters reflected the sense of resignation that was overtaking the Confederate Army. He wrote about stampedes of retreating soldiers and the exhausted country-side which could no longer supply the army. He was anguished over his cousin Ed Black, who was captured by Union forces at Third Winchester. And he wrote about another relative, Floyd J. McDonald, who died in Winchester of wounds received in action two months earlier.

Black managed to focus on some of the lighter moments of his experience, too. This group of letters gives evidence of his skill as a storyteller. He provided a striking character sketch of the irascible Jubal Early, who was "almost amiable" after hearing of Thomas Rosser's success capturing stores in New Creek, West Virginia, in late November. Black's narration of a discussion of the pros and cons of surgeons and quartermasters marrying during the war exhibits his droll wit.

"Good fortune attends me all the time, and I see no reason why it will not continue," Black wrote in a letter that dates from early November 1864. Although being a member of the medical corps offered no assurance against death or maiming by enemy fire, Black went through the war unscathed. Harvey Black would participate in the surrender of the Army of Northern Virginia on April 9, 1865, at Appomattox. After the surrender, he would return to Blacksburg to rejoin the family he had left four years earlier, stronger for the experience he had endured and ready to help rebuild a conquered society as a physician, educator, and hospital administrator.

Harrisonburg
Oct. 8, 1864 [1]

My dear Wife —

We have just reached this place, and will move on to New Market this evening. I learn that our advance passed through that place yesterday evening. We were thrown very much behind the army by having our Hospital at Waynesboro but will probably overtake them tomorrow. [2]

The Yankees commenced their retreat from this place and above on day before yesterday. They are retreating rapidly. There is little prospect of capturing many on the retreat. They seem to have left under the impression that we have received heavy reinforcements. We have now a good cavalry force and may be able to resist an attack — should they make one. [3]

They have burned nearly all the mills and barns, and in the neighborhood of Bridgewater a good many private houses. This was done — the houses — because of an officer being killed near [blank line] — said Apperson. Son of their Qr Master General Meigs. [4]

I have no news to write. Have not yet received any letters. They moved 110 of our wounded from this place. The Drs. of the Hospital are talking all around me about what the Yankees did. [5] Continue to write. I will get your letters after a while. Love to all.

Most affectionately   HB

....

New Market
October 9, 1864

My dear Wife —

I wrote you yesterday from Harrisonburg, and my object in writing today is to enclose a list of names of officers captured at Winchester, and among the list I have the pleasure of seeing the name of Ed Black of the 36 Va. Infy, so that the presumption is that Ed is all safe, though a prisoner. The list is taken from the "Whig" of the 7th. [6]

In answer to your enquiring as to when I first heard he was wounded, I think it was first from Mr. Alexander after we came out of Winchester — and afterwards at Woodstock.[7] Tell King that I will forward his letter to Mrs. Carson with a note explaining what I have seen in regard to his capture.[8] I know she will kindly make the search and write to him.

Before leaving Woodstock, I left a note with Mrs. Magruder[9] for Dr. Love[10] who would [do] all that a friend and a man of his fine professional ability could do. Besides, I have several lady acquaintances who I am sure would give special attention to any wounded relative I might. Among others is a Miss Russell whose brother is on duty with me at the request of his mother.[11] She is giving special attention to Lt. McDonald.[12]

I hope, however, all our fears are groundless and that Ed has gotten off with probably a slight wound.

While I write, we are passing through one of those stampedes with which we are becoming so familiar of late. Rosser drove the Yankees handsomely for two days, capturing some prisoners, horses, etc., but today below Woodstock one of his regiments gave way and for the last hour the road has been filled with cavalrymen, wagons & Negroes going to the rear. I learn that Rosser lost the ordinance wagons of his command & some others wagons probably, but few men.[13]

Our infantry is encamped near this place, and we are making no preparation to move. I hear some one remark outside of the tent that "they say the Yankees are going back."

I had the pleasure to receive last night four letters from you. I came on in advance of the train and staid at Genl. Early's Hd Qrs last night with Major Pitzer.[14] When I found the letters I was well compensated for my ride in getting them. I cant undertake to answer them now as some wounded are coming in, and we have not yet got our Hospital entirely fitted up. Remember me kindly to all.

Dr. Munsie[15] has just returned from Mt. Jackson and says that the Yankees came that far and that the stampede was another of those unnecessary and disgraceful affairs for which there was no reason. I regret that it has occurred with Rosser, for much was expected from him.

Most affectionately & devotedly   H.B.

McGuire rcd a letter from Winchester last night which says the Yankees have 5,000 wounded in Winchester.[16] So we hurt them badly. We left between 500 & 600 of which 175 were from previous fights.

....

[undated, ca. November 4-8, 1864][17]

Dear Mollie —

I sent by Dr. Templeton $200 to hand to you.[18] Have you money enough to buy what you want? If not let me know. I have more on hand.

Perfect quiet exists in our army though it is reported that the 6th Corps has been sent to H[arper's] Ferry.[19] It is thought that we will move down through the valley again before going into winter Qrs. but our stay can not be long as the country is too much exhausted to supply our army.

Gilmore serves [as] my chauffeur though evidently averse to going into the army.[20] I got my Mexican blanket from him and gave him another in its place. He established his reputation with our mess for a great talker and they were debating the question last night which could excel he or Mr. Lacy.[21] The latter came back last night but went in to the army today. I think it improbable he will change his quarters as McCarson has come to remain as chaplain.[22]

I have rcd your letter of 28th and 1st of Nov. They may be dull to you but not to me. Don't be uneasy about me, I dont think it will be my lot to be captured. Good fortune attends me all the time, and I see no reason why it will not continue, and especially to get home in a couple of months; fly time fly.

I think the linsey very pretty. Tell Aunt Cook that her facility in making something out of almost nothing is evidence that she is born to be rich, instead of poor, for it gains her the means to make the future. I think Lizzie just as well postpone taking music lessons until next spring. It will be difficult for her to go so often to your uncle Joe to practice and will probably give them trouble and annoyance.

I heard from Winchester a few days ago and heard that Lt. Taylor McDonald died about two weeks ago from typhoid fever after his wound had gotten nearly well.[23] He was kindly treated. I wrote to Floyd a few days ago in relation to it, giving the particulars as far as I could learn.[24]

Accept my best love and give love to all.

Ever yours, HB

....

Lacy's Spring
Dec. 3, 1864

My dear Wife

Your welcome letter of 29th ultimo rcd this morning. I thought of writing you yesterday but felt sure I would get a letter from you this morning and preferred to have one to answer. I was sorry to hear of your Aunt Mary's child having scarlet fever.[25] Hope the little fellow will get well. I believe all our children have had it. Return my regards to the Misses Spickard.[26]

Your remark that you approve of Genl. Early's opinion in regard to people getting married during the war I think is questionable.[27] I took dinner Thursday with Dr. McGuire, Straith[28] & Major Rogers[29] present, and we had the question extensively discussed.

McG & S contending that it was wrong; R and I that it was not, and especially for Quartermasters & Drs. I believe all agreed that every lady wished to be woed and wedded, and R & I contended that as the lady had a choice in the matter that no wrong was done, and especially if the war was to last a long time. The major said he would be influenced very much by the season of the year. If in the fall of the year, he would certainly marry; if in the spring, he might hesitate.

Poor Straith hardly knows that he is married as he staid at home but one day & night.

I did not know that Bob had applied for a furlough.[30] I think now with you it will be January before I get off. McGuire told me Thursday that a Medical Ex. Bd. will be established to examine the medical officers who have not been examined, and I see that he has my name down among those to comprise the Board, and if so, this will detain me for awhile.[31] Say nothing about this, however, for something may occur by which it will not be appointed or my name might be left out. Suffice it to say that I will go the first day that I have the permission.

Poor Daniel seems to be always wrong.[32] I heard the rumors some time ago but could hardly think that he was so destitute of common sense, if lost to every other feeling. I likewise heard that Geo. B. Bane was regarded with some suspicion or at least was a strong reconstructionist.[33] Do you hear any thing of it? Enquire cautiously.

I aint trying to get sick, but I would almost be for 30 days sojourn with my beloved.

Genl. Early is now in a delightful humor — made so by Rosser's capture at New Creek.[34] I was in his company for a couple of hours while at McGuire's, & he was almost amiable. This was a brilliant affair, splendidly managed and with the loss of but one man killed and probably 2 wounded. It was a complete surprise, and a Yankee trick.[35] Rosser advanced to the front with a few men with Yankee overcoats on, and when surrounding its pickets, [they were] taken for Yankees. In this way he captured all the pickets.

The Yankees in the garrison saw them but supposed they were their men. They even rode with most of the command to within a hundred yards of the garrison and deliberately watered their horses. After this the General ordered the bugles to sound the charge and the Yankees charged still believing they were their men, but with the yell our fellows hollered out, "By golly, they are rebels." The Col. (Latham)[36] ordered to arms, but in less than 5 minutes the work was over. [The] cavalry charged, and all surrendered except a few who attempted to escape. A good many Yankees were said to be killed as they attempted to run off. Col. Latham escaped, but all the other officers were captured. About 100 escaped on the way back through the carelessness of a drunken Major Massie.[37]

The results of the expedition were over 600 prisoners, 1000 horses, between 500 & 600 cattle, 1000 sheep, 10 or 12 wagons brought off and about 200 burned, 5 pieces of artillery brought off and 4 pieces spiked, the destruction of a large amount of stores of every kind; capture of some gold and green backs, the burning of two Railroad bridges, the workshop at New Creek and the very extensive Mechanics Shops at Piedmont. The latter alone Genl.

Rosser estimates as five millions of dollars and was the largest and most important shops on the B&O R.R.

I forgot to mention 8 battle flags. Genl. Rosser brought the men with him to Genl. Early who captured the flags, thinking the Genl. would make them a complimentary speech, but the presentation or rather the acceptance was in keeping with his usual contrary way of doing everything. Genl. Rosser said, "General, here are the 8 men with the 8 stands of colors which they captured." The Genl. replied, "Boys, did you capture these flags?" "Yes sir, we captured them." "Well, set them up in the Corner."

It was said to be the richest field of plunder that the boys have ever had. There were 6 full stores of dry goods, besides the sutler stores. Genl. Rosser allowed his men to bring off all they could carry, not to impede their movements.

As they were coming back, one fellow had bundles all around him. He was trotting along when a bolt of calico came loose and spun out along the road nearly its full length before he saw it. Genl. Rosser came along about this time and ordered the command to "Close up." The poor fellow said most imploringly, "Oh General, do let me wind up my calico. I have but one shirt in the world and that on my back, and I want to take just this little piece along to have me a couple made." The Genl. said, "Why bless my soul. You have nearly enough for your whole regt." They had a lively time of it.

Capt. Smith[38] who I am waiting on at McCarson's told me many little, interesting incidents as related by the Genl. last night; but my paper is most out. A good part of the trip was that Genl. Custer met Rosser at Moorefield, and the latter offered him battle, but he very quietly withdrew and declined it.[39]

It is late, bed time, and I must stop. "I think of you day and dream of you by night," but I won't get on the subject of love as I might willingly use up another sheet. I will only say how devotedly I love you—how I love to cherish it, the happiness it affords me, my sweet, sweet darling. Kiss the children for me, and accept a thousand for yourself.

With the fondest affection   H.B.

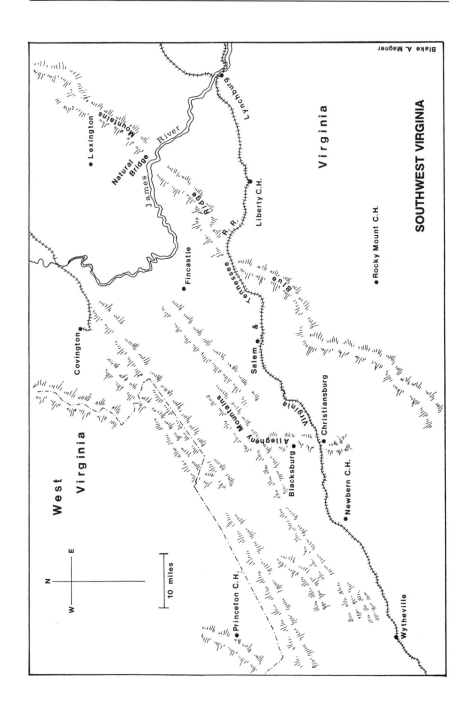

SOUTHWEST VIRGINIA

Blake A. Magner

Appendix A

Free and Slave Inhabitants in Blacksburg, Virginia, 1860

I n 1860, Blacksburg, Virginia, was little more than a village in size and scope. Founded in 1798 on a sixteen-block tract of 38 acres in Montgomery County, its boundaries were present-day Draper Road, Jackson Street, Wharton Street, and Clay Street. The town's chief function was to provide services and markets to the farming population outside its boundaries. Craftspersons, professionals, and merchants dominated its population. In the Appalachian region of Virginia, slavery was not the dominant force it was elsewhere in the state; only about 13% of Blacksburg's population were slaves. Perhaps most slaves in the town were domestic servants; few would have been field hands. Compared to most Appalachian market towns, Blacksburg had some distinction as an educational center. It contained a Methodist seminary, the Olin and Preston Institute, founded in 1851. Always facing economic difficulties, the seminary would be closed during the Civil War. It reopened after the war as the Preston and Olin Institute. When the Virginia Agricultural and Mechanical College (now Virginia Polytechnic Institute and State University) opened in 1872, it took over the single building of the Methodist seminary. [1]

Most Blacksburg residents were strongly pro-Confederate when the Civil War began, and many of its men volunteered to serve. One of those who enlisted in the Fourth Virginia Regiment in the heady days of April 1861 remembered the high spirits that animated Blacksburg residents at the time. John Howe recalled that

the people of Blacksburg gathered on the streets in excited groups taking leave of their loved ones; the ladies offering them gifts of tobacco pouches, sewing kits, pincushions, needle cases and other knickknacks designed for the pro- spective soldier. Most of the young ones were shouting and laughing, and some of the older ones were crying. But the boys were happy and gay with the prospect of going out in the world on their first great adventure. [2]

At least nineteen Blacksburg men of some seventy-five who were eligible ventured forth in that "great adventure"; most of them served in the Fourth Virginia Regiment. [3] Three of the nineteen would die of wounds or disease during the war, five others would survive their wounds, three would be incarcerated in Northern prisons, and one would desert to the Union. [4] When Harvey Black proclaimed his good fortune at not having "incurred a scratch" in the war, he knew as a surgeon better than anyone just how fortu- nate he had been.

Who were the people who marched away to war? Who were the people who gathered in the streets to send them off? The answers to these questions can be found in the 1860 census, taken on the eve of the Civil War. This Appendix analyzes and tran- scribes information obtained from two sources, the free schedules and the slave schedules for the town of Blacksburg in the 1860 census. For the free population, census records documented names, ages, occupations, and real estate and personal property holdings, along with a variety of other information. The slave schedules documented the number of slaves owned by household. Though the slaves themselves are not listed by name, they are listed by age and gender. They are also meticulously categorized by race, separating, for example, blacks from mulattos. [5]

The town's 1860 census showed that Blacksburg contained a total population of 406 people, including three free people of color and 52 African-American slaves. Of the 354 individuals listed in the free population schedules, all but 18 listed their birthplace as Virginia. Almost all of the rest were from northern rather than southern states. Three had been born in Pennsylvania, three in the District of Columbia, three in the not-yet-unified German states in Europe, two in Maryland, one in Alabama, one in Connecticut, one in Kentucky, one in Maine, one in Michigan, one in New York, and one in Rhode Island. For at least one Blacksburg resident, Mary

Kent Black, the place of birth was listed incorrectly; her birthplace is shown as Virginia even though she had been born in Illinois.

Most of those who listed occupations were engaged in crafts. The population included fourteen shoemakers, five blacksmiths, four wagonmakers, four cabinet makers, two saddlers, one carpenter, one hatter, one milliner, one plasterer, one brickmason, one potter, one silversmith, one tailor, one tanner, one tinner, one wagoner, and one weaver. Those providing services of one kind or another included five merchants, three clerks, two hotel keepers, two traders, two mail carriers, one constable, one deputy sheriff, one postmaster, one tollgate keeper, one bank cashier, and one bank teller. Ten people can be included among the professional classes: four teachers, three physicians, two ministers (one Old School Presbyterian and one Methodist), and one lawyer. [6] Finally, the town included eight people who described themselves as farmers, six who considered themselves laborers, and two who listed their occupation as students. Two women were listed as having occupations: Annie Lord, a teacher who had been born in Maine, and Fannie Zeigler, a Virginia-born milliner whose husband had come from the German state of Hesse Castle.

Census-takers reported their findings in terms of dwelling and family units. The "families" they reported on might more accurately be called households, in that they often contained apprentices and others not related to the heads of households. In the case of boarding houses or hotels, the relationship among members of a household was even more remote, causing distortion of statistical analyses such as household wealth. For the transcribed list below and the statistical summary that accompanies it, boarders living in the two hotels in Blacksburg have been broken away from the census "household" (in this case a hotel) and made separate households. [7] These households may contain one or more individuals, depending upon whether the boarders themselves seemed related. Where this was done, the smaller households containing boarders or families running hotels can be identified by aphabetical suffixes (e.g., 1041a) after their household numbers.

Using this methodology, the town included 68 households. Of these, 54 were non-slaveholding and 14 were slaveholding. The average total wealth of non-slaveholding households (combining real estate and personal property) was $1,739; the average wealth of slaveholding households was more than ten times that figure— $19,187. Harvey Black's household wealth, $19,320, was about the average for slaveholding families, though well above the average for all households of $5,331.

The average number of slaves held by slaveholding households was 3.7, though this figure is somewhat misleading. Only three households owned over five slaves (one owned six, another nine, and the third thirteen), while the rest owned four or fewer slaves. One household owned four slaves; four owned two slaves; three owned three slaves; and three households, including that of Harvey Black, owned one slave.

The 1860 Blacksburg Census Summarized Alphabetically by Head of Household

The first column lists the name of the head of a household. The second column contains the family or household number. The household size is shown in the third column. The last two columns show total wealth (real estate and personal property combined) and number of slaves owned. To see more information on any household, look up the family or household number in the list that follows this table.

Head of Household	Household Number	Household Size	Total Wealth	Slaves Owned
Alls, Thomas H.	1043	10	$1,280	0
Amiss, Elizabeth	988	7	$22,325	9
Angel, Benjamin	1015	4	$30	0
Argabright, Stewart	990	7	$300	0
Argabright, Susan	992	1	$3,100	0
Argabright, Wesley	989	8	$1,350	0
Barger, Elmira	1031	2	$30	0
Barton, Amos	1000	2	$50	0
Barton, Joseph	991	5	$25	0
Barton, Samuel	994	3	$550	0
Black, Edward	1036	4	$21,000	2
Black, Harvey	1003	7	$19,320	1
Bodell, David N.	1013	11	$2,150	0
Calbert, Robert H.	1004	3	$50	0
Camper, Andrew	1029	9	$150	0
Camper, Isaiah	1023	4	$300	0
Carden, George	1005	7	$30	0
Caves, Sarah	1035	9	$30	0
Croy, A. Jackson	1012	2	$30	0
Croy, Adam	1014	4	$1,200	0
Croy, Andrew	1008	3	$1,550	0

Head of Household	Household Number	Household Size	Total Wealth	Slaves Owned
Croy, Daniel A.	998	6	$100	0
Croy, Mary	1011	1	$860	0
Daugherty, Lucinda	1025	6	$75	0
Dawson, William H.	1010	9	$1,000	0
Effinger, William F.	1034	6	$950	0
Evans, James M.	997	13	$4,700	3
Fagg, William	1038	7	$75	0
Francisco, Robert L.	1020	7	$4,500	0
Galloway, William D.	1028	10	$100	0
Gilmore, John C.	1041a	1	$7,200	0
Gray, Nicholas	1032	3	$100	0
Green, William B.	986	3	$1,000	0
Harman, Joseph	1041d	2	$0	0
Harris, Thomas M.	1037	7	$150	0
Harvey, John M.	1026	2	$1,700	0
Harvey, Michael	1027	3	$0	0
Harvey, Thomas M.	1041c	1	$0	0
Helm, John B.	1018	7	$3,100	0
Henderson, James M.	982	5	$11,150	3
Hickman, William P.	1007	11	$17,000	2
Jackson, Thomas T.	985	6	$6,000	1
Jordan, John N.	1041	3	$150	0
Keister, Jacob	1030	7	$10,000	0
Kent, Sarah M.	1022	5	$1,400	2
Linkous, Mitchel	993	9	$150	0
Lord, Annie M.	982b	1	$0	0
Lybrook, John	1039	5	$23,550	2
Marron, John	1001	4	$200	0
Peck, William H.	1024	8	$51,600	3
Ronald, Charles A.	1040	4	$11,850	4

Head of Household	Household Number	Household Size	Total Wealth	Slaves Owned
Ronald, Nicholas M.	1041a	1	$15,500	0
Sanders, George	987	4	$75	0
Sheaf, George W.	999	9	$900	0
Shue, Joseph F.	1006	1	$350	0
Smith, Charles H.	983	9	$100	0
Smith, Leander	982a	2	$10,000	0
Speake, William F.	996	5	$5,600	0
Spickard, John C.	995	5	$1,875	1
Stanger, John A.	984	8	$950	0
Stanger, Thomas A.	1009	4	$900	0
Surface, Henry	1033	10	$450	0
Templeton, James A.	1019	5	$3,500	0
Thomas, Giles D.	1042	4	$56,200	6
Thomas, John M.	1016	2	$20,650	3
Thompson, Archibald	1002	6	$2,000	0
Wallenstein, Heirmann	1017	3	$7,500	0
Zeigler, Adolphus	1021	2	$2,450	0

The 1860 Blacksburg Census Transcribed in Order of Dwelling Numbers

Unless stated otherwise, all individuals listed Virginia as their place of birth.

Page 705; Dwelling number 1084; Family number 982:

Henderson, James M. White male, 50. Hotel keeper. Real estate, $3,150. Personal property, $8,000.

Henderson, Amanda M. White female, 38.

Henderson, James R. White male, 14. Attended school within the year.

Henderson, Catharine. White female, 11. Attended school within the year.

Henderson, John. White male, 6.

James M. Henderson owned three slaves: a 50-year-old black female; a 30-year-old mulatto female; and a 24-year-old mulatto male (Slave Schedules, 118).

Page 705; Dwelling number 1084; Family number 982a:

Smith, Leander. White male, 45. Brickmason. Personal property, $1,000.

Smith, Thomas R. White male, 40. Merchant. Real estate, $1,000. Personal property, $8,000.

Page 705; Dwelling number 1084; Family number 982b:

Lord, Annie M. White female, 23. Teacher. Born in Maine.

Page 705; Dwelling number 1085; Family number 983:

Smith, Charles H. White male, 55. Postmaster. Personal property, $100.

Smith, Nancy. White female, 49.

Smith, Amanda M. White female, 22.

Smith, Mollie. White female, 20.

Smith, Fannie. White female, 18. Attended school within the year.

Smith, Sarah. White female, 16. Attended school within the year.

Smith, Emma. White female, 14. Attended school within the year.

Smith, Nannie. White female, 11. Attended school within the year.

Smith, Susan. White female, 9.

Page 705; Dwelling number 1086; Family number 984:

Stanger, John A. White male, 40. Constable. Real estate, $800. Personal property, $150. Born in Kentucky.

Stanger, Mary. White female, 35.

Stanger, Henry. White male, 13. Attended school within the year.

Stanger, Bettie. White female, 11.

Stanger, Ellen. White female, 9. Attended school within the year.

Stanger, John. White male, 7. Attended school within the year.

Stanger, Robert. White male, 6.

Stanger, Annie. White female, 2.

Page 705; Dwelling number 1087; Family number 985:

Jackson, Thomas T. White male, 46. Physician. Real estate, $4,000. Personal property, $2,000.

Jackson, Luemma P. White female, 46.

Jackson, Mary E. White female, 18.

Jackson, Susan. White female, 16.

Jackson, Louisa. White female, 15. Attended school within the year.

Jackson, Catherine. White female, 66.

Thomas T. Jackson owned one slave, a 45-year-old black female (Slave Schedules, 118).

Page 705; Dwelling number 1088; Family number 986:

Green, William B. White male, 26. Farmer. Personal property, $1,000.

Green, Macah B. White female, 25.

Green, Benjamin H. White male, 20. Farmer.

Page 705; Dwelling number 1089; Family number 987:

Sanders, George. White male, 23. Shoemaker. Personal property, $75.

Sanders, Lioni. White female, 24. Person over 20 who can't read or write.

Sanders, [Unnamed]. White male, 1.

Broce, Julia V. White female, 17.

Page 705; Dwelling number 1090 unoccupied

Page 706; Dwelling number 1091; Family number 988:

Amiss, Elizabeth. White female, 70. Real estate, $9,325. Personal property, $7,000.

Wade, William A. White male, 33. Clerk.

Wade, Charlotte C. L. White female, 35.

Wade, Elizabeth. White female, 9.

Amiss, Louis F. J. White male, 42. Clerk. Real estate, $6,000.

Amiss, Mary W. White female, 30.

Amiss, Louis. White male, 1 month.

Elizabeth Amiss "and two others" owned nine slaves: a 41-year-old mulatto female; a 34-year-old mulatto male; a 21-year-old mulatto female; a 13-year-old mulatto female; an 11-year-old mulatto male; an 11-year-old black male; a 9-year-old black female; a 7-year-old mulatto male; and a 3-year-old mulatto male (Slave Schedules, 118).

Page 706; Dwelling number 1092; Family number 989:

Argabright, Wesley. White male, 43. Blacksmith. Real estate, $1,000. Personal property, $350.

Argabright, Sarah. White female, 42.

Argabright, Ida. White female, 17.

Argabright, William. White male, 15.

Argabright, Malinda. White female, 13. Attended school within the year.

Argabright, Henry. White male, 11.

Argabright, Susan. White female, 8.

Argabright, Margaret. White female, 2.

Page 706; Dwelling number 1093; Family number 990:

Argabright, Stewart. White male, 30. Blacksmith. Personal property, $300.

Argabright, Gabriella. White female, 28.

Argabright, Delia. White female, 7.

Argabright, Calvin. White male, 5.

Argabright, Biddy. White female, 4.

Argabright, Effie L. White female, 2.

Kipps, Elizabeth. White female, 18.

Page 706; Dwelling number 1094; Family number 991:

Barton, Joseph. White male, 65. Hatter. Personal property, $25. Born in Rhode Island.

Barton, Sarah. White female, 60.

Barton, James. White male, 33. Insane.

Barton, Joseph. White male, 21. Shoemaker.

Barton, Sarah. White female, 5. Attended school within the year.

Page 706; Dwelling number 1095; Family number 992:

Argabright, Susan. White female, 65. Real estate, $3,000. Personal property, $100. Person over 20 who can't read or write.

Page 706; Dwelling number 1096; Family number 993:

Linkous, Mitchel. White male, 63. Farmer. Personal property, $150.

Linkous, Jane. White female, 40.

Linkous, Mary A. White female, 18.

Linkous, James. White male, 17.

Linkous, William. White male, 14.

Linkous, Edmonia. White female, 11. Attended school within the year.

Linkous, Harrison. White male, 9. Attended school within the year.

Linkous, Elizabeth. White female, 7. Attended school within the year.

Linkous, Sarah. White female, 10 months.

Page 706; Dwelling number 1097; Family number 994:

Barton, Samuel. White male, 28. Cabinet maker. Real estate, $500. Personal property, $50.

Barton, Mary M. White female, 37.

Barton, James H. White male, 11 months.

Page 707; Dwelling number 1098; Family number 995:

Spickard, John C. White male, 56. Saddler. Real estate, $1,600. Personal property, $275.

Spickard, Nancy. White female, 48.

Spickard, Mollie W. White female, 21.

Spickard, Susan. White female, 20.

Spickard, Ellen. White female, 19.

Page 707; Dwelling number 1098; Family number 995 (continued):

John C. Spickard owned one slave, an 80-year-old black female (Slave Schedules, 118).

Page 707; Dwelling number 1099; Family number 996:

Speake, William F. White male, 29. Minister (Methodist Episcopal). Real estate, $5,000. Personal property, $600. Born in Maryland.

Speake, Mary A. White female, 25. Born in the District of Columbia.

Speake, Ida. White female, 4.

Speake, Annie. White female, 1.

Radcliffe, Willie. White female, 16. Born in the District of Columbia. Attended school within the year.

Page 707; Dwelling number 1100; Family number 997:

Evans, James M. White male, 41. Carpenter. Real estate, $3,000. Personal property, $1,000.

Evans, Mary W. White female, 37.

Evans, Margaret. White female, 17. Attended school within the year.

Evans, Charlotte F. White female, 15. Attended school within the year.

Evans, Tipton B. White male, 11. Attended school within the year.

Evans, William G. White male, 8. Attended school within the year.

Evans, Adonicam J. White male, 6. Attended school within the year.

Evans, Mary B. White female, 4.

Evans, Ann F. White female, 1.

Evans, Margaret. White female, 72.

Evans, Claiborne. White male, 50. Personal property, $700. Person over 20 who can't read or write. Insane.

Bell, William. White male, 22. Wagoner. Person over 20 who can read but can't write.

Bell, Sylvester. White male, 16. Attended school within the year.

James M. Evans "and his brother" owned two slaves, a 70-year-old mulatto male and a 70-year-old black male (Slave Schedules, 119).

Claiborne Evans owned one slave, a 42-year-old black female (Slave Schedules, 118).

Page 707; Dwelling number 1101; Family number 998:

Croy, Daniel A. White male, 40. Laborer. Personal property, $100.

Croy, Margaret A. White female, 29.

Croy, Harriet J. White female, 16. Attended school within the year.

Croy, Josephine E. White female, 14. Attended school within the year.

Croy, John M. T. White male, 5.

Croy, Andrew A. White male, 3.

Page 707; Dwelling number 1102; Family number 999:

Sheaf, George W. White male, 44. Shoemaker. Real estate, $800. Personal property, $100. Born in Pennsylvania.

Sheaf, Malinda. White female, 31.

Sheaf, Amos C. White male, 10. Attended school within the year.

Sheaf, William. White male, 6.

Sheaf, John. White male, 4.

Sheaf, Robert. White male, 3.

Sheaf, Edward. White male, 1.

Barton, Mary E. White female, 13. Attended school within the year.

Mares, Lucy. Black female, 11.

Page 707; Dwelling number 1103; Family number 1000:

Barton, Amos. White male, 24. Shoemaker. Personal property, $50.

Barton, Amanda. White female, 23.

Page 708; Dwelling number 1104; Family number 1001:

Marron, John. White male, 50. Blacksmith. Personal property, $200. Born in Maryland. Person over 20 who can read but can't write.

Marron, Elizabeth. White female, 54.

Marron, Emeline. White female, 18. Attended school within the year.

Marron, William. White male, 16. Blacksmith. Attended school within the year.

Page 708; Dwelling number 1105; Family number 1002:

Thompson, Archibald. White male, 50. Mail carrier. Real estate, $1,500. Personal property, $500.

Thompson, Sarah. White female, 45.

Page 708; Dwelling number 1105; Family number 1002 (continued):

Thompson, James. White male, 22. Shoemaker.

Thompson, John. White male, 20. Mail carrier. Attended school within the year.

Thompson, Nancy. White female, 17.

Thompson, Charles W. White male, 4.

Page 708; Dwelling number 1106; Family number 1003:

Black, Harvey. White male, 32. Physician. Real estate, $4,520. Personal property, $12,800.

Black, Mary. White female, 24.

Black, Kent. White male, 7.

Black, Elizabeth. White female, 5.

Black, Alexander. White male, 3.

Black, Charles W. White male, 11 months.

Kent, Germanicus. White male, 70. Real estate, $2,000. Born in Connecticut.

Harvey Black owned one slave, a 23-year-old black female (Slave Schedules, 118).

Page 708; Dwelling number 1107; Family number 1004:

Calbert, Robert H. White male, 28. Saddler. Personal property, $50.

Calbert, Mary F. White female, 25.

Calbert, Charles E. White male, 1 month.

Page 708; Dwelling number 1108; Family number 1005:

Carden, George. White male, 52. Shoemaker. Personal property, $30.

Carden, Mary A. White female, 46. Person over 20 who can read but can't write.

Carden, Charles. White male, 19. Shoemaker.

Carden, Margaret. White female, 21.

Carden, Nancy C. White female, 15. Attended school within the year.

Carden, Sarah E. White female, 15. Attended school within the year.

Carden, Harvey B. White male, 7.

Page 708; Dwelling number 1109; Family number 1006:

Shue, Joseph F. White male, 34. Silver smith. Personal property, $350.

Page 708; Dwelling number 1110; Family number 1007:

Hickman, William P. White male, 50. Minister (Old School Presbyterian). Real estate, $14,500. Personal property, $2,500.

Hickman, Margaret R. White female, 38.

Hickman, Eliza J. White female, 15. Attended school within the year.

Hickman, Mary C. White female, 13. Attended school within the year.

Hickman, James B. White male, 11. Attended school within the year.

Hickman, Emma S. White female, 9. Attended school within the year.

Hickman, J. Hoge. White male, 5.

Hickman, Kate L. White female, 3.

Hickman, Lula L. White female, 1.

Hickman, Maggie. White female, 1 month.

Smith, Lioni. White female, 22.

William P. Hickman owned two slaves, a 21-year-old black male and an 11-year-old black female (Slave Schedules, 118).

Page 708; Dwelling number 1111 unoccupied.

Page 709; Dwelling number 1112; Family number 1008:

Croy, Andrew. White male, 75. Wagon maker. Real estate, $1,500. Personal property, $50. Person over 20 who can read but can't write.

Croy, Sarah. White female, 64.

Croy, David. White male, 25. Wagon maker.

Page 709; Dwelling number 1113; Family number 1009:

Stanger, Thomas A. White male, 36. Deputy sheriff. Real estate, $400. Personal property, $500.

Stanger, Edmonia. White female, 35.

Stanger, Mary. White female, 3.

Stanger, John D. White male, 7 months.

Page 709; Dwelling number 1114; Family number 1010:

Dawson, William H. White male, 50. Teacher. Real estate, $800. Personal property, $200. Born in Michigan.

Dawson, Rosannah. White female, 39.

Dawson, William T. White male, 17. Shoemaker.

Dawson, Malissa J. White female, 15. Attended school within the year.

Dawson, Wesley M. White male, 13.

Dawson, Martha V. White female, 11. Attended school within the year.

Dawson, Sarah. White female, 9. Attended school within the year.

Dawson, Mary M. White female, 5.

Dawson, Maggie R. White female, 1.

Page 709; Dwelling number 1115; Family number 1011:

Croy, Mary. White female, 79. Real estate, $800. Personal property, $60. Person over 20 who can read but can't write.

Page 709; Dwelling number 1116; Family number 1012:

Croy, A. Jackson. White male, 30. Plasterer. Personal property, $30. Married within the year. Person over 20 who can't read or write.

Croy, Eliza F. White female, 21. Married within the year.

Page 709; Dwelling number 1117; Family number 1013:

Bodell, David N. White male, 48. Potter. Real estate, $1,750. Personal property, $400.

Bodell, Sophronia M. White female, 39.

Bodell, Mary E. White female, 16. Attended school within the year.

Bodell, Malinda E. White female, 14. Attended school within the year.

Bodell, Susan V. White female, 13. Attended school within the year.

Bodell, George W. W. White male, 11. Attended school within the year.

Bodell, Elizabeth F. White female, 8.

Bodell, Isabella B. E. White female, 6.

Bodell, Lilly F. White female, 5.

Bodell, W. Edgar. White male, 2.

Bodell, [Unnamed] White male, 2 weeks.

Page 709; Dwelling number 1118; Family number 1014:

Croy, Adam. White male, 68. Wagonmaker. Real estate, $1,100. Personal property, $100. Person over 20 who can't read or write.

Croy, Elizabeth. White female, 63.

Croy, Cornelius. White male, 30. Wagonmaker.

Croy, William D. White male, 20.

Page 709; Dwelling number 1119; Family number 1015:

Angel, Benjamin. White male, 36. Shoemaker. Personal property, $30. Born in the District of Columbia.

Angel, Eliza. White female, 41.

Angel, C. Robert. White male, 3.

Angel, W. Jordan. White male, 1 week.

Page 709; Dwelling number 1120; Family number 1016:

Thomas, John M. White male, 34. Merchant. Real estate, $5,000. Personal property, $15,650.

Thomas, Susan B. White female, 25.

John M. Thomas owned three slaves: a 23-year-old black female, a 14-year-old mulatto male, and a 5-year-old mulatto female (Slave Schedules, 118).

Page 710; Dwelling number 1121; Family number 1017:

Wallenstein, Heirmann. White male, 31. Merchant. Personal property, $7,500. Born in Wertenberg.

Wallenstein, Bettie. White female, 20. Born in Bavaria.

Wallenstein, Joseph. White male, 3 months.

Page 710; Dwelling number 1122; Family number 1018:

Helm, John B. White male, 54. Tinner. Real estate, $3,000. Personal property, $100.

Helm, Christina. White female, 50.

Lancaster, Josiah B. White male, 34. Trader.

Lancaster, Arabella. White female, 31.

Lancaster, William L. F. White male, 3.

Peterman, Michael G. W. White male, 29. Laborer.

Page 710; Dwelling number 1122; Family number 1018 (continued):

Campbell, Summerville. Mulatto female, 12.

Page 710; Dwelling number 1123; Family number 1019:

Templeton, James A. White male, 32. Physician. Real estate, $3,000. Personal property, $500.

Templeton, Margaret. White female, 30.

Templeton, Mary M. P. White female, 11.

Templeton, Howard. White male, 7.

Templeton, Emily. White female, 4.

Page 710; Dwelling number 1124; Family number 1020:

Francisco, Robert L. White male, 36. Cabinet maker. Real estate, $2,500. Personal property, $2,000. Born in Alabama.

Francisco, Keziah. White female, 30.

Francisco, Mary. White female, 8. Attended school within the year.

Francisco, Charles. White male, 6.

Francisco, Lucy. White female, 4.

Eakins, William. White male, 22. Cabinet maker.

Castle, Robert. White male, 53. Cabinet maker. Born in New York.

Page 710; Dwelling number 1125; Family number 1021:

Zeigler, Adolphus. White male, 31. Personal property, $250. Born in Hesse Castle.

Zeigler, Fannie. White female, 30. Milliner. Personal property, $2,200.

Page 710; Dwelling number 1126; Family number 1022:

Kent, Sarah M. White female, 50.

Kent, Ann E. White female, 31.

Kent, Mollie. White female, 16. Attended school within the year.

Ronald, Elizabeth. White female, 44. Personal property, $800.

Linkous, Josephus P. White male, 28. Clerk. Personal property, $600.

Sarah M. Kent owned two slaves, a 15-year-old black female and an 8-year-old black female (Slave Schedules, 118).

Page 710; Dwelling number 1127; Family number 1023:

Camper, Isaiah. White male, 33. Plasterer. Real estate, $250. Personal property, $50. Person over 20 who can't read or write.

Camper, Martha J. White female, 35 .

Camper, William P. White male, 3.

Camper, James T. White male, 1.

Pages 710-11; Dwelling number 1128; Family number 1024:

Peck, William H. White male, 46. Cashier, Farmers Bank. Real estate, $9,100. Personal property, $42,500.

Peck, Elizabeth M. White female, 41.

Peck, Robert W. White male, 18. Student. Attended school within the year.

Peck, John E. White male, 16. Student. Attended school within the year.

Peck, Charlotte C. White female, 13. Attended school within the year.

Peck, Josephus. White male, 10. Attended school within the year.

Peck, Mollie. White female, 8. Attended school within the year.

Peck, Charles. White male, 6.

William H. Peck owned 13 slaves: a 65-year-old black male; a 30-year-old mulatto female; a 21-year-old black male; an 18-year-old black female; a 16-year-old black male; a 14-year-old black female; a 12-year-old black female; an 8-year-old black female; a 6-year-old black female; a 4-year-old black male; two 2-year-old black males; and a 1-year-old black male (Slave Schedules, 118).

Page 711; Dwelling number 1129; Family number 1025:

Daugherty, Lucinda. White female, 53. Personal property, $75. Person over 20 who can't read or write.

Daugherty, Nancy A. White female, 20.

Daugherty, Henry T. White male, 18. Laborer.

Daugherty, Alice V. White female, 5.

Collins, Micapah. White male, 63. Laborer.

Bland, Sarah. White female, 56.

Page 711; Dwelling number 1130; Family number 1026:

Harvey, John M. White male, 31. Shoemaker. Real estate, $1,500. Personal property, $200.

Page 711; Dwelling number 1130; Family number 1026 (continued):

Harvey, Mary. White female, 20.

Page 711; Dwelling number 1130; Family number 1027:

Harvey, Michael. White male, 63. Tollgate Keeper.
Harvey, Mary. White female, 63.
Harvey, Sarah. White female, 26.

Page 711; Dwelling number 1131; Family number 1028:

Galloway, William D. White male, 49. Shoemaker. Personal property, $100.
Galloway, Elizabeth. White female, 42.
Galloway, Robert. White male, 20. Shoemaker.
Galloway, John C. White male, 18. Shoemaker.
Galloway, Vitiela M. White female, 16. Attended school within the year.
Galloway, Susan E. White female, 14. Attended school within the year.
Galloway, Everett O. White male, 12.
Galloway, William F. White male, 9.
Galloway, Charles M. White male, 5.
Galloway, [Unnamed]. White female, 1.

Page 711; Dwelling number 1132; Family number 1029:

Camper, Andrew. White male, 40. Weaver. Personal property, $150.
Camper, Catherine. White female, 40.
Camper, Mary P. White female, 16. Attended school within the year.
Camper, Floyd S. White male, 11. Attended school within the year.
Camper, Lucretia E. White female, 9. Attended school within the year.
Camper, Georgienne. White female, 7. Attended school within the year.
Camper, Nancy C. White female, 6.
Camper, Sarah V. White female, 4.
Camper, John H. White male, 1.

Page 711; Dwelling number 1133; Family number 1030:

Keister, Jacob. White male, 44. Farmer. Real estate, $8,300. Personal property, $1,700.

Page 711; Dwelling number 1133; Family number 1030 (continued):

Keister, Mary A. White female, 25.

Keister, Margaret J. White female, 16.

Keister, James W. White male, 14.

Keister, John T. White male, 11.

Keister, Charles. White male, 3.

Keister, Anderson T. White male, 1.

Page 711; Dwelling number 1134; Family number 1031:

Barger, Elmira. White female, 30. Personal property, $30.

Barger, Black. White male, 4.

Page 712; Dwelling number 1135; Family number 1032:

Gray, Nicholas. White male, 24. Personal property, $100.

Gray, Matilda. White female, 24.

Gray, Ann E. White female, 2 months.

Page 712; Dwelling number 1136; Family number 1033:

Surface, Henry. White male, 41. Blacksmith. Personal property, $450.

Surface, Emily. White female, 41.

Surface, Emily. White female, 17. Attended school within the year.

Surface, Sophronia. White female, 15. Attended school within the year.

Surface, George R. White male, 13. Attended school within the year.

Surface, Leoni J. White female, 11. Attended school within the year.

Surface, Samuel. White male, 9.

Surface, Edward A. White male, 6.

Surface, William N. White male, 4.

Surface, Joseph P. White male, 2.

Page 712; Dwelling number 1137; Family number 1034:

Effinger, William F. White male, 37. Tanner. Real estate, $900. Personal
property, $50.

Effinger, Maria N. White female, 30.

Effinger, William M. White male, 9.

Effinger, John P. White male, 5.

Page 712; Dwelling number 1137; Family number 1034 (continued):

Effinger, Mary J. White female, 3.

Effinger, Margaret S. White female, 2.

Page 712; Dwelling number 1138; Family number 1035:

Caves, Sarah. White female, 38. Personal property, $30. Person over 20 who can't read or write.

Caves, Ritchie J. White male, 12.

Caves, Robert. White male, 9.

Caves, Martha. White female, 7.

Caves, Henry. White male, 6.

Caves, Sarah A. White female, 4.

Caves, Amanda. White female, 2.

Caves, Isabella. White female, 1 month.

Newman, Nelly. White female, 45. Person over 20 who can't read or write.

Page 712; Dwelling number 1139; Family number 1036:

Black, Edward. White male, 25. Farmer. Real estate, $15,000. Personal property, $6,000. Property values for entire household. Married within the year.

Black, Jane. White female, 20. Married within the year.

Black, John. White male, 27. Farmer.

Black, Ann T. White female, 22.

Edward Black and "two others" owned two slaves, a 25-year-old black male and a 23-year-old mulatto female (Slave Schedules, 118).

Page 712; Dwelling number 1140; Family number 1037:

Harris, Thomas M. White male, 40. Trader. Personal property, $150.

Harris, Christina. White female, 36.

Harris, Robert H. M. White male, 19. Laborer.

Harris, James B. White male, 17. Laborer.

Harris, Willie. White female, 7. Attended school within the year.

Harris, Hart. White male, 5.

Harris, Charles. White male, 1.

Page 712; Dwelling number 1141 unoccupied.

Page 713; Dwelling number 1142; Family number 1038:

Fagg, William. White male, 55. Shoemaker. Personal property, $75. Person over 20 who can't read or write.

Fagg, Charlotte A. White female, 23.

Fagg, Elizabeth. White female, 19.

Fagg, Fannie. White female, 15. Attended school within the year.

Fagg, E. Jane. White female, 12. Attended school within the year.

Fagg, Septimus. White male, 8. Attended school within the year.

Fagg, C. Willis. White male, 6.

Page 713; Dwelling number 1143; Family number 1039:

Lybrook, John. White male, 40. Merchant. Real estate, $5,200. Personal property, $12,000.

Lybrook, Mary. White female, 24.

Lybrook, Virginia E. White female, 2.

Lybrook, George. White male, 1.

Evans, Jonathan B. White male, 32. Merchant. Real estate, $3,000. Personal property, $3,350.

Jonathan B. Evans owned two slaves, a 44-year-old black male and a 42-year-old black female (Slave Schedules, 118).

Page 713; Dwelling number 1144; Family number 1040:

Ronald, Charles A. White male, 32. Lawyer. Real estate, $1,350. Personal property, $10,000. Married within the year.

Ronald, Sally A. White female, 23. Married within the year.

Pace, George R. White male, 24. Teacher. Personal property, $500. Married within the year.

Pace, May F. White female, 17. Married within the year.

Charles A. Ronald owned 4 slaves, a 28-year-old black male; an 18-year-old black female; a 5-year-old mulatto male; and a 3-year-old mulatto male (Slave Schedules, 118).

Page 713; Dwelling number 1145; Family number 1041:

Jordan, John N. White male, 32. Hotel keeper. Real estate, $150.

Jordan, Isabella R. White female, 27.

Jordan, Betty H. White female, 1.

Page 713; Dwelling number 1145; Family number 1041a:

Ronald, Nicholas M. White male, 35. Teller (bank). Real estate, $8,000. Personal property, $7,500.

Page 713; Dwelling number 1145; Family number 1041b:

Gilmore, John C. White male, 28. Teacher. Personal property, $7,200. Born in Pennsylvania.

Page 713; Dwelling number 1145; Family number 1041c:

Harvey, Thomas M. White male, 28. Farmer.

Page 713; Dwelling number 1145; Family number 1041d:

Harman, Joseph. White male, 33. Tailor. Born in Pennsylvania.

Campbell, White. Mulatto male, 3.

Page 713; Dwelling number 1146; Family number 1042:

Thomas, Giles D. White male, 28. Real estate, $23,500. Personal property, $32,700.

Thomas, Matilda C. White female, 21.

Thomas, James W. White male, 3.

Thomas, Henry E. White male, 8 months.

Giles D. Thomas owned six slaves: a 30-year-old black male; a 25-year-old black male; a 22-year-old black male; a 22-year-old black female; an 18-year-old black female; and a 10-year-old black male (Slave Schedules, 118).

Page 713; Dwelling number 1147; Family number 1043:

Alls, Thomas H. White male, 43. Farmer. Real estate, $1,000. Personal property, $280.

Alls, Lucinda. White female, 33.

Alls, Margaret A. White female, 17.

Alls, Sarah E. White female, 15.

Alls, William T. White male, 12.

Alls, James H. White male, 8.

Page 713; Dwelling number 1147; Family number 1043 (continued):

Alls, Mary E. White female, 7.

Alls, Susannah. White female, 6.

Alls, Pamna. White female, 4.

Alls, [Unnamed]. White female, 10 months.

Page 713; Dwelling number 1148 unoccupied.

Page 713; Dwelling number 1149 unoccupied.

Relationships among the Black,
Kent, and Amiss Family Members
Mentioned in the Letters

The charts below do not attempt to list all of the members of the Black, Kent, and Amiss families or to put them in birth order, but only to list those mentioned in the letters or in the general and chapter introductions.

BLACK FAMILY

```
Alexander Black---------------Elizabeth McDonald
        |                |
        |                Harvey Black---Mary Irby Kent ("Mollie")
(siblings of HB)                 |
James Black              Alexander Black ("Alex")
Margaretta Black        Charles Black ("Charly")
                        Elizabeth Black ("Lizzie")--John S. Apperson
                        Kent Black ("Kentie")


Charles Black (uncle of HB)---Rhoda McDonald
        |
        Ann Black
        Edward Black
        Jane Black
        John Black
        Keziah Black---Robert Francisco


Susannah Black (aunt of HB)---Stephen McDonald
        |
Crockett McDonald (HB's double cousin)
```

KENT FAMILY

Germanicus Kent----------Arabella Amiss
                   |
            Cecelia Kent ("Ceal")---Robert White
            John Edwin Kent
            Lewis Amiss Kent
            Mary Irby Kent---Harvey Black

Elizabeth Kent ("Aunt Peck," sister of Germanicus Kent)---William
                                             Peck ("Uncle Will")
                                           |
                                     John E. Peck ("Ed")
                                     Robert W. Peck ("Bob")

AMISS FAMILY

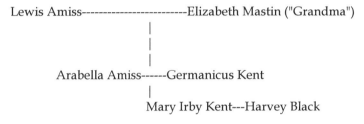

Lewis Amiss------------------------Elizabeth Mastin ("Grandma")
                   |
                   |
                   |
        Arabella Amiss------Germanicus Kent
                   |
                  Mary Irby Kent---Harvey Black

        Edwin J. Amiss ("Uncle Ed")----Sarah Peck
                   |
                  Elizabeth ("Lizzie") Amiss--William H. Palmer

        Charlotte Cooksey Amiss ("Aunt Cook")---William Wade
                                     ("Uncle Will")

Introduction

1. Harvey Black to Mollie Black, Hospital, Guiney Station, May 10, 1863, Black family papers, Special Collections Department, Virginia Polytechnic Institute and State University Libraries. Hereafter cited as Black family papers, Virginia Polytechnic Institute and State University Libraries. All further references to Black's Civil War letters in this Introduction and the chapter introductions are to letters in this collection. Later quotations from the letters will not receive endnotes. The Black family collection includes Harvey Black's Civil War letters and other correspondence, a prewar medical ledger, and a diary of his trip to the Northwestern frontier in 1849. A small collection of Harvey Black papers, containing two of Black's post-Civil War medical ledgers, is in the Special Collections Department of the Duke University Library.

2. Frank E. Vandiver, *Mighty Stonewall* (New York: McGraw-Hill, 1957), 483-84.

3. John S. Apperson, "Autobiography of John Samuel Apperson, M.D., " 86 1/2 (Apperson's pagination). Written in 1897-98 and never published, the autobiography exists partially in handwritten and partially in typescript format. The original manuscript is in the possession of Mrs. Barbara Rennie of Richmond, Virginia; a partial photocopy covering the Civil War years is in the possession of Glenn L. McMullen of Ames, Iowa. Hereafter cited as "Autobiography of John Samuel Apperson, M.D."

4. The account most historians have used as a primary source is Hunter McGuire, "Wounding and Death of Jackson," in Hunter McGuire and George L. Christian, *The Confederate Cause and Conduct in the War Between the States* (Richmond: L. H. Jenkins, n.d.), 219-29. McGuire published two earlier versions of his account: "Death and Wounding of Jackson," in the May 1866 issue of the *Richmond Medical Journal* (reprinted as Hunter McGuire, *Last Wound of the Late General Stonewall Jackson: The Amputation of the Arm and His Last Moments and Death* [Lynchburg, Virginia: Warwick House Publishing, 1991]); and "Death of Stonewall Jackson," *Southern Historical Society Papers* 14 (January-December 1886), 154-63. Most accounts of Jackson's wounding and the amputation of his arm mention Black in passing. In addition to McGuire's account and the account of Frank Vandiver cited above, see, for example, James Power

Smith, *With Stonewall Jackson in the Army of Northern Virginia* (published in *Southern Historical Society Papers* 43 [September 1920]), 53; Burke Davis, *They Called Him Stonewall: A Life of Lt. General T. J. Jackson, C.S.A.* (New York: Rinehart, 1954), 430-32; John Bowers, *Stonewall Jackson: Portrait of a Soldier* (New York: William Morrow, 1989), 346-47; and Byron Farwell, *Stonewall: A Biography of General Thomas J. Jackson* (New York: Norton, 1992), 512-13. Black's historiographical one-dimensionality has two sides. Though he is almost always mentioned in the story of Jackson's wounding, he is seldom mentioned in any other context. One recent exception is Robert K. Krick, *Stonewall Jackson at Cedar Mountain* (Chapel Hill: University of North Carolina Press, 1990), 381. Krick cites Black's comments on the ghastly and presumed mortal wound of Major R. Snowden Andrews at the Battle of Cedar Mountain in August 1862. Another brief reference to Black in a different context is Kenneth W. Noe, *Southwest Virginia's Railroad: Modernization and the Sectional Crisis* (Urbana: University of Illinois Press, 1994), 104. Hereafter cited as Noe, *Southwest Virginia's Railroad.* Noe quotes a speech Black may have made at the time of Virginia's succession from the Union.

5. The only treatment of Black's Civil War service is Glenn L. McMullen, "Tending the Wounded: Two Virginians in the Confederate Medical Corps," *Virginia Cavalcade* 40, no. 4 (Spring 1991): 172-83, which deals with Black and his assistant John S. Apperson during the Civil War. Hereafter cited as McMullen, "Tending the Wounded." A biographical article on Black by the same author will appear in the forthcoming *Dictionary of Virginia Biography*, to be published by the Library of Virginia. At present, the most complete biographical sketch of Black and the only source on his childhood is [John S. Apperson,] "Sketch of His [Dr. Harvey Black's] Life," in the *Annual Report of the Southwestern Lunatic Asylum at Marion, Virginia, for the Fiscal Year Ending September 30, 1888* (Richmond: J. H. O'Bannon, Superintendent of Public Printing, 1888), 35-41. Hereafter cited as [Apperson], "Sketch of His Life." A manuscript copy of the biographical sketch in Apperson's handwriting is in the Black family papers in the Virginia Polytechnic Institute and State University Libraries.

6. According to family sources, Black never spelled his first name with an "e," but the evidence for this is inconclusive. His personal papers contain no documents in which he signed his full name (his preference was for "H. Black"), and documents such as certificates presented to him by others consistently spell his name as "Harvey." His grave site in Blacksburg, Virginia, adds to the confusion: a monument spells his name as "Harvy" though his tombstone spells it as "Harvey."

7. The genealogy of the Black family is treated by Florence Black Weiland, *Fifty New England Colonists and Five Virginia Families* (Boothbay Harbor, Maine: Boothbay Register, 1965), 22-26; and Nannie Francisco Porter, *Blacks and Other Families* (n.p., n.d.), 1-24. Hereafter cited as

Weiland, *Fifty New England Colonists and Five Virginia Families* and Porter, *Blacks and Other Families.*

8. Black enrolled as a private in the First Virginia Infantry Regiment on November 24, 1846. He was detailed as a wardmaster in the regimental hospital in July 1847; in November 1847 he became a hospital steward in Sabtillo, Mexico. See Index to Compiled Service Records of Volunteer Soldiers Who Served in the Mexican War (U.S. National Archives Microcopy M616), no. 3; Compiled Service Records of Volunteer Soldiers Who Served in the Mexican War (Record Group 94, U.S. National Archives); U.S. Department of the Interior, Bureau of Pensions, Widow's Pension for Harvey Black's Mexican War service (1897), Black family papers, Virginia Polytechnic Institute and State University Libraries.

9. *Students at the University of Virginia: A Semi-Centennial Catalogue, with Brief Biographical Sketches* (Baltimore: Charles Harvey & Son, [1878?]), 5. Black's diploma is in the possession of Greer and Mary Kent Elliott of Blacksburg, Virginia. Mary Kent Elliott is the great-granddaughter of Harvey Black.

10. Harvey Black diary of a journey to the Northwestern frontier, entry for October 31, 1849, Black family papers, Special Collections Department, Virginia Polytechnic Institute and State University Libraries. Hereafter cited as Harvey Black diary, Black family papers, Virginia Polytechnic Institute and State University Libraries.

11. Harvey Black diary, November 1, 1849, Black family papers, Virginia Polytechnic Institute and State University Libraries.

12. Mary Irby Kent was born on April 27, 1836; she is said to be the first white, or non-Native American, child born in Rockford. See *Germanicus A. Kent, Founder of Rockford, Illinois, 1834* (n.p., n.d.), 2-6 (hereafter cited as *Germanicus A. Kent*); and the Lewis Amiss family Bible (photocopied pages, ca. 1900), in the Kent family papers, Special Collections Department, Virginia Polytechnic Institute and State University Libraries. Hereafter cited as Kent family papers, Virginia Polytechnic Institute and State University Libraries.

13. Their birthdates are June 9, 1853 (Kent); October 15, 1855 (Elizabeth); April 30, 1857 (Alexander); and August 23, 1859 (Charles). Genealogical files, Black family papers, Virginia Polytechnic Institute and State University Libraries.

14. For a list of the Blacksburg population in the 1860 census, see Appendix A. In that census, Harvey Black is shown as a 32-year-old physician with $4,520 in real estate and $12,800 in personal property. Also listed are his wife Mary (incorrectly identified as being born in Virginia), age 24; their three sons, Kent, 7; Alexander, 3; and Charles W., 11 months; and their daughter Elizabeth, 5. In the same household lived Mary's father, Germanicus Kent.   He was 70 years old at the time of the census and had $2,000 in real estate and no personal property listed (U.S. Census

Bureau, Population Schedules [Free] of the Eighth United States Census, 1860. National Archives Microcopy M653, no. 1363, Montgomery County, Virginia, 708). Microfilms from the 1860 census are hereafter cited as 1860 [state] Census, followed by roll number, county, and printed page number. Harvey Black owned one slave, a twenty-three-year-old female (U.S. Census Bureau, Population Schedules [Slave] of the Eighth United States Census, 1860, Virginia. National Archives Microcopy M653, no. 1394, Montgomery County, 118). The series is hereafter cited as 1860 Virginia Slave Schedules.

15. Harvey and Mollie Black were related to members of the following households in the Blacksburg census: Elizabeth Amiss, Edward Black, Robert L. Francisco, and William H. Peck. See Appendix A for further information on these households.

16. William Black moved to Ohio in 1814. His son, William Porter Black, had four sons who fought in the Civil War on the Union side; two of them were killed. See Chapter 3, note 31 for further information on the Black family of Ohio.

17. Black's father, mother, sister, and brothers settled in Ithaca Township, Richland County, Wisconsin. The 1860 census for Richland County shows Alexander Black, a 60-year-old farmer with $6,000 in real estate and $2,000 in personal property; his 52-year-old wife Elizabeth; their 28-year-old daughter Margaretta; and their sons James, 23; Oscar, 21; John Q., 16; and Winfield S., 13. James and Oscar are both listed as farmers in their own right, James with $1,200 in land and $300 in personal property, and Oscar with $1,600 in real estate and $50 in personal property (1860 Wisconsin census, no. 1428, Richland County, 135). The Black family was far from alone in settling Richland County in the 1850s. John Warren Hunt, *Wisconsin Gazetteer* (Madison, Wisconsin: Beriah Brown, 1853) noted that the county's population had risen from 903 in 1850 to about 3,000 three years later (190). Hunt wrote, "There are many large tracts of well-watered and rich land in the county—hence the name. The county is settling rapidly with an intelligent and enterprizing population, almost wholly Americans" (189). For additional information on the Black family of Wisconsin, see *History of Crawford and Richland Counties, Wisconsin, Together with Sketches of their Towns and Villages, Educational, Civil, Military and Political History; Portraits of Prominent Persons, and Biographies of Representative Citizens* (Springfield, Illinois: Union Publishing Company, 1884), 861-62, 895. This county history writes of Harvey Black's father: "Alexander Black was a man of rare courtesy, intelligence and integrity. Being prematurely gray, he had a more venerable appearance than his age would really suggest. It was always a pleasure to visit his hospitable home on the Willow, and enjoy the delightful society of this cultivated gentleman and his family. He possessed the courteous manners of the Virginian, and his intelligence always rendered him a most agreeable and entertaining companion" (895). On the Wisconsin Blacks, see also Weiland, *Fifty New*

England Colonists and Five Virginia Families; Porter, *Blacks and Other Families;* and *Atlas of Richland Co. Wisconsin, Drawn From Actual Surveys and the County Records* (Madison, Wisconsin: Harrison & Warner, 1874).

18. At this time, the First Brigade contained the 2nd, 4th, 5th, 27th, and 33rd Virginia Infantry Regiments and Rockbridge Artillery Battery.

19. On the Fourth Virginia, see James I. Robertson, Jr., *The Fourth Virginia Infantry* (Lynchburg, Virginia: H. E. Howard, 1982). Hereafter cited as Robertson, *Fourth Virginia.* Documents relevant to Black's Civil War service are included in two National Archives microfilm publications. His service in the Fourth Virginia Infantry Regiment is included in the Compiled Service Records of Confederate Soldiers Who Served in Organizations from the State of Virginia (National Archives Microcopy M324), no. 402. The series is hereafter cited as Compiled Service Records, Virginia. His service as a staff officer in the Second Corps Field Hospital is included in the Compiled Service Records of Confederate General and Staff Officers, and Nonregimental Enlisted Men (National Archives Microcopy M331), no. 24. This series is hereafter cited as Compiled Service Records, General and Staff Officers. Black was appointed as surgeon of the Fourth Virginia Infantry Regiment on May 1, 1861. His service record indicates that he was appointed as assistant surgeon to the Fifth Virginia Infantry Regiment in July 1861 to begin serving in September, but the transfer never took place. See the documents from July 31 to August 2, 1861, dealing with this matter. There is no record for Black among the Fifth Virginia Infantry service records.

20. Apperson appears in the 1860 Smyth County, Virginia, census as a 22-year-old student of medicine with neither real estate or personal property, living at 7 Mile Ford. He lived in the household of William Faris, a 39-year-old physician with $500 in real estate and $1,000 in personal property. Others in the household included Sarah M. Faris, 34; William F., 13; Laura J., 11; and Luther B. Faris, 8 (1860 Virginia Census, Smyth County, no. 1377, 950). For biographical information on Apperson, see "Biography of John Samuel Apperson," in Lyon G. Tyler, ed., *Men of Mark in Virginia, Ideals of American Life: A Collection of Biographies of Leading Men of the State* 3:6-9 (Washington, D.C.: Men of Mark Publishing Company, 1907); Clement A. Evans, ed., *Confederate Military History: A Library of Confederate States History, Expanded Edition* (Atlanta: Confederate Publishing Co., 1899), 3:704-05 (hereafter cited as *Confederate Military History*); McMullen, "Tending the Wounded."

21. In the confusing days preceding the surrender of the Army of Northern Virginia on April 9, 1865, Black and Apperson were separated. Apperson's name does not appear on the list of those who surrendered at Appomattox, though Black's name does. See *The Appomattox Roster: A List of the Paroles of the Army of Northern Virginia issued at Appomattox Court House on April 9, 1865* (New York: Antiquarian Press, 1962), 185-86. The list of hospital stewards and attendants attached to the Second Corps Field

Hospital on April 10, 1865, includes R. W. Thomas, W. Richardson, John A. Craig, T. Busick, J. W. Baker, and J. W. Russell. Apart from Black, no surgeons for the Second Corps Field Hospital are listed. For Apperson's activities during this period, see John S. Apperson diaries, no. 6, April 2-10, 1865, Apperson family papers, Special Collections Department, Virginia Polytechnic Institute and State University Libraries. Hereafter cited as Apperson diaries, Virginia Polytechnic Institute and State University Libraries.

22. "Autobiography of John Samuel Apperson, M.D.," 55.

23. Apperson diaries, no. 3, February 22, 1862, Virginia Polytechnic Institute and State University Libraries.

24. "Autobiography of John Samuel Apperson, M.D.," 56.

25. "Autobiography of John Samuel Apperson, M.D.," 61.

26. Apperson diaries, no. 4, April 23, 1863, Virginia Polytechnic Institute and State University Libraries.

27. Two recent biographies of McGuire are John W. Schildt, *Hunter Holmes McGuire: Doctor in Gray* (Chewsville, Maryland: John W. Schildt, 1986) and Maurice F. Shaw, *Stonewall Jackson's Surgeon Hunter Holmes McGuire: A Biography* (Lynchburg, Virginia: H. E. Howard, 1993). The first of these is hereafter cited as Schildt, *Hunter Holmes McGuire.* See also McGuire's service record (Compiled Service Records, General and Staff Officers, no. 171).

28. Hunter McGuire, "Prostatic Enlargement," *Transactions of the Nineteenth Annual Session of the Medical Society of Virginia Held at Norfolk, Virginia, October 23, 24, 25 and 26, 1888* (Richmond: J. W. Fergusson & Son, 1888), 200. Hereafter cited as McGuire, "Prostatic Enlargement."

29. U. S. War Department, *The War of the Rebellion: A Compilation of the Official Records of the Union and Confederate Armies,* series I, vol. 12, pt. 3, 344-45. Hereafter cited as *Official Records;* unless otherwise noted, all citations are to Series I. Another of Peale's reports on the events is in United States Surgeon General's Office, *Medical and Surgical History of the Civil War* (Wilmington, North Carolina: Broadfoot Publishing Company, 1990), 2:228. Hereafter cited as *Medical and Surgical History of the Civil War.* There is nothing in Black's service record about the incident. General Jackson's report on operations in the Shenandoah Valley, May 14-31, 1862, says only that "Dr. H. Black, acting medical director, discharged his duties well" (*Official Records,* 12, pt. 1:709). See also George H. Weaver, M.D., "Surgeons as Prisoners of War: Agreement Providing for their Unconditional Release during the American Civil War," *Bulletin of the Society of Medical History of Chicago* 4, no. 3 (January 1933): 249-61, and Samuel E. Lewis, "General T. J. Jackson (Stonewall) and His Medical Director, Hunter McGuire, M. D., at Winchester, May, 1862," *Southern Historical Society Papers* 30 (January-December 1902): 226-236. The latter is hereafter cited as Lewis, "Jackson and McGuire at Winchester."

30. See the discussion in Schildt, *Hunter Holmes McGuire*, 39.

31. John S. Apperson letter to Dr. Kent Black, December 26, 1898, quoted in Lewis, "Jackson and McGuire at Winchester," 234.

32. Wyndham B. Blanton, *Medicine in Virginia in the Nineteenth Century* (Richmond: Garrett & Massie, 1933), 82; "Names of Presidents and Vice-Presidents of the Medical Society of Virginia, From its Organization, Nov. 2d, 1870, through 1889," *Transactions of the Twentieth Annual Session of the Medical Society of Virginia Held at Roanoke, Virginia, September 3rd, 4th and 5th, 1889* (Richmond: J. W. Fergusson & Son, Printers, 1889), 342.

33. The address is printed in the *Transactions of the Fourth Annual Session of the Medical Society of Virginia, Held in Norfolk November 11th, 12th, 13th and 14th, 1873* (Richmond: Fergusson & Rady, Printers, 1874), 41-53.

34. *Transactions of the Fourth Annual Session of the Medical Society of Virginia, Held in Norfolk November 11th, 12th, 13th and 14th, 1873* (Richmond: Fergusson & Rady, Printers, 1874), 21.

35. *Virginia Agricultural and Mechanical College: Its History and its Organization* (n.p., [1874?]), 1-2; Lyle Duncan Kinnear, *The First 100 Years: A History of Virginia Polytechnic Institute and State University* (Blacksburg, Virginia: Virginia Polytechnic Institute Educational Foundation, 1972), 35-41.

36. [Apperson,] "Sketch of His Life," 37-38.

37. *Annual Report of the Virginia Eastern Lunatic Asylum for the Fiscal Year Ending September 30, 1877* (Richmond: R. F. Walker, Superintendent of Public Printing, 1877), 7-11; Shomer S. Zwelling, *Quest for a Cure: The Public Hospital in Williamsburg, Virginia, 1773-1885* (Williamsburg: Colonial Williamsburg Foundation, 1985), 55.

38. Certificate of election (1885), Black family papers, Virginia Polytechnic Institute and State University Libraries; Earl G. Swem and John W. Williams, *A Register of the General Assembly of Virginia, 1776-1918, and of the Constitutional Conventions* (Richmond: Davis Bottom, Superintendent of Public Printing, 1918), 206.

39. [Apperson,] "Sketch of His Life," 38-39. See also Black's summary of events in the *Annual Report of the Southwestern Lunatic Asylum at Marion, Virginia, to the General Assembly of Virginia, for the Fiscal Year Ending Sept. 30, 1887* (Richmond: Wm. Ellis Jones, Book and Job Printer, 1887), 7-8.

40. McGuire commented about Black's case in "Operative Treatment in Cases of Enlarged Prostate," *Virginia Medical Monthly* 15, no. 7 (October 1888): 445-56, and in "Prostatic Enlargement," 199-207.

41. U.S. Department of the Interior, Bureau of Pensions, Widow's Pension for Harvey Black's Mexican War service (1897), Black family papers, Virginia Polytechnic Institute and State University Libraries; [Apperson,] "Sketch of His Life," 40-41; and "Honorary Fellow Harvey-Black," in *Transactions of the Nineteenth Annual Session of the Medical Society*

of Virginia Held at Norfolk, Virginia, October 23, 24, 25 and 26, 1888 (Richmond: J. W. Fergusson & Son, 1888), 261.

42. In Blacksburg, the William H. Peck household owned thirteen slaves, the Elizabeth Amiss household owned nine slaves, and the Edward Black household owned two slaves. See Appendix A for further information.

43. Published primary documents by individual Confederate surgeons can be classified into three categories: letters, diaries, and reminiscences. Published collections of letters include Edmund Cody Burnett, ed., "Letters of a Confederate Surgeon: Dr. Abner McGarity, 1862-1865," *Georgia Historical Quarterly* 29 (1945): 76-114, 159-190, and 222-253; and 30 (1946): 35-70; Enoch L. Mitchell, ed., "Letters of a Confederate Surgeon [Urban G. Owen] in the Army of Tennessee to His Wife," *Tennessee Historical Quarterly* 4 (1945): 341-353; and 5 (1946): 60-81, 142-181; Franklin A. Doty, ed., "The Civil War Letters of Henry Mathers, Assistant Surgeon, Fourth Florida Regiment, C.S.A.," *Florida Historical Quarterly* 36 (1957): 94-124; and Spencer Glasgow Welch, *A Confederate Surgeon's Letters to His Wife* (New York: Neale Publishing Co., 1911). Published diaries of Confederate surgeons include Joseph Dill Alison, "I Have Been Through My First Battle and Have Had Enough of War to Last Me," *Civil War Times Illustrated* 5 (February 1967): 40-46; Joseph Dill Alison, "With a Confederate Surgeon at Vicksburg," *American History Illustrated* 3 (July 1968): 31-33; Louis Shaffner, "A Civil War Surgeon's Diary," *North Carolina Medical Journal* 27 (1966): 409-415; and Jim Stanbery, ed., "A Confederate Surgeon's View of Fort Donelson: The Diary of John Kennerly Farris," *Civil War Regiments: A Journal of the American Civil War* 1 (1991): 7-19. Reminiscences by Confederate surgeons include Simon Baruch, "A Surgeon's Story of Battle and Capture," *Confederate Veteran* 22 (January 1914): 545-548; Peter W. Houck, ed., *Confederate Surgeon: The Personal Recollections of E. A. Craighill* (Lynchburg, Virginia: H. E. Howard, 1989); Hunter McGuire, "Wounding and Death of Jackson," in *The Confederate Cause and Conduct in the War Between the States* by Hunter McGuire and George L. Christian (Richmond: L. H. Jenkins, n.d.); Aristides Monteiro, *War Reminiscences by the Surgeon of Mosby's Command* (Richmond: C. N. Williams, 1890); Edwin D. Newton, "My Recollections and Reminiscences," *The Southern Practitioner* 30 (October 1908): 474-489; Edwin D. Newton, "Reminiscences of the Medical Department, Confederate States Army and Field and Hospital Service, Army of Northern Virginia," *Southern Practitioner* 25 (January 1903): 36-43 and 26 (March 1904): 168-174; Arthur Howard Noll, ed., *Doctor Quintard: Chaplain CSA and Second Bishop of Tennessee, Being His Story of the War* (Sewanee, Tennessee: University Press of Sewanee, 1905), and William H. Taylor, *De Quibus: Discourses and Essays* (Richmond: Bell Publishers, 1908).

44. The standard work on medicine in the Confederacy is Horace H. Cunningham, *Doctors in Gray: The Confederate Medical Service* (Baton

Rouge: Louisiana State University Press, 1960). Hereafter cited as Cunningham, *Doctors in Gray*. Two other works by Cunningham on Confederate medicine are also useful: "The Confederate Medical Officer in the Field," *New York Academy of Medicine Bulletin* 34 (1958): 461-88; and *Field Medical Services at the Battles of Manassas* (Athens: University of Georgia Press, 1968). Other useful general works on medicine in the Confederacy include George W. Adams, "Confederate Medicine," *Journal of Southern History* 6 (1940): 151-156; Wyndham B. Blanton, *Medicine in Virginia in the Nineteenth Century* (Richmond: Garrett & Massie, 1933); Frank R. Freemon, "Administration of the Medical Department of the Confederate States Army, 1861 to 1865," *Southern Medical Journal* 80 (1987): 630-637; Courtney R. Hall, "Confederate Medicine," *Medical Life* 42 (1935): 443-508; Mary Louise Marshall, "Medicine in the Confederacy," *Bulletin of the Medical Library Association* 30 (1942): 279-299; Hunter McGuire, "Progress of Medicine in the South,"*Southern Historical Society Papers* 17 (January-December 1889): 1-12; Francis Peyre Porcher, "Confederate Surgeons," *Southern Historical Society Papers* 17 (January-December 1889): 12-21; Harris D. Riley, Jr., "Medical Furloughs in the Confederate States Army," *Journal of Confederate History* 2 (1989): 115-131; Harris D. Riley, Jr., "Medicine in the Confederacy," *Military Medicine* 118 (1956): 53-64 and 144-153; and Richard Boies Stark, "Surgeons and Surgical Care of the Confederate States Army," *Virginia Medical Monthly* 87 (1960): 230-241.

45. Apperson diaries, no. 4, November 21, 1862, Virginia Polytechnic Institute and State University Libraries.

46. Cunningham, *Doctors in Gray*, 133.

47. "Autobiography of John Samuel Apperson, M.D.," 69.

48. Apperson diaries, no. 2, July 21, 1861, Virginia Polytechnic Institute and State University Libraries.

49. Apperson diaries, no. 2, July 21, 1861, Virginia Polytechnic Institute and State University Libraries.

50. Cunningham, *Doctors in Gray*, 265.

One: "I See No Reason to Despond": April 4-May 2, 1862

1. "Autobiography of John Samuel Apperson, M.D.," 78.

2. After his defeat at Kernstown on March 23, Jackson slowly moved his army southward up the Valley Turnpike, with Turner Ashby's cavalry skirmishing with Union soldiers during the slow retreat. On April 2 he established his headquarters at Rude's Hill, overlooking the Shenandoah River and south of Mt. Jackson, about 40 miles south of Winchester on the Valley Pike.

3. Mr. Gardner is probably one of two brothers from Christiansburg, both members of Company G of the Fourth Virginia Regiment, the Montgomery Fencibles. Robert M. Gardner, who had enlisted in 1861 at

Christiansburg, was wounded at Kernstown on March 23, 1862. Fleming W. Gardner, who also enlisted in 1861 at Christiansburg, was mustered out of service on April 17, 1862 (for both Gardners, see Compiled Service Records, Virginia, no. 406; Robertson, *Fourth Virginia*, 51). The 1860 Montgomery County census shows Fleming W. Gardner as 18 years old and Robert as 16. Both lived in the household of Hamilton Gardner, a master shoe and bootmaker with $2,500 in real estate and $350 in personal property. Others in the household included Julia Ann Gardner, 46; Ellen J., 22; Lavinia C., 20; Edward M., 12; Rosabell M., 7; and Eliza W. Gardner, 4. John Williams, a 40-year-old boot and shoe maker, also lived in the household, as did Nancy R. Murphy, 76, who had $100 in personal property (1860 Virginia Census, no. 1363, Montgomery County, 559).

4. John C. Wade, a captain in Company G, enlisted in 1861 at Christiansburg; his term of enlistment expired on April 17, 1862 (Compiled Service Records, Virginia, no. 413; Robertson, *Fourth Virginia*, 78). The 1860 census for Christiansburg lists him as a 31-year-old deputy clerk with $900 in real estate. Jane H. Wade, 33; Emily E., 8; Joseph E., 6; William 3; and Mary L. Wade, 10 months, were also part of the household, as was Abram Ingle, a 57-year-old well digger (1860 Virginia Census, no. 1363, Montgomery County, 570-71). The letter mentioned by Black has not survived.

5. Camp Buchanan was located below Mount Jackson.

6. Turner Ashby served as Jackson's cavalry leader, commanding a cavalry brigade of 600 men. Flamboyant and daring, he was a legendary figure among both Confederate and Union soldiers. No Confederate reports of the skirmish in Edinburg could be located; for Union reports, see *Official Records*, 12:418-20. Union casualties in the skirmish are listed as three, well below the fifty casualties suggested by Black. Union General Nathaniel P. Banks reported that Ashby "received a shot through his cap, which he exhibited with some satisfaction to the people of Woodstock" (*Official Records*, 12:418).

7. Newtown, subsequently renamed Stephens City, was several miles south of Winchester. No references to this incident were found in the *Official Records* or other sources.

8. Colonel Samuel V. Fulkerson's brigade consisted of only two regiments, the 23rd and 37th Virginia.

9. Jackson relieved Richard Garnett of his command of the Stonewall Brigade on April 1 for his unauthorized withdrawal at Kernstown; Garnett was arrested and taken to Harrisonburg. On April 2, Brigadier General Charles S. Winder, a stern disciplinarian in Jackson's mold, assumed command of the Stonewall Brigade. Because there was a general feeling that Garnett had been unjustly arrested, Winder received a cool welcome from the brigade. Garnett's trial was never concluded; later given another brigade, he would be killed in action during Pickett's charge at Gettysburg on

July 3, 1863. Winder would be killed in action also, at Cedar Mountain on August 9, 1862.

10. Certain passage of a conscription act by the Confederate government caused the number of voluntary enlistments and reenlistments to rise during the weeks that Jackson's army was at Rude's Hill, with recruits eager to join celebrated units such as the Stonewall Brigade. The Conscription Act of April 16, 1862, required all white males between 18 and 35 to serve three years in the Confederate army; those already in Confederate service were required to serve out three years. There were a number of exemptions available, however, including the home production of nitre; see note 13 below.

11. The Grayson Dare Devils was the name taken by Company F of the Fourth Virginia. It consisted largely of farmers from Grayson County who prided themselves on their marksmanship.

12. "Davidson" is probably William Davidson Croy of the Fourth Virginia Regiment. He enlisted in the Montgomery Highlanders, later to become Company E, at Blacksburg in April 1861 (Compiled Service Records, Virginia, no. 404; Robertson, *Fourth Virginia*, 47). Davidson Croy is shown as being among Black's patients in his pre-Civil War medical account book (Harvey Black medical accounts, ca. 1855-60, Black family papers, Special Collections Department, Virginia Polytechnic Institute and State University Libraries, 339). Hereafter cited as Black medical account book, Virginia Polytechnic Institute and State University Libraries. Croy appears in the 1860 Blacksburg census as a 20-year-old living in the household of Adam Croy, a 68-year-old wagon maker with $1,100 in real estate and $100 in personal property. Others in the household include Elizabeth Croy, 63, and Cornelius Croy, also a wagon maker, 30 (1860 Virginia Census, no. 1363, Montgomery County, 709). Croy would desert at Second Manassas in August 1862; see Chapter 2, note 44.

13. Salt peter or nitre was used to make gunpowder; calcium nitrate deposits could be found in the limestone caves of the Appalachian region. The "home production" of nitre exempted men from military service. A July 31, 1862, report by I. M. St. John, Superintendent of the War Department's Niter and Mining Bureau, mentions six small nitre-producing caves in Wythe, Smyth, Pulaski, and Montgomery Counties (*Official Records*, Series IV, 2:28).

14. "Bill" is possibly a reference to William Marron, who is shown as living in Blacksburg near the Black family in the 1860 census. Marron, at that time a 16-year-old blacksmith, lived in the household of John Marron, also a blacksmith, age 50, with $200 in personal property and no real estate. Elizabeth Marron, 54, and Emeline Marron, 18, also lived in the household (1860 Virginia Census, no. 1363, Montgomery County, 708).

15. This is probably a reference to John M. Thomas, shown in the 1860 census as a 34-year-old merchant living in Blacksburg with his wife, Susan

B. Thomas, age 25. John M. Thomas had $5,000 worth of real estate and $15,650 in personal property (1860 Virginia Census, Montgomery County, no. 1363, 709). Thomas owned three slaves (1860 Virginia Slave Schedules, no. 1394, Montgomery County, 118). No further information on Thomas's Civil War activities could be located; indexes to several National Archives Civil War microfilm publications were searched without success. These publications included Confederate Papers Relating to Citizens or Business Firms (U.S. National Archives Microcopy M346); Union Provost Marshall's File of One-Name Papers re Citizens (U.S. National Archives Microcopy M345); and Records of the Nitre and Mining Bureau (U.S. National Archives Microcopy M258).

16. Enos Price, a 37-year-old stone cutter with no real estate and $400 in personal property, lived in the Matamoras area of Montgomery County with his wife Elizabeth M., age 36, and their children Jonas H., 16, a laborer; Noah E., 14; Ballard S., 8; Victoria J., 6; Araminta F., 3; and Elizabeth S., 8 months old (1860 Virginia Census, no. 1363, Montgomery County, 687). Like many of the residents of German descent living near Tom's Creek and Brush Mountain, Price opposed slavery. A year earlier, he had conspired with one of the slaves of Montgomery County physician James H. Otey (see note 17 below) to mount an insurrection against slaveholders and to sway public opinion against secession. See Cathleen Carlson Reynolds, "A Pragmatic Loyalty: Unionism in Southwestern Virginia, 1861-1865" (Master's thesis, University of Alabama at Birmingham, 1987), 26, for an account of this incident. One resident whose opinion wasn't swayed, D. W. L. Charlton, wrote in a letter of May 23, 1861: "We have our troubles here at home, we have Detected a Scoundrel one of the Prices in attempting to incite the Negroes in our County to Robbing and Murdering the Whites, but fortunately he was discovered by part of the Home guard and now have him secure in our jail, [but] we expect to have trouble yet at Prices Fork" (Charlton family papers, Special Collections Department, Virginia Polytechnic Institute and State University Libraries).

17. Dr. James Hervey Otey was born in Bedford County, Virginia, in 1825 and moved to Montgomery County in 1859. In the 1860 census, he is shown as a 35-year-old farmer and physician with $15,000 in real estate and $20,000 in personal property. Other members of his household listed in the census were his wife, Louisa, age 28; his son, Gordon, 2; and his daughters, Mary, 4, and Elizabeth, 10 months old (1860 Virginia Census, no. 1363, Montgomery County, 704). Dr. Otey owned 27 slaves (1860 Virginia Slave Schedules, no. 1394, Montgomery County, 118). The Otey family lived in Walnut Spring, an estate built by James Randal Kent for his daughter Louisa on the occasion of her marriage to Dr. Otey. On Walnut Spring, see J. Hoge, "The Hoge Otey House," *Mountainside* 1, no. 3 (1981): 28-30. Years later, Dr. Otey's daughter Elizabeth would marry one of Dr. Black's sons, Alexander Black. For biographical information on Otey, see *Hardesty's Historical and Geographical Encyclopedia, Illustrated . . . Special*

[Montgomery County] *Virginia Edition* (New York: H. H. Hardesty & Co., 1884), 410. Hereafter cited as *Hardesty's Encyclopedia.*

18. Giles J. Henderson is shown as a 40-year-old farmer with $25,000 in real estate and $12,500 in personal property in the 1860 Montgomery County census. In the same household are his wife Celinda M. H., age 37, and seven children: Susan, 15; Cornelia, 14; Eugene, 12; Nash, 8; Crosswell, 5; Ada, 4; and Sora, 2. Also living in the household was David Martin, 40, a carpenter with no real estate and $500 in personal property (1860 Virginia Census, no. 1363, Montgomery County, 748). Giles Henderson owned 19 slaves (1860 Virginia Slave Schedules, no. 1394, Montgomery County, 120). Nearby lived Thomas Henderson, a 73-year-old farmer with $7500 in real estate and $700 in personal property (1860 Virginia Census, no. 1363, Montgomery County, 748). Thomas Henderson may have been an uncle of Giles Henderson. See Anna Laura Henderson Tribble, *The Family Tree of Henderson* (Blacksburg, Virginia: n.p., 1981), [3]. It is unclear where Giles Henderson would have gone at this time. Later in the war he would serve in the 12th Congressional District Mounted Guard, a unit raised to support the duties of conscription officers (Compiled Service Records, Virginia, no. 211). For a possible reference to Henderson's service in such a unit, see Chapter 6, note 34.

19. Montgomery White Sulphur Springs, located about 5 miles from Blacksburg, was incorporated as a resort in Montgomery County in 1856, with Harvey Black's name listed among the incorporators. It was made a general hospital in May 1862. See Dorothy H. Bodell, *Montgomery White Sulphur Springs: A History of the Resort, Hospital, Cemeteries, Markers, and Monument* (Blacksburg, Virginia: Pocahontas Press, 1993), 7. Hereafter cited as Bodell, *Montgomery White Sulphur Springs.* For its hospital records, see U.S. National Archives Record Group 109, Box 27 (War Department Collection of Confederate Records, Hospital Rolls, Virginia and Miscellaneous).

20. John E. ("Ed") and Robert W. ("Bob") Peck, who are mentioned a number of times in the Black letters, were apparently the cousins of Mollie Black. Their father was William H. Peck ("Uncle Will"), shown in the 1860 Blacksburg census as a 46-year-old cashier at the Farmer's Bank. (William H. Peck may have also been referred to as "King"; see Chapter 4, note 3.) His wife was Elizabeth M. Peck ("Aunt Liz"), age 41. In addition to Ed and Bob Peck, other members of the household included Charlotte C., 13; Josephus, 10; Mollie, 8; and Charles, 6. The family possessed $9,100 in real estate and $42,500 in personal property (1860 Virginia Census, no. 1363, Montgomery County, 710). William H. Peck is shown as owning 13 slaves (1860 Virginia Slave Schedules, no. 1394, Montgomery County, 118). Ed Peck, 16 years old in the 1860 census, enlisted in Company E of the Fourth Virginia Regiment at Rude's Hill on April 1, 1862; Bob Peck, 18 in the census, had enlisted in Company E at Blacksburg a year earlier in April 1861. Both would be wounded at Groveton in August 1862. Ed Peck would also

be wounded at Payne's Farm in November 1863 and imprisoned twice, at Old Capitol Prison from November 1863 to March 1864 and at Elmira Prison from May 1864 to March 1865 (Compiled Service Records, Virginia, no. 410; Robertson, *Fourth Virginia*, 67). The exact relationship between Mollie Black and the Pecks is unclear, but William Peck may have been the brother of Sarah Peck Amiss, who was the mother of Elizabeth Amiss Palmer, another of Mollie Black's cousins (see Chapter 2, note 48).

21. Jackson's Valley Army, now numbering 6,000 men, left the Mount Jackson area on April 17, moving south to Harrisonburg, then east to Conrad's Store (now Elkton) at the foot of Swift Run Gap in the Blue Ridge Mountains. They arrived there on April 19.

22. The incident described by Black took place on April 17. Ashby and his men were burning the bridge on the North Fork of the Shenandoah River when they were attacked by Union cavalry. Ashby was charged by four Union soldiers when one of their bullets hit his horse; he escaped to the safety of Southern cannons at Rude's Hill before the horse collapsed. See Edward A. Moore, *The Story of a Cannoneer Under Stonewall Jackson* (Freeport, New York: Books for Libraries Press, 1971), 41-42, for another account of this incident. Ashby would be killed in action near Harrisonburg on June 6, 1862.

23. John David Ridley enlisted in Company E, Fourth Virginia Infantry, in April 1861 at Blacksburg. He was commissioned 2nd Lieutenant on July 1, 1861, and was detached from the regiment on recruiting duty the next month. He would be made regimental adjutant on April 22 and would die of wounds from an artillery shell in 1865 (Compiled Service Records, Virginia, no. 411; Robertson, *Fourth Virginia*, 70). Ridley could not be located in the Montgomery County census, nor does he appear as a head of household in the published census index, Ronald Vern Jackson, ed., *Virginia 1860 Federal Census, Excluding Present Day West Virginia* (North Salt Lake, Utah: Accelerated Indexing Systems International), 1984. Hereafter cited as Jackson, *Virginia 1860 Federal Census*.

24. The Conscription Act required the reorganization of companies and regiments, with company and regimental officers elected by their men.

25. The Montgomery Highlanders was the name given to Company E of the Fourth Virginia.

26. John Black was Harvey Black's cousin, the son of Charles Black. He is shown in the 1860 Blacksburg census as a 27-year-old farmer living in the same household as a brother and two sisters. His brother Edward, a 25-year-old farmer, and sisters Jane E., 20, and Ann T. Black, 22, are shown as having a combined value in real estate of $15,000 and personal property of $6,000 (1860 Virginia Census, no. 1363, Montgomery County, 712). The 1860 slave schedules show Edward Black and "2 others" as owning two slaves (1860 Virginia Slave Schedules, no. 1394, Montgomery County, 118). John Black enlisted in Company E of the Fourth Virginia Regiment in

April 1861 at Blacksburg. He was discharged for medical reasons on April 24, 1862 (Compiled Service Records, Virginia, no. 402; Robertson, *Fourth Virginia*, 40). Edward Black would enlist in Company F of the 36th Virginia Infantry on May 13, 1862 (Compiled Service Records, Virginia, no. 821).

27. This may refer to Black's April 22 letter, above. If there was an April 21 letter, it has been lost.

28. Charles Andrew Ronald enlisted in Company E of the Fourth Virginia in April 1861 in Blacksburg as its captain. He was promoted to Lieutenant Colonel on February 20, 1862, and to Colonel on April 23, 1862. He would be wounded at Kearneysville, [West] Virginia, on October 16, 1862, and would resign from Confederate service almost a year later on September 11, 1863 because of the wound's continuing effects (Compiled Service Records, Virginia, no. 411; Robertson, *Fourth Virginia*, 71). Ronald was a well-known attorney who had served as Montgomery County Commonwealth Attorney and as a representative in the House of Delegates in the 1850s. His eloquence led to his nickname as the "Patrick Henry of the Southwest." Ronald would serve 18 months as regimental commander before resigning (*Hardesty's Encyclopedia*, 411; Robertson, *Fourth Virginia*, 10-11). The 1860 Blacksburg census lists Ronald as a 32-year-old lawyer with $1,350 in real estate and $10,000 in personal property. In the same household were his wife, Sally A. Ronald, 23; George R. Pace, a 24-year-old teacher with $500 in personal property; and May F. Pace, 17 (1860 Virginia Census, no. 1363, Montgomery County, 713). George Pace was also a member of the Fourth Virginia; see Chapter 2, note 12. Charles Ronald owned 4 slaves, according to the 1860 census (1860 Virginia Slave Schedules, no. 1394, Montgomery County, 118).

29. Robert Davison Gardner enlisted in the Pulaski Guards, later to become Company C of the Fourth Virginia Infantry, as a 1st Lieutenant in April 1861 at Newbern. He was promoted to Captain on July 25, 1861, and to Lieutenant Colonel on April 22, 1862. He would be wounded at Fredericksburg in December 1862 and would retire from service on April 9, 1864 (Compiled Service Records, Virginia, no. 406; Robertson, *Fourth Virginia*, 51). For Black's comments on Gardner's wounding at Fredericksburg, see Chapter 2, note 59. Gardner is shown in the 1860 census as a 29-year-old carpenter with $800 in real estate and $150 in personal property, living in Newbern. Elizabeth J. Gardner, 28, and William S. Gardner, a 32-year-old carpenter, also lived in the household (1860 Virginia census, no. 1373, Pulaski County, 697).

30. A lawyer and newspaper editor before the war, William Terry enlisted in the Wythe Grays, later to become Company A of the Fourth Virginia Regiment, as a lieutenant in April 1861 at Wytheville. He was promoted to captain on May 13, 1861, and to Major on April 22, 1862. Terry would be wounded three times, at Groveton in August 1862, at Payne's Farm in November 1863, and at Fort Stedman in March 1865.

Promoted to Colonel in September 1863, he would become a Brigadier General, commanding the Stonewall Brigade, on May 19, 1864 (Compiled Service Records, Virginia, no. 412; Robertson, *Fourth Virginia*, 76). For a biographical sketch of Terry, focusing on his Civil War service, see *Confederate Military History*, 3:673-74. Terry is shown in the 1860 census as a 35-year-old lawyer living in Wytheville with $23,000 in real estate and $45,000 in personal property. In the same household were Emma, 30; Benjamin, 6; William, 4; and John Terry, 2. William H. Boldin, like Terry a lawyer, was another member of the household (1860 Virginia census, no. 1385, Wythe County, 746).

31. Matthew Davis Bennett enlisted in Company E in April 1861 at Blacksburg. He was appointed 1st Lieutenant on July 1, 1861, and was promoted to Captain on April 22, 1862. He would be wounded twice—at Groveton in August 1862 and at Winchester in September 1864. Promoted to Major on February 19, 1864, he would resign from Confederate service on February 23, 1865 (Compiled Service Records, Virginia, no. 402; Robertson, *Fourth Virginia*, 39). The 1860 Montgomery County census shows him as a 26-year-old farmer in the McDonald's Mill area living in the household of Davis M. Bennett, a 75-year-old farmer with $9,000 in real estate and $7,660 in personal property. Prudence Bennett, 63, also lived in the household (1860 Virginia Census, no. 1363, Montgomery County, 749). Davis Bennett owned 8 slaves (1860 Virginia Slave Schedules, no. 1394, Montgomery County, 120).

32. John Thomas Howe enlisted in Company E in April 1861 at Blacksburg. He was elected 2nd Lieutenant on April 22, 1862. He would be wounded and captured at Gettysburg on July 3, 1863, and would spend 18 months in a Union prison, gaining release on January 8, 1865 from Johnson's Island Prison in Ohio (Compiled Service Records, Virginia, no. 407; Robertson, *Fourth Virginia*, 57). John T. Howe is listed in the 1860 Montgomery County census as an 18-year-old farmer. No real estate or personal property are listed under his name (1860 Virginia Census, no. 1363, Montgomery County, 670). For Howe's experiences in the Civil War, see Daniel Dunbar Howe, *Listen to the Mockingbird: The Life and Times of a Pioneer Virginia Family* (Boyce, Virginia: Carr Publishing Co., 1961), 43-100. Hereafter cited as Howe, *Listen to the Mockingbird*.

33. James G. Wall enlisted in Company E in April 1861 at Blacksburg, and was elected 2nd Lieutenant on April 22, 1862. Two years later, in April 1864, he would be reported as absent without leave. He was dropped from the rolls of the Fourth Virginia after May 2, 1864 (Compiled Service Records, Virginia, no. 413; Robertson, *Fourth Virginia*, 79). Wall is shown in the 1860 census for Montgomery County as a 25-year-old laborer with $400 in real estate and $300 in personal property. Elizabeth A., 25, Franklin T., 5; James W., 4; and Edward Wall, 2, lived in the same household (1860 Virginia Census, no. 1363, Montgomery County, 744).

34. Joseph M. Barton enlisted in Company E at Blacksburg in April 1861. He was appointed Fourth Corporal on September 8, 1861 and was elected 2nd Lieutenant on April 22, 1862. Barton would die in Winchester on April 8, 1863; his cause of death is not shown in his service record (Compiled Service Records, Virginia, no. 402; Robertson, *Fourth Virginia*, 39). The 1860 census for Blacksburg shows Barton as a 21-year-old shoemaker living in the household of Joseph Barton, a 65-year-old hatter with $25 in personal property. Sarah, 60; James, 33; and Sarah Barton, 5, also lived in the household (1860 Virginia Census, no. 1363, Montgomery County, 706).

35. Robert G. Newlee enlisted as Captain of Company L of the Fourth Virginia in July 1861 at Blacksburg. Company L, which had no nickname, was made up largely of Blacksburg residents. Newlee resigned from Confederate service on April 21, 1862 (Compiled Service Records, Virginia, no. 409; Robertson, *Fourth Virginia*, 65). He is shown in the Blacksburg census for 1860 as a 40-year-old farmer with $4,000 in real estate and $1,000 in personal property. Martha J. Newlee, 27, and Melvina D. Newlee, 4 months, lived in the same household (1860 Virginia Census, no. 1363, Montgomery County, 698). Newlee owned one slave (1860 Virginia Slave Schedules, no. 1394, Montgomery County, 116). For a muster roll of Company L during Newlee's tenure as its captain, see the Newlee family papers, Special Collections Department, Virginia Polytechnic Institute and State University Libraries.

36. Henry Jackson Keister enlisted in Company L in July 1861 at Blacksburg and was elected 2nd Lieutenant on April 22, 1862. He would be promoted again, to 1st Lieutenant, in February 1863, wounded at Gettysburg on July 3, 1863, and promoted to Captain in November 1863 (Compiled Service Records, Virginia, no. 408; Robertson, *Fourth Virginia*, 59). The 1860 Montgomery County census shows Keister as a 25-year-old farmer with neither real estate nor personal property. He lived in the same household as Sarah Keister, 63, with $2,600 in real estate and $600 in personal property, and Mary Long, 30 (1860 Virginia Census, no. 1363, Montgomery County, 699).

37. There were two William H. Thomases in the Fourth Virginia, one in Company E and the other in Company L. Black refers to the latter, born in 1837, who had enlisted as a corporal in July 1861 at Blacksburg and was promoted to 2nd Lieutenant on April 22, 1862. He would be promoted to 2nd Lieutenant in July 1862, be assigned to the Ordnance Bureau in August 1862, and resign from Confederate service on October 9, 1862 (Compiled Service Records, Virginia, no. 412; Robertson, *Fourth Virginia*, 76). Thomas is shown in the 1860 Montgomery County census as 24 years old, with no occupation, real estate, or personal property listed. He lived in the household of William Thomas, a 64-year-old farmer with $42,000 in real estate and $31,250 in personal property. Lucretia H. Thomas, 57, and Julia Thomas, 16, were also in the household (1860 Virginia Census, no.

1363, Montgomery County, 699). The elder William Thomas owned 14 slaves (1860 Virginia Slave Schedules, no. 1394, Montgomery County, 120).

38. John T. Jernell, who had enlisted in Company E at Blacksburg in April 1861, was discharged on April 23, 1862 (Compiled Service Records, Virginia, no. 407; Robertson, *Fourth Virginia*, 58). Jernell may be John T. Journelle in the 1860 Montgomery County census; the family spelled its name both ways. Journelle is shown as a 22-year-old farmer living in the household of Lewis Journelle, a 65-year-old farmer with $6,000 in real estate and $775 in personal property. Others in the household included Melvina, 53; Mollie J., 32; Harriet, 27; Eliza B., 24; Hamilton P., 20; Lewis M., 18; Jasper N., 16; Amanda C., 12; and Jackson M. Journelle, 8 (1860 Virginia Census, no. 1363, Montgomery County, 743).

39. George T. Richardson enlisted in Company E at Blacksburg in April 1861 and was discharged on April 23, 1862. He would re-enlist in the Fourth Virginia on October 28, 1863, and would be wounded at the Battle of Payne's Farm on November 27 of the same year (Compiled Service Records, Virginia, no. 411; Robertson, *Fourth Virginia*, 70). Richardson, a 22-year-old laborer in the 1860 Montgomery County census, is shown as having no real estate or personal property. He lived in the same household as John H. Richardson, a 25-year-old laborer with $30 in personal property (1860 Virginia Census, no. 1363, Montgomery County, 746).

40. John Choice Galloway enlisted in Company E in Blacksburg in April 1861. He was discharged on April 23, 1862 (Compiled Service Records, Virginia, no. 406; Robertson, *Fourth Virginia*, 51). Galloway is shown in the 1860 Blacksburg census as an 18-year-old shoemaker living in the household of William D. Galloway, a 49-year-old shoemaker with $100 in personal property. Others in the household included Elizabeth, 42; Robert, 20, also a shoemaker; Vitiela M., 16; Susan E., 14; Everett O., 12; William F., 9; Charles M., 5; and an unnamed female, 1 (1860 Virginia Census, no. 1363, Montgomery County, 711).

41. As noted above, John Black was discharged a day later, on April 24.

42. George T. McDonald enlisted in Company E at Blacksburg in April 1861 and was discharged on April 23, 1862 (Compiled Service Records, Virginia, no. 409; Robertson, *Fourth Virginia*, 62). McDonald is shown as a 20-year-old farmer in the 1860 census living in the McDonald's Mill area of Montgomery County. He lived in the household of Edward McDonald, a 48-year-old farmer with $8,200 in real estate and $2,200 in personal property. Others in the household included Catharine, 46; Elizabeth, 22; John, 18; Sarah, 16; Mark M., 14; Martha V., 13; Catharine S., 11; and Naomi R. McDonald (1860 Virginia Census, no. 1363, Montgomery County, 759). Edward McDonald owned one slave (1860 Virginia Slave Schedules, no. 1394, Montgomery County, 121).

43. James E. Caldwell enlisted in Company E at Blacksburg in April 1861 and was discharged on April 23, 1862 (Compiled Service Records, Virginia, no. 408; Robertson, *Fourth Virginia*, 43). Caldwell is listed as a 27-year-old plasterer in the 1860 census. He lived in the household of Hugh Caldwell, a 56-year-old farmer with $850 in real estate and $225 in personal property. Sarah E., 51; Lewis H., 21; Montgomery T., 16; Giles, 12; and Orlanda Caldwell, 10, made up the rest of the household (1860 Virginia Census, no. 1363, Montgomery County, 755).

44. The man discharged on April 23 whom Black forgot is apparently William Hale, also of Company E, who enlisted in April 1861 at Blacksburg. Hale was wounded at Manassas on July 21, 1861, and was discharged at Swift Run Gap, April 23, 1862 (Compiled Service Records, Virginia, no. 406; Robertson, *Fourth Virginia*, 54). He is listed in the 1860 Montgomery County census as a 25-year-old merchant with $1,000 in personal property. He lived in the household of John Hale, a 50-year-old farmer with $3,500 in real estate and $1,300 in personal property. Sarah Hale, 46; Jacob, 23, with $200 in personal property; Daniel, an 18-year-old farmer; L. Don, 15; Z. Montgomery, 12; Mary M., 9; and Sarah C. Hale, 3, were also members of the household (1860 Virginia Census, no. 1363, Montgomery County, 744).

45. Banks occupied Harrisonburg with 19,000 men.

46. Ridley was made Adjutant on April 22, 1862 (Compiled Service Records, Virginia, no. 411; Robertson, *Fourth Virginia*, 70).

47. Robert L. Francisco enlisted in Company E of the Fourth Virginia at Blacksburg in April 1861 and was detailed as a Quartermaster Sergeant on August 14 of the same year. In June 1862 he would be made a Captain and Assistant Quartermaster (Compiled Service Records, Virginia, no. 405; Robertson, *Fourth Virginia*, 50). Francisco was married to Harvey Black's cousin Keziah, a sister of John and Edward Black. The 1860 census for Blacksburg shows him as a 36-year-old cabinet maker, born in Alabama, with $2,500 in real estate and $2,000 in personal property. In the same household were his wife, Keziah, age 30; and their children, Mary, 8; Charles, 6; and Lucy, 4. Two other cabinet makers also lived in the household: William Eakins, 22, and Robert Castle, 53 (1860 Virginia Census, no. 1363, Montgomery County, 710). Nannie Francisco Porter, a daughter of Robert Francisco, later wrote of the postwar relationship among John Black, Edward Black, and her father. "Each evening just after supper the two brothers came to visit their sister Kizzie and her husband and as the three men were Confederate soldiers, my father a Captain in Stonewall Jackson's Brigade, Lt. Edward Black under Gen. Joseph Johnston, and John Black Commander of the Home Guards, many were the war stories told by these veterans until the whole family were convulsed with laughter or sat in sorrowing silence as some tragic experience was related" (Porter, *Blacks and Other Families*, 15).

48. Albert Gallatin Pendleton enlisted as captain of the Smyth Blues, later organized as Company D of the Fourth Virginia Infantry, in April 1861 at Marion and was promoted to Major on January 31, 1862. Robertson notes that Pendleton had earlier been in line to command the Fourth Virginia, but that he had made a number of enemies in the regiment. The observation that he had "started home" must relate to a furlough rather than a discharge. No mention is made in Pendleton's service record of being discharged, though he later joined the Quartermaster's Department (Compiled Service Records, Virginia, 410; Robertson, *Fourth Virginia*, 10, 67). The 1860 census for 7 Mile Ford, Smyth County, shows Pendleton as a 23-year-old attorney with no real estate or personal property. He lived in a hotel (or boarding house) operated by Archibald B. Sprinkle, a 49-year-old hotel keeper with $8,500 in real estate and $10,000 in personal property. Twenty-nine others lived in the hotel (1860 Virginia census, no. 1377, Smyth County, 1058-59).

49. Dr. Joseph Crockett enlisted in the Wytheville Grays (Company A of the Fourth Virginia Infantry) on April 17, 1861, at Wytheville and was appointed assistant regimental surgeon on May 4, 1861. As Assistant Regimental Surgeon, Crockett replaced Harvey Black when the latter was on leave. John Apperson was critical of Crockett's manner in his diary entry for February 2, 1862, during one such instance: "Sick call is rather indefinite now. Dr. Crockett has no system in anything he does. He declares he will have sick call at 7 o'clock but is never seen till some hours after" (Apperson diaries, no. 3, Virginia Polytechnic Institute and State University Libraries.) Crockett would be mortally wounded at the battle of Gaine's Mill on June 27, 1862, taking part in a charge against a Union battery (Compiled Service Records, Virginia, no. 404; Robertson, *Fourth Virginia*, 46; *Official Records*, 11, pt. 2:578, 991). Crockett appears as a 27-year-old physician living in his father's household in Wytheville in the 1860 census. His father, Robert Crockett, was a 56-year-old physician with $35,000 in real estate and $54,800 in personal property. Others in the household were Catharine, 30; Mary, 50; and Robert Crockett, a 24-year-old lawyer (see note 50 below). Neither Joseph nor Robert is shown as having property in their own names. Nannie McKee, 9, was also a member of the household (1860 Virginia census, no. 1385, Wythe County, 737-38).

50. Joseph Crockett's brother was Robert Crockett, Jr., who enlisted in the Wythe County Grays on April 17, 1861 — the same company and date as Dr. Crockett. Robert Crockett, Jr. was a 24-year-old lawyer when he enlisted. Robert Crockett was elected a 2nd Lieutenant on April 22, 1862, the day before this letter was written. He would be wounded at Second Manassas on August 30, 1862, then detailed as an enrolling officer on September 1, 1863. He later served as a Captain in the 14th Virginia Cavalry (Compiled Service Records, Virginia, no. 404; Robertson, *Fourth Virginia*, 46). See note 49 above for census information on Crockett.

51. Apperson refers to Abe as "Dr. B's man" in his diary entry for May 22, 1862: "Passing by Hamburg I saw Dr. B's man Abe—sick. I gave him some medicine" (Apperson diaries, no. 3, Virginia Polytechnic Institute and State University Libraries). Other than this brief reference, neither Abe nor Taylor could be identified.

52. John S. Apperson joined Company D of the Fourth Virginia in April 1861 at Marion. He was named regimental hospital steward by Harvey Black in June 1861. He applied to be reappointed as a hospital steward for the Fourth Regiment on March 4, 1862. On that date, Apperson wrote in his letter of application that he had been a "student of medicine for two years and . . . acting Steward for the 4th Regt. Va Vol's for nine months, and desire to continue in the position, that I may the better qualify myself for the practice of medicine hereafter." A day later, Harvey Black wrote to Samuel P. Moore, Confederate Surgeon General, that Apperson "has been discharging the duties of this office since June last, and I take pleasure in recommending him to your most favorable consideration. . ." See Letters Received by the Confederate Adjutant and Inspector General (U.S. National Archives Microcopy M474), no. 2, A-129. Hereafter cited as Letters Received by the Confederate Adjutant and Inspector General. Apperson was reappointed on April 12, 1862 (Compiled Service Records, Virginia, no. 402; and Apperson diaries, no. 3, May 1, 1862, Virginia Polytechnic Institute and State University Libraries).

53. General Richard S. Ewell had a long private conference with Jackson on April 28. On April 30 his division of 8,000 men would be moved into the camp at Swift Run Gap only hours after Jackson had vacated it to move southward.

54. "Ed" is probably a reference to Edward Black, Harvey Black's cousin.

55. William P. Hickman, age 50, is shown as an Old School Presbyterian minister in the 1860 Blacksburg census. He lived near the Harvey Black family with his wife Margaret, age 38, and eight children: Eliza J., 15; Mary C., 13; James B., 11; Emma S., 9; J. Hoge, 5; Kate L., 3; Lula L., 1; and Maggie, 1 month. Lioni Smith, 22, also lived in the household. Hickman is shown as having $14,500 in real estate and $2,500 in personal property (1860 Virginia Census, no. 1363, Montgomery County, 708). He owned two slaves (1860 Virginia Slave Schedules, no. 1394, Montgomery County, 118). Hickman is also listed in Black's account book, with the accounts listed there ending in 1860 (Black medical account book, Virginia Polytechnic Institute and State University Libraries, 305). He would be killed in action at the Battle of Cloyd's Farm on May 9, 1864, having joined a volunteer company organized to support Confederate forces at that engagement. See Ellison A. Smyth, *A History of the Blacksburg Presbyterian Church: Its First 150 Years* (Blacksburg, Virginia: n.p., 1982), 55.

56. New Orleans surrendered to Capt. David Farragut on April 25.

57. Dr. Robert L. Dabney, a Presbyterian minister, had been chaplain of the 18th Virginia Regiment when Jackson appointed him Assistant Adjutant General for the Valley Army on April 22, 1862 (Compiled Service Records, General and Staff Officers, no. 70).

58. "Aunt Liz" is Elizabeth Peck.

59. Benjamin F. Whitescarver, a 35-year-old surveyor, enlisted in Company E in April 1861 at Blacksburg. He was detailed as a Quartermaster Sergeant on June 6, 1861, and was appointed Captain and Assistant Quartermaster on July 19, 1861 (Compiled Service Records, Virginia, no. 413; and Robertson, *Fourth Virginia*, 80). Whitescarver could not be located in the 1860 Montgomery County census.

60. Robert L. Francisco would be appointed Captain in the Quartermaster Department on July 11, 1862, to report to the Fourth Virginia Regiment (Compiled Service Records, General and Staff Officers, no. 98).

61. Mary Hart Preston was the wife of Robert T. Preston, at that time Colonel of the 28th Virginia Regiment (he was mustered out on April 29, 1862). Robert and Mary Preston lived in Solitude, a house now part of the campus of Virginia Polytechnic Institute and State University. See John Frederick Dorman, *The Prestons of Smithfield and Greenfield in Virginia* (Louisville: The Filson Club, 1982), 264-265. Hereafter cited as Dorman, *The Prestons of Smithfield and Greenfield*. In the 1860 Montgomery County census, Robert Preston is listed as a 57-year-old farmer with $44,830 in real estate and $37,500 in personal property. Mary Preston, 57, and James P. Preston, 22, also lived in the household, as did Patrick Bohan, a 62-year-old gardener (1860 Virginia Census, no. 1363, Montgomery County, 702). Preston owned 33 slaves (1860 Virginia Slave Schedules, no. 1394, Montgomery County, 117). Robert Preston was later active in the Home Guard in Montgomery County, to judge from documents dating from August and September 1863 (*Official Records*, 29, pt. 2:667, 717, 744).

62. John C. Spickard is listed in the 1860 census as a 56-year-old saddler in Blacksburg, whose real estate was valued at $1,600 and whose personal property was valued at $275 . His wife, Nancy, age 48, and three daughters (Mollie, 21; Susan, 20; and Ellen, 19) were in the same household (1860 Virginia Census, no. 1363, Montgomery County, 707). Spickard owned one slave (1860 Virginia Slave Schedules, no. 1394, Montgomery County, 118). A circingle (or surcingle) is a belt used to bind a saddle or pack to a horse's back.

63. Jackson's Valley Army, having left Swift Run Gap on April 30, marched through heavy mud and quicksand to Port Republic, taking three days to make the sixteen-mile march. On May 3, they would march east over Brown's Gap, arriving at Mechum's Station, presumably to abandon the Shenandoah Valley and head to Richmond from there.

64. Charles Black was two years old at the time this letter was written. Nothing certain is known about the nature of his illness, except that he

survived it. Given Black's description, however, one might speculate that the infant was suffering from a streptococcal infection.

65. "Squire Peck" is likely William H. Peck, the father of John and Edward Peck. The house to which Black refers is possibly the house of Germanicus Kent, who was living with the Black family until his death in March 1862.

66. Apperson's diary entry for this same date echoes Black's concern about imminent action. He wrote from near Port Republic: "Today we have been at the same place. Various orders have come and we are ready to move. . . . The enemy is reported to be in cannon shot of us—movements are active" (Apperson diaries, no. 3, May 2, 1862, Virginia Polytechnic Institute and State University Libraries). As Harvey Black notes in the next paragraph, Federal forces kept beyond range and "nothing was done."

67. Black's account of the march to Mechum's Station is graphic but probably not overstated in its description of the difficulties the Valley Army encountered. As James I. Robertson, Jr., has written, "men and horses floundered in the mud as the army crept through the Blue Ridge and then veered southward toward Mechum's River Station and Virginia Central Railroad. Averaging little more than five miles a day, the army half crawled and half waded through the quagmire for three days." See James I. Robertson, Jr., *The Stonewall Brigade* (Baton Rouge: Louisiana State University Press, 1963), 85.

68. John Apperson commented in his diary on the large number of sick men in the Fourth Virginia during this march. Writing from Brown's Gap on May 3, he wrote, "The sick list is always large on a march, larger in the 4th Reg't than in any other from what I learn. Orders from Gen. Winder put all those complaining in the rear of their respective Regiments in charge of the asst Surg. Some 38 of our Reg't had to march in that way and a delapidated set they were. Rheumatic patients, and those affected with Bronchial diseases, Diarrhea, Dysentery, and all other diseases almost had some victims" (Apperson diaries, no. 3, May 3, 1862, Virginia Polytechnic Institute and State University Libraries).

69. On the night of Saturday, May 3, the Valley Army boarded westbound trains that would take them to Staunton. From there they would march farther westward to meet up with General Edward Johnson's forces. Johnson's brigade of 3,000 men would join Jackson's forces on May 5. On May 8, the Confederates would defeat a Union army at McDowell, Virginia, 35 miles west of Staunton.

70. In using the term "contrabands," Black was alluding to the practice of Union officials to designate slaves as contrabands of war, a practice begun by General Benjamin Butler at Fort Monroe, Virginia, in May 1861. The term contrabands became a general slang term for blacks and slaves.

71. Charlotte Cooksey L. Wade ("Aunt Cook"), age 35 in the 1860 census, was the aunt of Mollie Black and the wife of William A. Wade, age 33. The Wades lived with Elizabeth Amiss, age 70, shown as having real estate valued at $9,325 and personal property valued at $7,000. Elizabeth Amiss was Charlotte Wade's mother and Mollie Black's grandmother on her mother's side of the family. In the same household were Elizabeth Wade, daughter of William and Charlotte Wade, 9; and three members of the Amiss family: Louis, 42, a clerk with $6,000 in real estate; Mary, age 30; and Louis, one month old. William Wade's occupation is given as clerk; he had no personal property or real estate listed in his own name (1860 Virginia Census, no. 1363, Montgomery County, 706). Elizabeth Amiss and "two others" owned nine slaves, according to the 1860 slave schedules (1860 Virginia Slave Schedules, no. 1394, Montgomery County, 118).

Two: "Their Loss is Much Greater than Ours in Numbers, But Not Equal to Ours in Worth": August 31-December 15, 1862

1. Sunday, August 31st was a day for the Stonewall Brigade to treat its wounded and bury its dead. Some of its members were engaged in burial detail after the battles of Groveton and Second Manassas, and wounded men were still being located on the battlefield. The next day, September 1, the Brigade would witness action again at the Battle of Chantilly, or Ox Hill. For a graphic portrayal of the trials of the Confederate medical staff at Groveton and Second Manassas, see Horace H. Cunningham, *Field Medical Services at the Battles of Manassas* (Athens: University of Georgia Press, 1968), 85-89. Hereafter cited as Cunningham, *Field Medical Services at the Battles of Manassas*. The location of Cross Hospital has not been determined; no hospital with that name could be located at or near the Manassas battlefield. It is likely that the hospital was a temporary one set up at the house or farm of an individual named Cross. The most likely candidate in Prince William County is John Cross, a 46-year-old farmer with $1,450 in real estate and $1,075 in personal property living in Groveton. Others in the Cross household were Elizabeth, 48; Susan, 21; Abbe, 20; John P., 19; Hamilton, 17; Ebin, a 12-year-old male; Barzilio, a 10-year-old male; Atossa, a 9-year-old female; Golia, a 6-year-old female; and Rinaldo, a 4-year-old male. John P. and Hamilton Cross are shown as being farm laborers (1860 Virginia Census, no. 1373, Prince William County, 429).

2. Jackson's Division at Second Manassas consisted of the Stonewall (First) Brigade, commanded by William Smith Hanger Baylor, Jones's (Second) Brigade, Taliaferro's (Third) Brigade, and Starke's (Fourth) Brigade. The Stonewall Brigade went into the Second Manassas Campaign with only 635 men. Its already thin ranks were further decimated during the three days of fighting, suffering 415 casualties—67 killed and 348 wounded (*Official Records*, 12, pt. 2:561). The word "took" in the phrase

"Stonewall Brigade took a prominent part" was apparently copied over with another word, indecipherable except to say that it ends with the letters "ted."

3. According to the report of Captain Jonathan B. Evans on the Fourth Virginia's involvement at Groveton and Second Manassas, the regiment suffered a total of 97 dead and wounded from the two battles, a figure that echoes Black's estimate of "near 100" casualties. Sixteen men were killed and 60 wounded on August 28 at Groveton; 2 were killed and 19 wounded on the 29th and 30th at Manassas (*Official Records*, 12, pt. 2:662).

4. Andrew J. Cromer, a member of Company E of the Fourth Virginia Regiment, enlisted in April 1861 at Blacksburg. He was killed at Second Manassas on August 30, 1862 (Compiled Service Records, Virginia, no. 404; Robertson, *Fourth Virginia*, 47). Cromer is shown in the 1860 census for Montgomery County as a 20-year-old farmer with $125 in personal property. He lived in the household of William Cromer, a 49-year-old farmer with $1,200 in real estate and $1,800 in personal property. Samuel W., an 18-year-old farmer; Charles D., a 16-year-old farmer; Virginia A., 13; Evelina A., 11; Franklin W., 9; and Susan O. Cromer, 6, were also members of the household. In addition, Nancy Pharis, 35; and James Fisher, a 17-year-old farmer, lived in the household (1860 Virginia Census, no. 1363, Montgomery County, 620).

5. Miles F. Adams of Company E enlisted on March 12, 1862 at Blacksburg, and was killed at Groveton on August 28, 1862 (Compiled Service Records, Virginia, no. 402; Robertson, *Fourth Virginia*, 37). Adams appears in the 1860 census for Montgomery County as an 18-year-old laborer living with his parents, John W. Adams, a 40-year-old blacksmith with $400 in personal property, and Nancy J. Adams, also 40. Siblings in the household included Giles M., 15 (also listed as a laborer); William J., 14; Harriet E., 11; Nancy J., 5; John W., 2; and Lucretia, 4 months (1860 Virginia Census, no. 1363, Montgomery County, 747).

6. The service records of both Robert and Ed Peck indicate that they were wounded at Groveton on August 28, 1862, but do not give details on their wounds (Compiled Service Records, Virginia, no. 410).

7. David Tobias ("Tob") Robinson (or Robison), a member of Company E, enlisted in September 1861 at Camp Harman. He was wounded in the hip on August 30, 1862, at Second Manassas. He would later be wounded and captured at Gettysburg on July 3, 1863. Exchanged in August 1863, he would be promoted to 2nd Lieutenant on March 8, 1864 (Compiled Service Records, Virginia, no. 411; Robertson, *Fourth Virginia*, 70). David Robinson is listed in the 1860 Montgomery County census as an 18-year-old farmer with no real estate or personal property in his name. He lived in the household of Matthew Robinson, a 56-year-old farmer with $7,500 in real estate and $1,250 in personal property. Margaret Robinson, 58, also lived in the household (1860 Virginia Census, no. 1363,

Montgomery County, 699). These may have been his grandparents; to judge by a later reference connecting "Nan" to David Robi(n)son, his mother may have been Ann Robison, 38, with $500 in real estate and $100 in personal property in the McDonald's Mill area. In the same household lived Julina and Susannah Bowles, both 28 (1860 Virginia Census, no. 1363, Montgomery County, 748). See Chapter 4, note 16.

8. Charles Carden enlisted in Company E in April 1861 at Blacksburg, and is shown as being on duty through April 1862 (Compiled Service Records, Virginia, no. 403; Robertson, *Fourth Virginia*, 43, where his name is given as Charles Carder). Charles Carden is shown as a 19-year-old shoemaker in the 1860 Blacksburg census. He lived in the household of George Carden, a 52-year-old shoemaker with no real estate and $30 in personal property listed. In the same household were George Carden's wife, Mary A. Carden, 46, and four other children: Margaret, 21; Nancy C., 15; Sarah E.,15; and Harvey B. Carden, 7 (1860 Virginia Census, no. 1363, Montgomery County, 708).

9. Adam Cunningham of Company E had joined the Fourth Virginia on March 13, 1862, at Blacksburg, and was wounded at Groveton on August 28, 1862. Cunningham would be captured at Spotsylvania on May 12, 1864 and imprisoned at Elmira Prison, where he would die on September 18 of the same year (Compiled Service Records, Virginia, no. 404; Robertson, *Fourth Virginia*, 47). He is shown in the 1860 Montgomery County census as a 36-year-old laborer with $30 in personal property living in the same household with Martha J. Cunningham, 35; and M. D. Taylor, a 5-year-old female (1860 Virginia Census, no. 1363, Montgomery County, 747).

10. Joseph Henderson, a member of Company E, enlisted in April 1861 at Blacksburg. He was elected sergeant on April 22, 1862, and was wounded at Groveton on August 28, 1862. He would receive another wound at Chancellorsville on May 3, 1863, desert on September 20 of that year, and take an oath of allegiance to the Union later in the same month (Compiled Service Records, Virginia, no. 407; Robertson, *Fourth Virginia*, 56). Henderson is listed in the 1860 Montgomery County census as a 17-year-old laborer living in the household of Ephriam E. Sites, a 48-year-old farmer with $1,800 in real estate and $450 in personal property. Others in the Sites household included Barbara, 39; S. Jackson, 20; Sarah J., 18; Mary J., 14; Simon P., 10; John E., 6; and Lavinia A. Sites, 1 month. Mary Shanks, 72, and Catharine Shanks, 68, also lived in the household (1860 Virginia Census, no. 1363, Montgomery County, 752).

11. William C. Slusser enlisted in Company L in July 1861 at Blacksburg as a sergeant. Promoted to 3rd Lieutenant on December 6, 1861 and to 1st Lieutenant on April 22, 1862, he was killed at Groveton on August 28, 1862 (Compiled Service Records, Virginia, no. 412; Robertson, *Fourth Virginia*, 73). The 1860 Montgomery County census shows him as a 30-year-old farmer living in the household of John B. Slusser, a 57-year-old

farmer with $15,000 in real estate and $4,350 in personal property. Elizabeth Slusser, 56, and John H. Slusser, 19, were also in the household, as were Nancy Hamlin, 34, and John Martin, 15 (1860 Virginia Census, no. 1363, Montgomery County, 745).

12. George R. Pace, who enlisted in Company L in July 1861 at Blacksburg, was wounded at Groveton on August 28, 1862. He would later be wounded at Chancellorsville on May 3, 1863 (Compiled Service Records, Virginia, no. 410; Robertson, *Fourth Virginia*, 66). Pace lived in the household of Charles Ronald; see Chapter 1, note 28.

13. David Earhart (or Earheart), a member of Company L, enlisted at Blacksburg on April 16, 1862. His name is spelled both as "Earhart" and "Earheart" in his service record, which doesn't record his wound at Second Manassas. Earhart would be killed at Chancellorsville on May 3, 1863 (Compiled Service Records, Virginia, no. 405; Robertson, *Fourth Virginia*, 49). He does not appear in the 1860 Montgomery County census, though a David Earheart appears in nearby Giles County as a 26-year-old Pearisburg merchant with $400 in real estate and $3,500 in personal property. Earheart lived in the household of Henry G. Dennis, a 40-year-old merchant with $2,300 in real estate and $5,100 in personal property listed in his name. Others in the Dennis household included Mary Dennis, 38; twins Emma and Mary, 11; Joseph, 8; Sally, 5; John, 3; and Edwin, 5 months. John W. Mullins, a 22-year-old clerk with $180 in personal property, and Sarah Dougherty, a 23-year-old domestic, also lived in the household (1860 Virginia census, no. 1345, Giles County, 915).

14. In choosing not to amputate Ed Peck's arm, Black was certainly aware that he was not taking the easy and obvious course of action, and he justified it by citing other surgeons' opinions. The most common treatment for serious wounds to the extremities was amputation, a treatment necessitated by the large number of wounded men who had to be treated quickly and by the increased danger from infections caused by probing the wound and possibly leaving foreign matter in it. It is unclear how long Peck had to recuperate; there is no mention of a long sick furlough in his service record.

15. The most likely candidate for Mr. Hutchinson is Melville B. Hutchinson, shown in the 1860 census as a 51-year-old farmer in Loudoun County with $3,300 in real estate and $2,140 in personal property living in the Pleasant Valley area. Others in the same household included Lusinda, 50; Elemuel F., 27; Maria, 24; Lucey E., 22; Mary C., 20; George C., 18; Charles L, 17; Lidia A., 14; and Rorinda E. Hutchinson, 12 (1860 Virginia Census, no. 1359, Loudoun County, 323). John Apperson refers to a Mr. Hutchinson of Loudoun County, presumably the same person, in his diary entry for October 16, 1862: "I traded horses today with Major Mercer. I expect that I made a bad exchange. The horse I had I got from Mr. Hutchinson in Loudoun County, Va., a large horse that travelled very finely but the number of his years were too many for me, or too many for

him to see many more" (Apperson diaries, no. 3, Virginia Polytechnic Institute and State University Libraries).

16. John A. English is listed in the 1860 Loudoun County census as a 39-year-old farmer in Middleburgh with $15,500 in real estate and $8,740 in personal property. In the household lived his wife Henrietta C., 38, and daughter Ina J., 13 (1860 Virginia Census, no. 1359, Loudoun County, 552-53).

17. "Dr. Powell" is possibly John S. Powell, a 29-year-old physician in Occoquan, Prince William County in the 1860 census. He is shown as having no real estate and $200 in personal property. He lived in the household of William Selectman, a 52-year-old farmer with $10,100 in real estate and $11,330 in personal property. Others in the household included Elizabeth, 53; George A., a 21-year-old farm laborer; William H., a 19-year-old clerk; and Redman Selectman, a 16-year-old farm laborer. John H. Hammill, a 35-year-old merchant, lived in the household as well (1860 Virginia Census, no. 1373, Prince William County, 546). Powell had earlier been an Assistant Surgeon in the 49th Virginia Infantry. He enlisted on July 19, 1861, and resigned Feb. 1, 1862 for reasons of health (Compiled Service Records, Virginia, no. 920).

18. After Second Manassas, a number of Confederate hospitals were moved to Aldie, in Loudoun County. See Cunningham, *Field Medical Services at the Battles of Manassas*, 108 n. 97.

19. Black's use of the term "assistant" probably refers to assistant surgeon in this instance, and thus would not include stewards and nurses.

20. In expressing concern about being made a prisoner of war, Black, of course, was alluding to a situation that was rapidly changing because of the negotiations that had taken place during and after the Confederate occupation of Winchester the previous spring.

21. Matthew Davis Bennett was wounded at Groveton on August 28, 1862 (Compiled Service Records, Virginia, no. 402).

22. Hugh Augustus White enlisted in the Liberty Hall Volunteers, a Rockbridge County company, on June 8, 1861, at Lexington. This company would later be organized as Company I of the Fourth Virginia Infantry; most of its members were college students and professors from Washington College in Lexington. A divinity student, White was promoted to Sergeant on September 13, 1861, and to Captain in April 1862. He was killed in action on August 30, 1862, at Second Manassas (Compiled Service Records, Virginia, no. 413; *Official Records*, 12, pt. 2:819). White could not be found in the 1860 Virginia census.

23. Andrew E. Gibson enlisted in Company D in April 1861 at Marion. He was appointed regimental quartermaster on June 6, 1861, and was promoted to Captain on February 26, 1862. He died on August 29, 1862, of wounds received the day before (Compiled Service Records, Virginia, no. 406; *Official Records*, 12, pt. 2:819). Gibson appears in the 1860 Smyth

County census as a 22-year-old merchant with no real estate or personal property. He lived in the town of Marion, in the household of Edward S. Watson, a 53-year-old lawyer. Others in the household were Virginia C. Watson, 45; Sarah A. Gibson, 43, with $3,500 in real estate and $10,000 in personal property; Mary A. Gibson, 20; and James J. McMahon, a 35-year-old Presbyterian minister (1860 Virginia Census, no. 1377, Smyth County, 1052).

24. William Smith Hanger Baylor, commanding the Stonewall Brigade, was killed August 30 at Second Manassas. A native of Augusta County, Virginia, Baylor was Commonwealth Attorney for the city of Staunton when the war began. He had been put in command of the 5th Virginia Infantry at its reorganization in April 1862. After Winder's death at Cedar Mountain on August 9, Baylor was placed in command of the Stonewall Brigade. Baylor's death came before his promotion to brigadier general could be approved. In the words of General Jackson, Baylor "fell in front of his brigade while nobly leading and cheering it on to the charge" (*Official Records*, 12, pt. 2:647).

25. John Neff, also killed on August 30, commanded the 33rd Virginia Infantry. He was killed while taking part in a regimental charge (*Official Records*, 12, pt. 2:657). The son of a Dunkard minister, Neff was also a member of this pacifist sect. He had joined the Confederate army against his parents' wishes.

26. The 27th Regiment, commanded by Andrew Jackson Grigsby, had only 65 men present at the Battle of Groveton on August 28; of these, 4 were killed and 24 were wounded. The regiment suffered no casualties on the 29th, and lost one killed and one wounded on the 30th, by which time its strength had dwindled to 45 men (*Official Records*, 12, pt. 2:662-63).

27. William Terry was wounded in his arm and side at Groveton on August 27, 1862 (Compiled Service Records, Virginia, no. 412; Robertson, *Fourth Virginia*, 76).

28. John Hall Fulton, a member of Company A, enlisted in April 1861 at Wytheville as a 3rd Lieutenant. He was promoted to 1st Lieutenant on May 13, 1861, and to Captain on April 22, 1862. His wound came at Groveton on August 28, 1862. Later severely wounded at Chancellorsville on May 3, 1863, he would have a leg amputated and would be released from Confederate service on August 1, 1863 (Compiled Service Records, Virginia, no 405; Robertson, *Fourth Virginia*, 51). Fulton appears in the 1860 census for Wythe County as a 24-year-old lawyer with $100 in personal property, living in Wytheville. James T. Gleaves, Jr., also a lawyer, is in the same household. Gleaves was 26 and had $2,900 in personal property (1860 Virginia census, no. 1385, Wythe County, 740).

29. Benjamin Drake Fulton of Company A enlisted in April 1861 at Wytheville and was promoted to 2nd Lieutenant on April 22, 1862. He was wounded at Groveton on August 28, 1862. He would be killed in

action nearly two years later, at Spotsylvania on May 12, 1864 (Compiled Service Records, Virginia, no. 405; Robertson, *Fourth Virginia*, 51). Fulton appears as 19 years old and living in the household of his father, A. S. Fulton, a 59-year-old judge with $25,000 in real estate and $12,000 in personal property, in Wythe County. Others in the household were Sallie, 45; Andrew K., a 28-year-old farmer; Mary, 16; William, 4; and Betsey Fulton, 50. Betsy Greene, 30; John W. Greene, a 29-year-old merchant with $500 in personal property; and Andrew Greene, 2, also lived in the household (1860 Virginia census, no. 1385, Wythe County, 759).

30. Although Brigadier General Richard S. Ewell had a leg amputated after having a knee shattered at Groveton, he would return to Confederate service in May 1863 to replace Jackson as commander of the Second Corps of the Army of Northern Virginia.

31. Black's reference to the fighting "before Richmond" is an allusion to the Seven Days Campaign, which lasted from June 25 to July 1, 1862.

32. Rev. Foushee Tebbs enlisted on July 1, 1862 as the Fourth Virginia Regiment's chaplain. Tebbs would be absent from service due to illness from December 20, 1862 to April 8, 1863, when he resigned (Compiled Service Records, Virginia, no. 412; Robertson, *Fourth Virginia*, 76). John Apperson, who referred to him as "Parson Tibbs," records his leaving in his diary entries for April 7 and 8, 1863. On April 8, Apperson recorded that "Parson Tibbs left this morning. I gave him some directions . . . as he went towards Charlottesville, Va" (Apperson diaries, no. 4, Virginia Polytechnic Institute and State University Libraries). Tebbs is shown in the 1860 Rockbridge County census as F. C. Tebbs, a 38-year-old Methodist preacher with $300 in personal property, living in Lexington (1860 Virginia census, no. 1378, Rockbridge County, 21).

33. On September 19, two days after the Battle of Antietam, the Army of Northern Virginia began its march back to Virginia. The Stonewall Brigade reached Martinsburg, Virginia (now West Virginia) on September 25, passed through the town, and went into camp about a mile beyond it.

34. Edwin J. Amiss, a 50-year-old farmer in the 1860 census for Montgomery County, owned real estate valued at $43,600 and personal property valued at $45,000. His wife was 44-year-old Sarah S. Amiss (1860 Virginia Census, no. 1363, Montgomery County, 753). Amiss owned 21 slaves (1860 Virginia Slave Schedules, no. 1394, Montgomery County, 121). Edwin and Sarah Amiss were the parents of Elizabeth Amiss Palmer, Mollie Black's cousin; see note 48 below.

35. The number of stragglers—men falling from the ranks during a march, disappearing, or deserting—was very high during the invasion of Maryland. Several factors contributed to the magnitude of straggling, including lack of proper shoes, a poor diet consisting largely of green corn, and a reluctance on the part of some soldiers to turn the war from a defensive to an offensive struggle by invading the North.

36. The Battle of Antietam, or Sharpsburg, on September 17 resulted in nearly 25,000 total casualties on both sides, making that battle the most costly single day in the war. Union forces in the battle numbered 75,316; Confederate forces numbered 37,330. Union casualties numbered 2,108 killed, 9,549 wounded, and 753 missing. Confederate casualties were 2,700 killed, 9,024 wounded, and 2,000 missing.

37. The *Official Records* cites a reconaissance from Shepherdstown on September 25, but no reports give further details (*Official Records*, 19, pt. 1:1).

38. Black served as acting medical director for his division between the time this letter was written and mid-November 1862, in Dr. Robert T. Coleman's absence (see note 39 for information on Coleman and note 41 for more information on the division). It is unclear exactly when Black's duties as chief surgeon of the division began; his service record is silent on the matter. John Apperson, who resumed writing in his diaries on October 8, 1862, after a gap of several months, noted on that date that "Dr. Black has been called to the post of Chief Surgeon of the Division and I am still with him" (Apperson diaries, no. 3, Virginia Polytechnic Institute and State University Libraries).

39. Dr. Robert T. Coleman was appointed surgeon to the 21st Virginia Infantry on July 16, 1861; by the Battle of Antietam on September 17, 1862, he had become Chief Surgeon of the 1st Division, retaining that position at least through 1863 (Compiled Service Records, General and Staff Officers, no. 59; *Official Records*, 12, pt. 1:403; 21:677; 27, pt. 2:517). John Apperson wrote of Coleman in his diary entry for November 13, 1862: "Dr. Coleman arrived today . . . He is an insinuating man and one of the most loquacious I ever saw. Really I think from appearance talking is part of his being. A nice gentleman though he is, and one whose energy and pleasing qualifications fit him well for the post he fills" (Apperson diaries, no. 4, Virginia Polytechnic Institute and State University Libraries). None of the Robert Colemans listed as heads of households in Jackson, *Virginia 1860 Federal Census* were physicians. For a biographical sketch of Coleman, see William B. Atkinson, M.D., ed., *The Physicians and Surgeons of the United States* (Philadelphia: Charles Robson, 1878), 286-87. Coleman was one of the surgeons who would assist in the amputation of General Jackson's arm at Chancellorsville.

40. Apperson, who continued to work under Black when he was Acting Division Surgeon, also thought the position a pleasant one. He wrote in his diary from division headquarters on October 21, 1862: "I have not been outside of the limits of the camp today. Camp has some charms like those of home itself to me. I have nearly every convenience that I wish, and hence am contented. I fear when Dr. Coleman returns from Richmond that he will take the place of the Division Surgeon and Dr. B will return to the regiment" (Apperson diaries, no. 3, Virginia Polytechnic Institute and State University Libraries).

41. The First Division of Jackson's Corps of the Army of Northern Virginia at the time of the Maryland Campaign consisted of Winder's (Stonewall) Brigade of the 2nd, 4th, 5th, 27th, and 33rd Virginia Infantry Regiments; Taliaferro's Brigade of the 47th and 48th Alabama and the 10th, 23rd, and 37th Virginia; Jones' Brigade of the 21st, 42nd, and 48th Virginia Infantry and 1st Virginia Battalion; and Starke's Brigade of the 1st, 2nd, 9th, 10th, and 15th Louisiana Infantry and Coppens' Louisiana Battalion (*Official Records*, 19, pt. 1:808). The Louisiana Brigade had joined the division on or around August 12, 1862 (*Official Records*, 19, pt. 1:1014). During the action at Antietam, two successive changes in command due to casualties put Grigsby in charge of the Division and Gardner in charge of the Stonewall Brigade, though it is unclear how long either of them remained in these respective positions (*Official Records*, 19, pt. 1:1012). Grigsby would later retire from Confederate service after being passed over for command of the Stonewall Brigade by Jackson; Gardner would be placed in command of the Fourth Virginia.

42. Charles A. Ronald would be seriously wounded in the thigh at Kearneysville three weeks after this letter was written on October 16. John Apperson recorded the scene: "We went out and found Colonel Ronald badly wounded in the left thigh by a fragment of a shell—it passed on the side but [word scratched out] on the outer side of the femoral artery and perhaps imbedded itself in the substance of some of the muscles of the thigh" (Apperson diaries, no. 3, October 16, 1862, Virginia Polytechnic Institute and State University Libraries). Though Ronald did not retire from Confederate service until September 1863, his command of the Fourth Virginia was effectively ended with this wound.

43. Alexander Crawford enlisted in Company L of the Fourth Virginia in July 1861 at Blacksburg. Detailed as a nurse in the Winchester hospitals from December 1861 to April 1862, he was killed August 28, 1862 at Groveton (Compiled Service Records, Virginia, no. 404; Robertson, *Fourth Virginia*, 46). Crawford could not be located in the 1860 Virginia census for Montgomery County or nearby counties.

44. Davidson Croy's service record shows him deserting at Second Manassas in August 1862; no further record of him is noted (Compiled Service Records, Virginia, no. 404). In a manuscript volume of Tobias Robinson listing members of Company E, William Davidson Croy is shown as deserting on August 28, 1862. Robinson's annotation next to his name is "Gone to Yankees" (David Tobias Robinson, "Company 'E' 4th Va. Inftry" [photocopy], Special Collections Department, Virginia Polytechnic Institute and State University Libraries, 9-10). Apparently Croy did not join another Virginia Confederate regiment at a later date; the only listing for him in the Index to Compiled Service Records, Virginia is in Company E of the Fourth Virginia.

45. Brothers James H. and John W. Thompson had both enlisted in Company E of the Fourth Virginia in April 1861. James transferred to the

28th Virginia on September 1, 1861. John would transfer to the 14th Virginia Cavalry on September 28, 1862, several days after this letter was written (Compiled Service Records, Virginia, no. 412; Robertson, *Fourth Virginia*, 76). The 1860 Blacksburg census lists James as a 22-year-old shoemaker and John as a 20-year-old mail carrier. They lived in the household of their father, Archibald Thompson, referred to as "Arch" in these letters. Thompson was a 50-year-old mail carrier with $1,500 in real estate and $500 in personal property. Sarah , 45; Nancy, 17; and Charles W. Thompson, 4, lived in the household as well (1860 Virginia Census, no. 1363, Montgomery County, 708). The Thompsons were close neighbors of the Blacks.

46. The illegible word may be "McMorrison" or an initial and a surname, such as "M. M____in." No suitable candidates could be located. No one named "McMorrison" appears in Jackson, *Virginia 1860 Federal Census*, nor are there any McMorrisons at all in the Montgomery County census. No McMorrison appears in the Index to Compiled Service Records, Virginia.

47. George W. Sheaf, shown in the 1860 census as a 44-year-old shoemaker born in Pennsylvania, lived in Blacksburg near the Black family. He had $800 in real estate and $100 in personal property. Others in the same household included his wife Malinda, 31; Amos C., 10; William, 6; John, 4; Robert, 3; and Edward, 1. Mary E. Barton, 13, and Lucy Mare, 11, also lived in the household, the latter a free black (1860 Virginia Census, no. 1363, Montgomery County, 707). George Sheaf had earlier served in Company E of the Fourth Virginia Regiment. He enlisted August 27, 1861, and was detailed as a drummer on November 29, 1861. He was discharged from service for a disability on March 3, 1862 (Compiled Service Records, Virginia, no. 411; Robertson, *Fourth Virginia*, 72).

48. William H. Palmer was at that time a Major in the First Virginia Infantry, having enlisted as a private on April 2, 1861. In October 1862, he would be detached from the First Virginia to serve on the staff of General A. P. Hill, and would later became Hill's chief of staff (Compiled Service Records, General and Staff Officers, no. 193). Palmer was born and raised in Richmond. He married Sarah Elizabeth Amiss of Blacksburg in 1856. She was the daughter of Edwin J. Amiss and Sarah (Peck) Amiss, and a cousin of Mollie Black. William H. Palmer appears in the 1860 Henrico County census as a 24-year-old merchant with $400 in personal property, living in a boarding house in Richmond, in Henrico County's 1st ward. Others in his family were Sarah E., 24; Laelia, 2; and Florence, 10 months (1860 Virginia census, no. 1352, Henrico County, 137). In 1861, the Palmers had a home in Montgomery County, Mountain View, near Blacksburg. After the war, they lived in Richmond and made Mountain View their summer home. For biographical information on Palmer, including his military record, see *History of Virginia*, vol. 5, *Virginia Biography*, (Chicago

and New York: The American Historical Society, 1924): 91-92, and *Hardesty's Encyclopedia*, 410.

49. Kent, the Blacks' oldest child, was nine years old at the time of this letter.

50. Elizabeth Black was six years old, soon to be seven, at this time.

51. Alexander Black was five years old when this letter was written.

52. "Ceal" is Cecelia L. Kent White, Mollie Black's sister, who was living in Unionist Marion County, Virginia. She was married to the Methodist educator William R. White, president of the West Virginia Conference Seminary in Fairmont, Virginia, from 1856 to 1863. Fairmont, in Marion County, was in that part of the state that would soon become West Virginia, and White would become that state's first Superintendent of Public Instruction in 1864. From 1852 to 1855 he had been Principal of the Olin and Preston Institute in Blacksburg. For biographical information on White, see George Wesley Atkinson, ed., *Prominent Men of West Virginia* (Wheeling, West Virginia: W. L. Callin, 1890), 732. W. R. White is shown in the 1860 Virginia census for Marion County as a 29-year-old high school teacher born in the District of Columbia. C. L. White, a 21-year-old female born in Illinois, lived in the same household. White is listed as having $5,000 in real estate and $350 in personal property (1860 Virginia Census, no. 1361, Marion County, 562).

53. Belle Boyd, the celebrated Confederate spy, may have been in transit after being imprisioned in Washington's Old Capitol Prison at this time. John P. Sherbourne's Special Orders No. 175, dated August 29, 1862, refers to turning over Belle Boyd, "now confined in Old Capitol Prison" to Major Gen. Dix to be sent through the lines to the south (*Official Records*, Series II, 4:461).

54. Apperson was also impressed by the depth of anti-Confederate sentiment in Martinsburg, as he noted in his diary entry for October 18, 1862, during an expedition of the Stonewall Brigade to destroy the Baltimore and Ohio Railroad facilities there. Apperson wrote: "The citizens of Martinsburg are the most unsound and bitter enemies we have travelled among — the citizens of Maryland not excepted. Not a handkerchief waves to us here but often a curl of the lips from some Yankee love-stricken woman" (Apperson diaries, no. 3, Virginia Polytechnic Institute and State University Libraries).

55. Between this letter and the next, there is a gap of almost two months. During this period, Black returned to the Fourth Virginia Regiment as its surgeon, then was placed in charge of hospitals at Winchester. He came back to the regiment before it moved toward Fredericksburg. According to Apperson, Black was asked in early December to take charge of hospitals for the Second Corps — possibly a reference to the Second Corps Field Hospital, which would be established several weeks later

(Apperson diaries, no. 4, November 14, 19, and December 2, 1862, Virginia Polytechnic Institute and State University Libraries).

56. John Apperson described the initial action of the Battle of Fredericksburg as experienced by the medical staff in his diary entry for December 13: "This morning the whole earth was shrouded in a canopy of snow and fog. Nothing could be seen more than a few hundred yards. We ate breakfast and put things in order to move as soon as it may be necessary. The two armies lay last night within 400 yards of each other, face to face. Precisely at 20 min. to 10 o'clock the first gun fired and the fight soon became general. Dr. Black moved after up above Mr. Yerby's and pitched his hospital tents and by noon the wounded commenced coming in" (Apperson diaries, no. 4, Virginia Polytechnic Institute and State University Libraries). By the end of December 14, the medical staff had been treating the wounded for two days. As Apperson remarked, "no one rests where one of our medical officers is" (Apperson diaries, no. 4, December 14, 1862, Virginia Polytechnic Institute and State University Libraries).

57. A. P. Hill's Light Division suffered 2,122 total casualties at Fredericksburg — 231 killed, 1,474 wounded, and 417 missing (*Official Records*, 21:648).

58. The entire Second Corps, including A. P. Hill's Division, suffered 3,415 casualties at Fredericksburg, according to Jackson's report of January 31, 1863. Three hundred forty-four men were killed, 2,889 wounded, and 526 missing (*Official Records*, 21:635). The Stonewall Brigade had 74 casualties — 4 killed, 69 wounded, and 1 missing (*Official Records*, 21:678). Casualties in the Fourth Virginia were light — none killed and 12 wounded (*Official Records*, 21:562). For the activities of the Fourth Virginia in the battle, see the report of William H. Terry, *Official Records*, 21:681-83.

59. Robert D. Gardner, in command of the Fourth Virginia, suffered a severe facial wound when he was struck by an artillery shell on December 13, 1862 (Compiled Service Records, Virginia, no. 406; *Official Records*, 21:677). Brigadier General E. F. Paxton, commander of the Stonewall Brigade, wrote on December 24, 1862: "Lieutenant-Colonel Gardner, after having passed unhurt and distinguished for his gallantry through all the battles of the campaign ... fell, at the head of his regiment, severely, if not fatally, wounded" (*Official Records*, 21:678). William Terry was given command of the Fourth Virginia; Gardner would be retired from Confederate service on April 9, 1864.

60. Lieutenant General James Longstreet commanded the First Army Corps. He reported his casualties at Fredericksburg as 251 killed, 1,516 wounded, and 120 missing, for a total of 1,894 (*Official Records*, 21:572). Clearly, Black's reference is to the number killed rather than to total casualties.

61. Because of a lack of hospital facilities in and around Fredericksburg, the wounded were sent by railroad to Richmond. Lafayette Guild,

Medical Director of the Army of Northern Virginia, reported on December 12 that "all the farm houses in this vicinity are filled with poor refugees from the bombarded town of Fredericksburg, and our limited transportation has precluded our having a sufficiency of tents; therefore, it will be necessary to have the wounded rapidly conveyed to Richmond, after the primary operations have been performed" (*Official Records*, 21:577). Apperson's diary entry for December 15 noted that "the wounded of this hospital are being sent away—taken to the R Road and sent to Richmond and then distributed to the hospitals" (Apperson diaries, no. 4, Virginia Polytechnic Institute and State University Libraries).

Three: "I Had Hoped that None of Our Near Relations Would Engage in the War on the Yankee Side": April 1-July 19, 1863

1. Apperson diaries, no. 4, December 18 and 19, 1862, Virginia Polytechnic Institute and State University Libraries.

2. "Muster Roll of Steward[s], Wardmaster[s], Cooks, Nurses, Matrons, and Detached Soldiers, Sick, in the Hospital of 2nd Corps, A N Va, Guiney's Station, April 1 - 31 May 1863," RG 109 (War Department Collection of Confederate Records), Box 20—Hospital Rolls, Virginia and Miscellaneous, Guiney's Station, U.S. National Archives. (Hereafter cited as Muster Roll, 2nd Corps Hospital, U.S. National Archives.) A total of 57 attendants are listed, although the hospital's surgeons are not included on the list. This is the most complete of four muster rolls of the hospital in the National Archives. The others date from December 31, 1862 and February 1-March 31, 1863 (two copies).

3. Keziah Shepherd appears in the 1860 census for Spotsylvania County as a 38-year-old female living in Fredericksburg in the household of M. W. Bailey, 60, an agent for the Adams Express, with no real estate and $300 in personal property. Thomas A. Wall, a 30-year-old clergyman with no real estate or personal property, lived in the household also (1860 Virginia Census, no. 1380, Spotsylvania County, 287).

4. Apperson diaries, no. 4, March 7, 1863, Virginia Polytechnic Institute and State University Libraries.

5. Charles W. Sydnor to "Miss Mollie," February 1, 1863, Charles W. Sydnor papers, Southern Historical Collection, University of North Carolina, Chapel Hill. Sydnor had been a medical student in Winchester before he joined the Second Corps Field Hospital as a steward (Compiled Service Records, General and Staff Officers, no. 240). Sydnor appears in the 1860 Frederick County census as a 28-year-old medical student living in Cedar Creek. He lived in the household of Richard M. Sydnor, a 73-year-old farmer. Others in the same household were Margaret, a 53-year-old housewife; Ann H., 23; George F., a 19-year-old farm hand; Silas H., 17; and Emma C. Sydnor, 13. None of the family members are shown as having real estate or personal property (1860 Virginia census, no. 1347,

Frederick County, 678-79). In a later letter, Sydnor remarked about the burdens the hospital staff faced during periods of action. "You know when an engagement is going on and a long time after, our department is kept very busy with the wounded," he wrote on April 30, 1863, near Fredericksburg (Sydnor to "Miss Mollie," Sydnor papers, University of North Carolina).

6. See note 31 below for information on Black's Ohio relatives in the Union. Though there is no evidence that either Harvey or Mollie Black bore ill will toward their Union brothers and cousins, one other member of the Black family certainly did. According to Nannie Francisco Porter, Ann Black, angered by the treatment of her brother Ed in a Union prison, would refuse to see members of the Black family of Ohio when they visited Blacksburg after the war. Porter writes that "Miss Nannie" Black "prided herself on being an unreconstructed rebel." After the war a well-appointed carriage came to her front gate. The visitors "inquired if that was the original home of John Black and when the hostess stated it was, they descended from the carriage and introduced themselves as descendants of William Black." At that point, Nannie Black told a servant "to show them out as they were Yankees" (Porter, *Blacks and Other Families*, 17).

7. Black wrote this letter on April Fool's Day, a day on which he apparently was the object of several gentle pranks. John Apperson noted in his diary entry for this date: "When I rose the cooks and workers were trying their skill at deception on each one as he made his appearance. Dr. Black had many calls unsolicited by him from the duped" (Apperson diaries, no. 4, Virginia Polytechnic Institute and State University Libraries).

8. The nature of Mollie Black's illness is unknown.

9. The records for births for Montgomery County list no births to Elizabeth A. Palmer and William Palmer during this period ("Register of Births, 1853-68," Montgomery County Courthouse, Christiansburg, Virginia). A long and somewhat disjointed section regarding a mistake in Black's bank account immediately after this sentence has been excised to facilitate the flow of the letter.

10. The reference to the force that Burnside had in North Georgia is unclear. Union General Ambrose Burnside was relieved of the command of the Army of the Potomac after the Union debacle at Fredericksburg. He was made commander of the Army of the Ohio, serving in that capacity from March 25 to December 12, 1863. He commanded no force in North Georgia during this period.

11. Major General J. E. B. ("Jeb") Stuart, commanding Lee's Cavalry, had already become famous for his daring raids and exotic manner. Stuart's cavalry troops had engaged Union General William W. Averell's cavalry at Kelly's Ford, Virginia on March 17; during April he guarded the Rappahannock river.

12. John Apperson commented on this incident in his diary entry for March 30, 1863. He wrote: "Today the Provost General made a descent upon a sutler's establishment and confiscated his entire stock and put him in the ranks. The offence was smuggling whiskey. Some 20 gallons was found among his goods, packed in rice and corn. About $1800 worth was sent to the Hospital. Among other things a box of tobacco. This pleased the lovers of the weed" (Apperson diaries, no. 4, Virginia Polytechnic Institute and State University Libraries).

13. This is Black's only reference to smallpox in those letters that have survived. Apperson mentions a smallpox ward in the Second Corps Field Hospital in his diary entries for January 3, 13, and 18, 1863. He also mentions deaths from smallpox in his entries for March 7 and April 1, 1863 (Apperson diaries, no. 4, Virginia Polytechnic Institute and State University Libraries).

14. "Kiz" is Keziah Francisco, Robert Francisco's wife.

15. No record of John Thompson's marriage could be located in Montgomery County marriage records. "Arch" is Archibald Thompson, John Thompson's father. See Chapter 2, note 45.

16. Black had apparently left the Chancellorsville area on May 8. John Apperson wrote in his entry for his diary that day: "Dr. Black received orders to send off all the wounded that could bear transportation and then move his hospital back to Guiney. Dr. went ahead and asked me to stay in the back. Nearly a hundred wagons reported to carry the wounded to Hamilton's Crossing." Later in the same entry he grew philosophical about the battlefield he was leaving: "Tomorrow we leave this field of late conflict and go back to a quiet retreat. Many are the scenes we have witnessed here; many are the sad reflections that must follow us after this. Here the distinction between the wealthy and poor, the learned and ignorant, the distinguished and the unknown are merged into one common lot. The friend and foe lay side by side suffering similar agonies at each other's hands." By the morning of May 10, however, Apperson was less concerned with speculative questions than with the condition of his feet, writing that "this morning we left camp and came in across the Telegraph Road towards Guiney Station. Yesterday my feet were so sore that it was with much difficulty that I could walk. This morning I feel much better" (Apperson diaries, no. 4, Virginia Polytechnic Institute and State University Libraries).

17. Major General Isaac Trimble had been wounded at Second Manassas and slowly recovered from the lingering effects of the wound until the Gettysburg Campaign. His Division—"Stonewall" Jackson's old division containing the Stonewall Brigade—was commanded temporarily by Brigadier General Raleigh E. Colston at Chancellorsville.

18. Chancellorsville is often viewed as Lee's greatest triumph. With only half the strength of Major General Joseph Hooker's Army of the

Potomac—60,000 as opposed to 130,000 men—Lee still split his Army of Northern Virginia twice in a daring attempt to outmaneuver Hooker. Lee left a small force at Fredericksburg and, driving the Union army back to Chancellorsville, placed 20,000 men there to demonstrate against the Union front. In the meantime, Jackson's Second Corps, numbering 26,000 men, marched through the Wilderness and around Hooker's army to attack it from the rear. Jackson emerged from the Wilderness at dusk on May 2; Hooker was caught off guard by Jackson's attack as he thought the Confederates were in retreat. The Union Army withdrew across the Rapidan River on May 5 and 6.

19. Total Union casualties for the Chancellorsville campaign were 17,287—1,606 killed, 9,762 wounded, and 5,919 missing. Total Confederate losses were 12,764—1,665 killed, 9,081 wounded, and 2,018 missing.

20. Dr. Graham is John Alexander Graham, a Rockbridge County physician who was surgeon of the Fifth Virginia Infantry. See Lee A. Wallace, Jr., *5th Virginia Infantry* (Lynchburg, Virginia: H. E. Howard, 1988), 121. He is likely the same person referred to by John Apperson in his diary entries for January 4, 1863, and January 9, 1863: "Dr. Graham is here on a visit to his brother who is very sick in the hospital" and "Dr. Graham came from the camp of the first Brigade" (Apperson diaries, no. 4, Virginia Polytechnic Institute and State University Libraries). None of the John Grahams listed in Jackson, *Virginia 1860 Federal Census* were physicians. No service record for Graham could be found among those for members of the Fifth Virginia Infantry.

21. The house was Major J. Horace Lacy's summer house, Ellwood, near the border between Spotsylvania and Orange counties. Lacy was the brother of the Reverend Beverly Tucker Lacy (see note 71 below), who buried "Stonewall" Jackson's amputated arm at Ellwood. The house was used for treating the wounded after Chancellorsville and, indeed, continued to be used for several months past this time. George M. Neese described the structure in his journal entry for November 11, 1863: "The house stands on Wilderness Run, in a lonely place about half a mile south of the Culpepper plank road; it is a good-sized farmhouse, built of wood, square, with two porticos and painted a dove color. From the apex of the roof a hospital flag still flutters in the cold November wind." See George M. Neese, *Three Years in the Confederate Horse Artillery* (New York and Washington: Neale Publishing Company, 1911), 236-37. Hereafter cited as Neese, *Three Years in the Confederate Horse Artillery*. Lacy was not occupying the house at the time. Rather, he was headquartered in Dublin, Virginia, as inspector of field transportation for the Department of Western Virginia. See A. Wilson Greene, *J. Horace Lacy: The Most Dangerous Rebel of the County* (Richmond: Owens Publishing Company, 1988), 16. His other home, Chatham in Stafford County, was in Union hands at this time. Lacy is shown in the 1860 census as a 37-year-old farmer with $140,000 in real estate and $180,000 in personal property in Stafford Court House, Stafford

County, Virginia. In the same household were Betty Lacy, 31; Agnes, 8; William J., 6; Elizabeth B., 4; Graham G., 1; and Fanny L. Lacy, 12 (1860 Virginia Census, no. 1375, Stafford County, 874).

22. Adam J. Wilson was a member of Company L of the Fourth Virginia Regiment who had enlisted in Blacksburg in July 1861. Detailed as a nurse, he was wounded on May 3, 1863, at Chancellorsville, and his right arm was amputated (Compiled Service Records, Virginia, no. 414; Robertson, *Fourth Virginia*, 81). The 1860 census for Montgomery County shows him as 15 years old and living in the household of Zedekial Wilson, 57, a farmer with $6,500 in real estate and $10,300 in personal property. In the same household were Eliza J., 37; Susan, 22; Margaret E., 20; Adam J., 15; and Elkana J. Wilson, 14. Collom Spickard, 25, and Mary Spickard, 24, also lived in the same household (1860 Virginia Census, no. 1363, Montgomery County, 744).

23. Harvey A. Jamison enlisted in Company C of the Fourth Virginia Regiment at Newbern on April 17, 1862 (Compiled Service Records, Virginia, no. 407; Robertson, *Fourth Virginia*, 58). Jamison had been a medical student for two years prior to his military service and was detailed as a steward. His service record shows him as being a steward in the Field Hospital of the Second Corps of the Army of Northern Virginia on November 1, 1862, several months prior to its official origin (Compiled Service Records, General and Staff Officers, no. 139; Muster Roll, 2nd Corps Hospital, U.S. National Archives). Jamison appears as Hearvey Jamison in the 1860 census for Pulaski County. He is shown as an 18-year-old laborer living in the town of Newbern, in the household of Hearvey A. Jamison, a 45-year-old farmer with $13,000 in real estate and $5,750 in personal property. Others in the household were Maria, 39; John, a 20-year-old laborer; Mary, 16; Ruth, 13; Maria, 12; Anna, 6; Susan, 4; and Ida Jamison, 2 (1860 Virginia census, no. 1373, Pulaski County, 737).

24. Harvey Black owned one slave, according to the 1860 census—a twenty-three-year-old female (1860 Virginia Slave Schedules, no. 1394, Montgomery County, 118). Though her name is not given in the census, other sources show her name as Adeline or Adaline. She was originally owned by Black's father Alexander. A bill of sale in the Black family papers documents the fact that William P. Peyton "in consideration of the sum of three hundred dollars . . . bargained & sold to Alex. Black a Negro girl named Adaline a slave for life" on March 8, 1845 (Black family papers, Virginia Polytechnic Institute and State University Libraries). Alexander Black may have sold or given the slave to Harvey Black when he moved to Wisconsin in 1854.

25. Jackson was brought to the home of Thomas Coleman Chandler—specifically, a small building in this estate, the "office"—to recuperate on May 4. Chandler, shown in the 1860 census as a 62-year-old farmer with $14,000 in real estate and $39,500 in personal property, owned Fairfield at Guineys in Caroline County. Others in the household included Mary E.,

43; Mary K., 21; James, 11; Lucy, 9; Elizabeth, 7; and Mannie Chandler, 5. Henry H. Chandler, a 23-year-old farmer with $4,000 in personal property, and Elizabeth Chandler, 21, also lived in the household (1860 Virginia Census, no. 1339, Caroline County, 731).

26. Jackson died of pneumonia around 3 on the afternoon of May 10, 1863, the day this letter was written. Black's statement anticipating Jackson's death echoed the diary entry of John Apperson after he had learned of that death. Apperson wrote on May 10: "[N]ews had come that Genl. Jackson was no more. Oh! What a blow this was! What a loss—how disheartening. But God gave him to us and He has taken him from us, and we should trust to him to raise another in his stead. His death will cause a nation to mourn, for no man of the war has so entirely won the affection of the people as Jackson" (Apperson diaries, no. 4, Virginia Polytechnic Institute and State University Libraries).

27. Lee's communication of May 3 is recorded in the *Official Records*: "I have just received your note, informing me that you were wounded. I cannot express my regret at this occurrence. Could I have directed events, I should have chosen for the good of the country to be disabled in your stead. I congratulate you upon the victory, which is due to your skill and energy" (*Official Records*, 25, pt. 2:769).

28. "Retta" is Margaretta Black, Harvey Black's sister, who was about 31 years old at the time this letter was written. She lived in Richland County, Wisconsin, and is shown in the 1860 Wisconsin census as living in the household of her parents. See Introduction, note 17 for census information on the Black family of Wisconsin.

29. Harvey Black had four brothers in Richland County, Wisconsin, whose ages would have made them eligible for military service. James (the oldest), Oscar, John Q., and Winfield S. Black were between 26 and 16 years old at the time of this letter. None appear in the list of Wisconsin Union soldiers, *Wisconsin Volunteers: War of the Rebellion, 1861-1865* (Madison, Wisconsin: Published by the State, Democrat Printing Company, 1914).

30. Lewis Amiss Kent, Mollie Black's younger brother, was born in Rockford, Illinois, in 1842. Though he spent most of his youth in Blacksburg, he enrolled in Beloit College in Wisconsin in the late 1850s, and enlisted in the Union Army when war broke out in 1861. Lewis Kent was a member of the Sixth Wisconsin Regiment. He took part in a number of battles in which the Stonewall Brigade was engaged on the Confederate side, including Second Manassas, Groveton, Antietam, Chancellorsville, and Gettysburg. At the Battle of Five Forks in 1865, Kent was made the regimental commander. For Kent's story, see William J. K. Beaudot, "A Virginian in the Iron Brigade: The Civil War Experiences of Lewis Amiss Kent of Blacksburg, Virginia," *Blue & Gray* 7, no. 4 (April 1990): 26-30. The uncle to whom Harvey Black referred was probably Aratus Kent, a

Presbyterian minister and missionary in Northern Illinois and the first president of Beloit College.

31. William Black, one of the two founders of Blacksburg, moved to Ohio in 1814. His son, William Porter Black, had four sons who fought in the Civil War on the Union side; at least two were killed. According to Florence Black Weiland, Cyrus and Adam Black died in action, Cyrus as a member of the First Kentucky Infantry, which along with others from Ohio he helped to raise. Two other brothers, Josiah and William Black, enlisted in Temperance County, Wisconsin, and Shawnee County, Kansas, respectively (Weiland, *Fifty New England Colonists and Five Virginia Families*, 11). Cyrus Black's service record, showing him being killed in action at Stone River on December 31, 1862, can be found in Compiled Service Records of Volunteer Union Soldiers Who Served in Organizations from the State of Kentucky (U.S. National Archives Microcopy M397), no. 153. On Josiah Black, see Index to Compiled Service Records of Volunteer Union Soldiers Who Served in Organizations from the State of Wisconsin (U.S. National Archives Microcopy M559), no. 3. There were three William Blacks in Kansas Union regiments: William A. C. Black in the 19th Kansas Cavalry; William G. Black in the 8th Kansas Infantry; and William R. Black in the 11th Kansas Cavalry. See Index to Compiled Service Records of Volunteer Union Soldiers Who Served in Organizations from the State of Kansas (U.S. National Archives Microcopy M542), no. 1. It is uncertain which of these was Harvey Black's relative. On Adam Black, see *Official Roster of the Soldiers of the State of Ohio in the War of the Rebellion, 1861-1866* (Akron: The Werner Printing and Manufacturing Co., 1891), 11:785; *History of Clark County, Ohio* (Chicago: W. H. Beers, 1881), 312; and Index to Compiled Service Records of Volunteer Union Soldiers Who Served in Organizations from the State of Ohio (U.S. National Archives Microcopy M552), no. 9. A private in the 8th Ohio Cavalry Regiment, Adam Black died at Front Royal, Virginia, on October 13, 1864, and was buried in Winchester, Virginia.

32. The Sixth Wisconsin Regiment was in First Corps, Fourth Brigade of the Army of the Potomac. Its next major assignment would be at Gettysburg.

33. Black's care of Union soldiers was not unusual. An instance of this after the Battle of Fredericksburg is mentioned in a report of Major D. B. Bridgford, Chief Provost-Marshall of the Second Corps, written on January 9, 1863: "December 16, received 109 prisoners of war, which I paroled and sent to Guiney's Depot, under command of Captain Upshaw, with instructions to have them forwarded by railroad to Richmond, if possible, which orders were carried into effect. During the same day I went through Drs. H. Black's and W. H. Whitehead's hospital, where I paroled 23 Federal prisoners. A considerable number of wounded prisoners were sent to Richmond" (*Official Records*, 21:641). Apperson mentions several instances of the hospital stewards being allowed to operate on Union patients after

Chancellorsville, including a momentous operation in his own career, one which he undertook in a less than charitable frame of mind: "Today I performed my first important operation. Took off a Yankee's leg below the knee. Dr. Wilkerson stood by. I felt no embarrassment whatever. Mrs. Jones gave me a true history of Yankee vandalism. It is truly distressing. No people can prosper whose propensity for wanton destruction of property and oppressing defenseless women is so great. How the blood is made to boil at such atrocities — such acts of inhumanities" (Apperson diaries, no. 4, May 7, 1863, Virginia Polytechnic Institute and State University Libraries). Even camaraderie among Union and Confederate surgeons after battles was apparently not uncommon. Spencer Glasgow Welch, surgeon for the Thirteenth South Carolina Infantry, speaks of visiting with Yankee surgeons on May 4, 1863, on the Chancellorsville battlefield. See Spencer Glasgow Welch, *A Confederate Surgeon's Letters to His Wife* (New York: Neale Publishing Co., 1911), 52.

34. Black probably had little to worry about. Major General George Stoneman commanded the newly-formed Cavalry Corps of the Army of the Potomac, with 10,000 cavalrymen. Stoneman's Raid, lasting from April 29 to May 8, had been designed to damage the communication and supply lines of the Army of Northern Virginia before the main action at Chancellorsville would begin. Delayed two weeks because of flooding of the Rappahannock River, Stoneman's Raid accomplished little apart from the destruction of some railroad track. Stoneman was relieved of his command after the Chancellorsville campaign.

35. Longstreet had been placed in an independent command — that of the Department of Virginia and North Carolina — in February 1863, with the assignment of protecting Richmond from the east. Thus he did not take part in the Chancellorsville campaign. He reported to Lee's headquarters on May 9, and rejoined the reorganized Army of Northern Virginia soon thereafter as commander of the First Corps. See note 49 below.

36. The "Edmund Hurt" to whom Black refers is probably Wilson A. Hurt, a medical student who enlisted in Confederate service on April 1, 1863 and who was appointed as a hospital steward at the General Hospital, Howard's Grove, in Richmond on May 14, 1863 (Compiled Service Records, General and Staff Officers, Roll no. 137). The 1860 Virginia census index includes one Wilson Hurt as a head of household, probably not the same person. That Wilson Hurt was a 23-year-old farmer living in Abingdon with $150 in personal property. Laura Hurt, a 20-year-old housekeeper, lived in the same household (1860 Virginia census, no. 1397, Washington County, 410).

37. John P. Ellsberry enlisted in the 3rd Alabama Regiment on April 26, 1861, at Montgomery, Alabama. He was attached to the Second Corps Field Hospital as a steward on April 15, 1863 (Compiled Service Records, Alabama, no. 105; Compiled Service Records, General and Staff Officers, no. 86; Muster Roll, 2nd Corps Hospital, U.S. National Archives).

Ellsberry had a medical degree; John Apperson referred to him as "Dr. Elsbury" in his diaries (Apperson diaries, no. 5, Virginia Polytechnic Institute and State University Libraries, February 12 and 17, 1864). Elsberry appears in the 1860 Alabama census as a 20-year-old doctor with neither real estate or personal property, living in Hayneville. He lived in the household of B. T. Howe, a 32-year-old farmer with $5,020 in personal property. S. H. Howe, a 23-year-old female, William W., 6; and E. A. Howe, 4, also lived in the household (1860 Alabama census, no. 14, Lowndes County, 529).

38. William W. Drane had also been in the 3rd Alabama; he had enlisted on April 15, 1861 as a druggist (Compiled Service Records, Alabama, no. 105; Muster Roll, 2nd Corps Hospital, U.S. National Archives). Black's petition to appoint Drane as a steward can be found in Letters Received by the Confederate Adjutant and Inspector General's Office, no. 106, letter 324-D. In the petition, Black says Drane was placed on special duty April 25, 1863. Drane's name does not appear in Ronald Vern Jackson, ed., *Alabama 1860 Census Index* (Bountiful, Utah: Accelerated Indexing Systems, 1981).

39. "Dr. Powell" is probably Dr. John W. Powell, chief surgeon in A. P. Hill's corps and Hill's personal physician (see Hill's report of January 1, 1863 in *Official Records*, 21:648). Powell's service record says only that he was Surgeon, McCreary's S. C. Infantry (Compiled Service Records, General and Staff Officers, no. 201).

40. Palmer, at that time Gen. A. P. Hill's chief of staff, had been severely injured when his horse was killed on the evening of May 3 at Chancellorsville. This took place in the same chain of events in which Jackson was wounded. For Palmer's account of the incident, see W. H. Palmer, "Another Account of It," *Confederate Veteran* 13, no. 5 (May 1905): 232-33. Palmer was removed from service for several months. The nature of his wife's illness is unknown.

41. The letter mentioned hasn't survived.

42. Nothing is known about the nature of Charlotte Cooksey Wade's illness at this time.

43. Henry Earheart (whose last name Black consistently misspelled as "Earhart") enlisted in Company L of the Fourth Virginia in July 1861. He was detailed as an agent to scout for medical supplies on December 31, 1862 (Compiled Service Records, Virginia, no. 405; Robertson, *Fourth Virginia*, 49). Earheart (spelled "Earhart") is shown as being attached to the Second Corps Field Hospital on January 1, 1863, as an agent (Muster Roll, 2nd Corps Hospital, U.S. National Archives). He appears in the 1860 Montgomery County census as a 24-year-old farmer with neither real estate or personal property in his own name. He lived in the household of George Earheart, a 66-year-old farmer with $31,500 in real estate and $27,500 in personal property. Nancy, 58, and Elizabeth Earheart, 18, also

lived in the household (1860 Virginia Census, no. 1363, Montgomery County, 746). George Earheart owned 17 slaves, according to the 1860 slave schedules (1860 Virginia Slave Schedules, no. 1394, Montgomery County, 120).

44. Union forces under U. S. Grant led unsuccessful assaults against Vicksburg on May 19 and 22, though it would ultimately fall on July 4, 1863.

45. Dr. Jonathan T. Evans is listed in the 1860 census for Montgomery County as a 44-year-old physician at Montgomery White Suphur Springs. He had real estate valued at $9,000 and personal property valued at $1,000. He was married to Virginia Evans, age 32, who is shown as having $3,800 in personal property in her own name (1860 Virginia Census, no. 1363, Montgomery County, 736). Jonathan T. Evans may be the brother in the "James M. Evans & bro." who owned 2 slaves, according to the slave schedules. Virginia Evans is also shown as a slaveholder, owning 3 slaves (1860 Virginia Slave Schedules, no. 1394, Montgomery County, 119). For a biographical sketch of Dr. Evans, see *Hardesty's Encyclopedia*, 406-07.

46. A ring pessary was a metal ring inserted vaginally in women having prolapse of the cervix.

47. "Mary H." is probably Mary Harvey, shown in the 1860 Blacks-burg census as 20 years old and living with her husband, John M. Harvey, a 31-year-old shoemaker with $1,500 in real estate and $200 in personal property (1860 Virginia Census, no. 1363, Montgomery County, 711).

48. C. H. Smith is shown in Harvey Black's account book as paying $20.00 for the rent of a house and lot on March 2, 1863; the payment is listed under the account of "Germanicus Kent's Estate" (Black medical account book, Virginia Polytechnic Institute and State University Libraries, 577). Germanicus Kent, Mollie Black's father, had died on March 1, 1862. Other accounts in Black's account book relate to Charles H. Smith, probably the same person (48, 366, 377). The 1860 Blacksburg census shows Smith as the town's 55-year-old postmaster with $100 in personal property. In the same household lived his wife Nancy, 49, and seven daughters: Amanda M., 22; Mollie, 20; Fannie, 18; Sarah, 16; Emma, 14; Nannie, 11; and Susan, 9 (1860 Virginia Census, no. 1363, Montgomery County, 705).

49. On May 20, Lee proposed to Jefferson Davis that the infantry of the Army of Northern Virginia be reorganized into three corps (*Official Records*, 25, pt. 2:810-11). To make the reorganization an equitable one, one division was taken from the First Corps, commanded by Longstreet, and one from the Second Corps, commanded by Richard Ewell after Jackson's death. The addition of a third division completed the Third Corps, with A. P. Hill in command of it. The new Corps was announced on May 30 (*Official Records*, 25, pt. 2:840).

50. It is difficult to determine exactly who Bettie and Lizzie are. It is possible that two Elizabeths — Mollie Black's cousin Elizabeth Palmer and

the Blacks' daughter Elizabeth, or Lizzie—are being distinguished from each other by nicknames.

51. Black may have referred to Reverend Charles Miller, at one time chaplain of the Fourth Virginia. Miller was appointed chaplain of the Fourth on July 19, 1861, and resigned December 9, 1861 (Compiled Service Records, General and Staff Officers, no. 178). Miller had been ordained as a Presbyterian minister in 1854, and he served in the Kimberlin Church of Giles County, Virginia, from 1853 to 1862. From 1862 to 1890 he served as pastor of the White House Church near Radford ("Memorial of Rev. Charles A. Miller," April 20, 1893, in Rev. Charles A. Miller family Papers, Special Collections Department, Virginia Polytechnic Institute and State University Libraries). Another possible identification is the son of Grief Miller, whom some sources identify as Charles Miller. According to Mary Apperson, there were once 3 tanneries in Blacksburg, "one on the present site of the William Preston Hotel owned by Mr. Grief Miller g. father of Mr. Warren Miller" (Mary E. Apperson, "Told to me by my mother Lizzie Black Apperson, 1936" [notebook], 87. Apperson family papers, Special Collections Department, Virginia Polytechnic Institute and State University Libraries). Hereafter cited as Mary Apperson notebook, Virginia Polytechnic Institute and State University Libraries. Charles Miller could not be found in the 1860 Virginia census.

52. "Mr. Coleman" is possibly James D. Coleman, shown in the 1860 Caroline County census as a 45-year-old minister and farmer in Bowling Green, with $41,250 in real estate and $66,171 in personal property. In the same household were Heuldah C. Coleman, a 33-year-old female, and three children: Alice C., 11; James D., 10; and Lucie B. Coleman, 1. Eliza McEwen, a 27-year-old teacher, also lived in the household (1860 Virginia Census, no. 1339, Caroline County, 739).

53. Dr. Thomas Verner Moore was a prominent Presbyterian cleric who was minister of the First Presbyterian Church in Richmond. See Alfred Nevin, ed., *Encyclopedia of the Presbyterian Church in the United States of America* (Philadelphia: Presbyterian Encyclopedia Publishing Co., 1884), 542-43; *Official Records*, Series II, 5:966. The 1860 Virginia census shows him as a 42-year-old minister with $2,500 in real estate and $20,000 in personal property. He lived in the Second Ward of Richmond. In the same household were Mathilda G. Moore, a 32-year-old domestic; James B., a 17-year-old fisherman; John M., 15; Lillie L., 13; Frank D., 11; Fannie B., 6; and Thomas V. Moore, Jr., 3. Other members of the household were Frances V. Cox, an 18-year-old seamstress; Frances F. Gwathney, 55; Robert W. Gwathney, 16; and Rachel Brice, a 50-year-old black servant (1860 Virginia Census, no. 1352, Henrico County, 425).

54. Dr. James Armstrong Duncan was a Methodist minister who was editor of the *Richmond Christian Advocate* from 1861 to 1863 and pastor of the Broad Street Church in Richmond from 1863 to 1866. See Nolan B. Harmon, ed., *The Encyclopedia of World Methodism* (Nashville: United

Methodist Publishing House, 1974), 727. Duncan appears in the 1860 Virginia census as a 30-year-old Methodist minister with no real estate or personal property. Duncan lived in a boarding house in Richmond's First Ward. Others in his household were Sally, 25; Eppy, 4; and David Duncan, 2 (1860 Virginia Census, no. 1352, Henrico County, 137).

55. Apparently neither sermon was published at the time; neither is listed in *Confederate Imprints: A Bibliography of Southern Publications from Secession to Surrender*, eds. T. Michael Parrish and Robert M. Willingham, Jr. (Austin: Jenkins Publishing Co., n.d). Hereafter cited as *Confederate Imprints*.

56. Several brief and disjointed paragraphs regarding social activities immediately preceding this sentence have been excised to preserve the flow of the letter.

57. After crossing the Potomac River, the Army of Northern Virginia encamped at Darkesville, West Virginia, during its retreat from Gettysburg. Several reports were written at Darkesville on July 19, 1863 (*Official Records*, 27, pt. 2:576-86).

58. Jordan's Springs, in Frederick County, Virginia, served as a hospital center both before and after the Gettysburg campaign. Lafayette Guild, Medical Director of the Army of Northern Virginia, wrote to Surgeon General S. P. Moore, June 22, 1863, directing that "all our sick and wounded be collected at Jordan's Springs preparatory to their removal up the Valley to Staunton." He added that "Jordan's Springs is a very suitable place for a hospital; the patients are very well cared for and are comfortable" (*Official Records*, 27, pt. 3:916).

59. The Stonewall Brigade went into Gettysburg with 1,450 effectives and suffered 330 casualties—35 dead, 208 wounded, and 87 missing (*Official Records*, 27, pt.2:506). According to the report of Maj. William Terry on the Fourth Virginia Infantry's activities at Gettysburg, written on July 16, 1863, total casualties for the regiment were 138, with 12 killed, 65 wounded, and 61 missing (*Official Records*, 27, pt. 2:522-23). A later return of casualties in the Army of Northern Virginia shows the figures for the Fourth Virginia as 8 killed and 78 wounded, with none captured or missing (*Official Records*, 27, pt. 2:341). Terry and his regiment were singled out for praise by Stonewall Brigade commander J. A. Walker in his report of August 17: "I should especially notice the gallant and efficient conduct of Maj. William Terry, commanding the Fourth Virginia Regiment, who gallantly led his regiment almost to the breastworks of the enemy, and only retired after losing three-fourths of his command" (*Official Records*, 27, pt. 2:519).

60. Colonel Ronald's original company was Company E.

61. Jonathan B. Evans enlisted in Company L of the Fourth Virginia Regiment in July 1861 at Blacksburg. Mustered in as a Second Lieutenant, he was promoted to First Lieutenant on December 6, 1861, and was elected

Captain on April 22, 1862. He would be killed at Payne's Farm on November 27, 1863 (Compiled Service Records, Virginia, no. 405; Robertson, *Fourth Virginia*, 49). In the 1860 census for Blacksburg, he is shown as a 32-year-old merchant living in the same household as the John Lybrook family. He had real estate valued at $3,000 and personal property valued at $3,350 (1860 Virginia Census, no. 1363, Montgomery County, 713). Evans owned two slaves (1860 Virginia Slave Schedules, no. 1394, Montgomery County, 118).

62. Captain Bennett's company was Company E.

63. Robert M. Harris enlisted at Blacksburg in Company E in April 1861. From September 1861 to December 1862 he is shown as being in various hospitals. On October 1, 1863, he would be promoted to Corporal (Compiled Service Records, Virginia, no. 406; Robertson, *Fourth Virginia*, 55). Harris is shown as a 19-year-old laborer in the 1860 census for Blacksburg. He lived in the household of Thomas M. Harris, a 40-year-old trader with $150 in personal property. Christina Harris, 36; James B., a 17-year-old laborer; Willie, a 7-year-old female; Hart, a 5-year-old male; and Charles Harris also lived in the household (1860 Virginia Census, no. 1363, Montgomery County, 712).

64. George Barger enlisted in Company E in April 1861 at Blacksburg. He was wounded at First Manassas on July 21, 1861, and was detailed as a nurse in a Winchester hospital in December 1861. In September 1862, he was detailed as an ambulance driver. He would transfer to the 14th Virginia Cavalry on August 13, 1863 (Compiled Service Records, Virginia, no. 402; Robertson, *Fourth Virginia*, 38). The 1860 census for Montgomery County shows Barger as a 21-year-old farmer with no real estate or personal property. He lived in the household of Mary Barger, 54, with $6,000 in real estate and $750 in personal property. Others in the household were M. Jane, 33; Jackson, 23; and Montgomery, 16 (1860 Virginia Census, no. 1363, Montgomery County, 696).

65. Andrew J. Hoge enlisted in Company E in April 1861 at Blacksburg and was promoted to Corporal in June 1863. He was killed at Gettysburg on July 3, 1863, by an artillery shell (Compiled Service Records, Virginia, no. 407; Robertson, *Fourth Virginia*, 56). An unidentified photograph of the slain soldier is shown in Francis Trevelyan Miller, ed., *The Photographic History of the Civil War* (New York: The Review of Reviews Co., 1911), 9:205. Captioned "But While Life Lasts, To Fight," the photograph identifies Hoge only as a Confederate sharpshooter posted at the "Devil's Den" at Gettysburg, reported as missing in action but actually killed. For the story of Hoge's death and the identification of the photograph, see Nellie Jane Hoge, "The Tragedy of Devil's Den," *Confederate Veteran* 33, no. 1 (January 1925): 20. Hoge is shown in the 1860 Montgomery County census as a 16-year-old student living with his parents, James Hoge, a 42-year-old farmer with $30,600 in real estate and $16,900 in personal property, and Eliza J. Hoge, 40. Others in the household were Annie,

18; George Tyler, 12; Robert H., 9; James, 6; Jane N., 4; and Joseph E. Hoge, one month old (1860 Virginia Census, no. 1363, Montgomery County, 746). James F. Hoge owned 18 slaves (1860 Virginia Slave Schedules, no. 1394, Montgomery County, 120).

66. Robert H. Calbert (or Calvert) enlisted in Company E of the Fourth Virginia on August 31, 1861 at Camp Harman. He was killed at Gettysburg on July 3, 1863 (Compiled Service Records, Virginia, no. 403; Robertson, *Fourth Virginia*, 43). The 1860 census for Blacksburg shows him as a 28-year-old saddler, with $50 in personal property. His 25-year-old wife, Mary F., and 1-month-old son, Charles E., lived in the same household (1860 Virginia Census, no. 1363, Montgomery County, 708).

67. John Kent Ewing enlisted in Company G in April 1861 at Christiansburg. He rose in rank from corporal (July 30, 1861) to sergeant (December 4, 1861). On April 22, 1862, he was elected Second Lieutenant and was promoted to First Lieutenant on May 3, 1863. Severely wounded at Gettysburg on July 3, 1863, he was left within enemy lines where he died from his wounds (Compiled Service Records, Virginia, no. 405; Robertson, *Fourth Virginia*, 49). For a studio photograph of Ewing, shown among other Confederate and Union soldiers who were killed and wounded at Gettysburg, see Champ Clark, *Gettysburg: The Confederate High Tide* (Alexandria, Virginia: Time-Life Books, 1985), 154. Ewing appears in the 1860 Montgomery County census as a 22-year-old clerk with $1,000 in personal property and no real estate. He lived in the household of David Shifflebarger, a 52-year-old farmer with $1,825 in personal property. The household included Mary, 53; Paris, a 33-year-old laborer; Minero, 27; Miranda, 24; Mahulda, 23; Mandola, 20 (the last four all females); Magarme, a 19-year-old (male) wagoner; and Malachi Shufflebarger, a 14-year-old male. Thomas Dobyns, a 23-year-old merchant with $4,000 in personal property, also lived in the household (1860 Virginia Census, no. 1363, Montgomery County, 702).

68. Hamilton D. Wade enlisted in Company G of the Fourth Virginia in April 1861 at Christiansburg. Mustered in as First Sergeant, he was successively promoted to the rank of Second Lieutenant on April 22, 1862, First Lieutenant on July 1, 1862, and Captain on May 3, 1863. By the war's end, he would be placed in command of the Fourth Virginia. Wade was twice wounded — at Groveton in August 1862 and at Payne's Farm in November 1863 (Compiled Service Records, Virginia, no. 413; Robertson, *Fourth Virginia*, 78). For a biographical sketch of Hamilton Wade, see "Capt. H. D. Wade," *Confederate Veteran* 16, no. 8 (August 1908): 412-13. Wade appears in the 1860 census for Christiansburg as a 24-year-old farmer with no real estate and $1,800 in personal property. He was living in the household of Mary Wade, 73 years old with $7,500 in real estate and $30,000 in personal property. Mary Morrison, 40, and Juliet Morrison, 42, also lived in the household (1860 Virginia Census, no. 1363, Montgomery County, 702).

69. The Fourth Virginia included two Sam Sniders. The more likely of the two to be delivering letters for Black is Samuel K. Snider, who enlisted in Company L in July 1861 at Camp Harman and was detailed as a nurse from August 1861 to October 1862. In February 1863 he was appointed hospital steward for the regiment (Compiled Service Records, Virginia, no. 412; Robertson, *Fourth Virginia*, 74). Samuel E. Snider also enlisted in Company L in July 1861; he was captured at Spotsylvania on May 12, 1864 and imprisoned at Elmira Prison until March 1865 (Compiled Service Records, Virginia, no. 412; Robertson, *Fourth Virginia*, 74). Neither Snider could be located in the 1860 Montgomery County census.

70. According to the report of Richard S. Ewell, the Second Corps got to Hagerstown on July 11. Unable to cross the Potomac immediately, they awaited a possible attack by Union forces: "On the 11th, we were moved into line between Hagerstown and Williamsport, our right joining the left of the Third Corps, and began fortifying, and in a short time my men were well protected. Their spirit was never better than at this time, and the wish was universal that the enemy would attack" (*Official Records*, 27, pt. 2:448). That attack never came, though William Terry must have anxiously expected it. No other mentions of the "Fort Terry" anecdote could be located. Terry himself didn't allude to the event in his report on Gettysburg and its aftermath, dated July 16, 1863 (*Official Records*, 27, pt. 2:522-23).

71. The Rev. Beverly Tucker Lacy, chaplain to the Second Corps of the Army of Northern Virginia, was the pastor of the Fredericksburg Presbyterian Church in December 1862 when General Jackson summoned him to his headquarters and asked him to organize the work of the Second Corps chaplains. Lacy was commissioned as a chaplain on March 28, 1863 (Compiled Service Records, General and Staff Officers, no. 151). See also W. G. Bean, "Stonewall Jackson's Jolly Chaplain, Beverly Tucker Lacy," *West Virginia History* 29, no. 2 (January 1968): 80. Hereafter cited as Bean, "Stonewall Jackson's Jolly Chaplain." The sermon Black heard apparently was never published; nothing by Lacy appears in *Confederate Imprints*. Lacy mentioned the Second Corps Field Hospital in a short article published in the *Central Presbyterian* on April 30, 1863. He wrote: "Saturday morning I spent about two hours in visiting the three wards at the Receiving Hospital near Guiney's Station. I read the scriptures, gave a short talk and prayed in each ward." Lacy found the sick and wounded "much interested and sensibly affected" by his message ("Religion in the Army," *Central Presbyterian*, April 30, 1863, 2). Beverly Tucker Lacy was the brother of J. Horace Lacy; see note 21 above. Beverly Tucker Lacy could not be found in Jackson, *Virginia 1860 Federal Census*.

72. Lacy may have preached at Blacksburg during the years from 1852 to 1857, a period in which he served as a Presbyterian minister in nearby Salem, Virginia (Bean, "Stonewall Jackson's Jolly Chaplain," 77).

73. The "enclosed scrap" has not survived.

74. Bob White cannot be identified, though there is a possibility that he may have been William Ryland White, Cecilia ("Ceal") L. White's husband (see Chapter 2, note 52). The reasoning behind this is that both William R. White and Lewis A. Kent were from Union states and relatives of Mollie Kent; White relayed information (though incorrect) on Kent.

75. Lewis Kent was in the Sixth Wisconsin rather than the Fifth. The Sixth Regiment was also engaged at Chancellorsville.

76. A Rockaway was a four-wheeled carriage open at the sides, named after the city in which it was manufactured, Rockaway, New Jersey.

77. "Grandma" is Elizabeth Amiss; see Chapter 1, note 71.

Four: "Very Unexpectedly I Find Myself Back at Orange": September 22–November 25, 1863

1. For Union reports on the series of inconclusive cavalry skirmishes with Jeb Stuart's cavalry at Madison Court House, White's Ford, Orange Court House, Racoon Ford, Liberty Mills, and Robertson's Ford lasting from September 21-23, 1863, see *Official Records*, 29, pt. 1:140-43. Stuart, who had a horse shot from under him in one of the skirmishes, did not write a report on them; the only report from the Confederate side came from Lee (*Official Records*, 29, pt. 2:742-43). Edward Johnson commanded "Stonewall" Jackson's old division in the Second Corps; Cadmus M. Wilcox commanded a division in A. P. Hill's Third Corps.

2. Gen. Braxton Bragg, commanding the Confederate Army of Tennessee, met the Union Army of the Cumberland under Gen. William S. Rosecrans in a two-day battle at Chickamauga, Georgia, on September 19-20. The battle was waged over control of the strategically-important city of Chattanooga, Tennessee. Both armies suffered heavy casualties—18,454 for Bragg, 16,170 for Rosecrans. Though the battle was a tactical victory for Bragg, he failed to pursue Rosecrans and the Union held Chattanooga. Confederate General John B. Hood, who commanded several divisions at Chickamauga, was severely wounded. Surgeons had to amputate Hood's right leg and his survival was, as Black speculated, in doubt. Apparently, rumors of Hood's death were rife; Robert E. Lee wrote from his headquarters at Orange Court House on September 23 that he was "grieved to learn of the death of General Hood" (*Official Records*, 29, pt. 2:743). Hood survived and returned to duty in winter 1864.

3. The identity of "King," who is mentioned several times in these letters, cannot be determined for certain. Perhaps the most likely "King" is William Peck, the father of Bob Peck. Black makes frequent references to "King" (see the letters of January 29, 1864, February 7, 1864, and October 9, 1864), who appears to be close to the Black family. It would also explain why "Bob" would stay all night with Black, then go in to the "regiment," by

which Black meant the Fourth Virginia. See Chapter 1, note 20 for information on the Peck family. Other possibilities for "King" include Zachariah King and Green King. The Montgomery County 1860 census includes a Zachariah King, a 59-year-old farmer with $1,600 in real estate and $200 in personal property, with a son named Robert. In the Zachariah King household were Elizabeth King, 57; William A., a 27-year-old farmer; Robert H., a 24-year-old farmer; Edie W., a 16-year-old farmer; and Floyd R. King, 12 (1860 Virginia Census, no. 1363, Montgomery County, 582). Although Robert H. King may have been the "Bob" that "King" was visiting, no Robert King appears among the soldiers of the Fourth Virginia Infantry. Another possibility is that King is the husband of Mrs. Green King, mentioned in Mollie Black's letter of December 22, 1863 (see Chapter 5, note 40). Green King could not be located in Jackson, *Virginia 1860 Federal Census.*

4. Fitzhugh Lipscomb is shown as being a 52-year-old brickmason with $2,500 in real estate and $3,700 in personal property in the Orange County census of 1860. In the same household were Martha, age 49, and Junie Lipscomb, age 39 (1860 Virginia Census, no. 1669, Orange County, 673). For a photograph of the house of "local merchant Fitzhugh Lipscomb," built circa 1855, see Ann L. Miller, *Antebellum Orange: The Pre-Civil War Homes, Public Buildings and Historic Sites of Orange County, Virginia* (Orange, Virginia: Orange County Historical Society, 1988), 22. Hereafter cited as Miller, *Antebellum Orange.*

5. Marry M. Williamson, 55 years old and a head of household in the 1860 Orange County census, managed a boarding house in Orange County. She had $3,000 in real estate and $7,600 in personal property. Living in her household were Sally, age 24; Roberta, 19; and Joseph Williamson, 14. Mildred J. Dade, 37; Molly O. Dade, 20; and Francis T. Barbon, a 73-year-old female, probably boarders, also lived in the household (1860 Virginia Census, no. 1669, Orange County, 672).

6. Dr. Edwin D. Newton was appointed an assistant surgeon in the Fourth Georgia Regiment on April 27, 1861; he resigned June 12, 1861. Newton was with the 7th Georgia in 1862. He apparently served with the Second Corps Field Hospital at some point in 1863, but his service record does not record it (Compiled Service Records, General and Staff Officers, no. 186). The evidence for this statement comes from an order issued by Lafayette Guild on September 27, 1863, stating that "Surgeon E. D. Newton [has been] ... relieved from temporary duty with Surgeon H. Black in charge of Hospital Department of the 2nd Army Corps and will report to Surgeon Joseph E. Clagett for duty" (Letters Sent, Medical Director's Office, Army of Northern Virginia, 1863-5, Record Group 109, Ch. VI, 642:3, U.S. National Archives). This source is hereafter cited as Letters Sent, Medical Director's Office, 1863-65, U.S. National Archives. Newton later wrote two articles on his reminiscences of Confederate service in the Army of Northern Virginia: "Reminiscences of the Medical Department,

Confederate States Army and Field and Hospital Service, Army of Northern Virginia," *Southern Practitioner* 25 (January 1903): 36-43 and 26 (March 1904): 168-174; and "My Recollections and Reminiscences," *Southern Practitioner* 30 (October 1908): 474-489. The second of these is hereafter cited as Newton, "My Recollections and Reminiscences." Neither article mentions Black or the Second Corps Field Hospital. Newton's name does not appear in Jackson, *Virginia 1860 Federal Census* or in Ronald Vern Jackson, ed., *Georgia 1860 Census Index* (North Salt Lake, Utah: Accelerated Indexing Systems International, 1986).

7. This is probably a veiled reference to Daniel H. Hoge, a prominent Montgomery County lawyer. In the 1860 census, he is shown as a 49-year-old farmer with $31,125 in real estate and $37,500 in personal property. Other members of the household included A. Hawes (a 36-year-old female); Alice G., 12; Daniel D., 10; Elliott C., 8; James H., 6; John H., 5; Huldal A. H., 3; and Samuel H. Hoge, 1 month (1860 Virginia Census, no. 1363, Montgomery County, 771-2). According to the 1860 slave schedules, Hoge owned 35 slaves (1860 Virginia Slave Schedules, no. 1394, Montgomery County, 122). Hoge was known by 1864 to be a Unionist and a member of the Unionist organization the Heroes of America (see Chapter 7, note 32). Hoge would serve as a U.S. Congressman from 1865 to 1867. For a short biography of him, see James Hoge Tyler, *The Family of Hoge* (n.p.: 1927), 60-61.

8. John Buford's report of September 23 mentions 100 Confederate prisoners and "severe" casualties in the Third Union Cavalry Division (*Official Records*, 29, pt. 1:141). Other reports on the same series of skirmishes show about 100 Union casualties (*Official Records*, 29, pt. 1:142-43).

9. "No Name" is likely a reference to the novel of that name by the British novelist Wilkie Collins. Originally published in England in 1862, *No Name* was published in 1863 by West & Johnston of Richmond, and it may have been this edition to which Black had access (*Confederate Imprints*, 538).

10. Robert E. Lee made Brandy Station the headquarters for his Army of Northern Virginia in late October 1863.

11. Crockett McDonald was the son of Stephen McDonald and Susan (or Susannah) Black McDonald, the latter the sister of Harvey Black's father. Crockett McDonald was born in Wyoming County, Virginia (later West Virginia) in 1839, making him twelve years younger than Black. Their relationship was a complex one. Charles Black, an uncle of Harvey Black, had married Rhoda McDonald, who was the sister of Stephen McDonald—making Harvey Black and Crockett McDonald double cousins. See [F. V. McDonald], *Genealogy of the MacDonald Family: Edition B, Comprising all Names Obtained up to February, 1876* (New Haven: Tuttle, Morehouse & Taylor, 1876), 33, 97. Hereafter cited as *Genealogy of the MacDonald Family*. Susannah Black McDonald moved the family from

Wyoming County to Livingston County, Missouri, after Stephen McDonald's death in 1851. In the 1860 census for Livingston County, Susannah is shown as 57 years old and living in Chillicothe, Missouri. She had $7,000 in real estate and $3,500 in personal property. Both she and her son Kemper, age 23, are shown as having "farming done" as an occupation. Kemper's real estate value is shown as $3,000 and personal property value as $1,000. Others in the family included Crockett, age 21; and Whitten, age 13 (1860 Missouri Census, no. 630, Livingston County, 958). Crockett McDonald apparently returned to West Virginia sometime prior to November 1863 to get married; he would marry Ella (or Ellen) V. Hall in Princeton, West Virginia, on November 5, 1863 (*Genealogy of the MacDonald Family*, 97). Although it is unclear exactly why Mollie Black might have seen him at this time, it is possible that he crossed Confederate lines to visit relatives in Southwest Virginia prior to his wedding. Crockett McDonald, who apparently did not serve on either side in the Civil War, would take his new wife to Missouri. At the time of the 1870 census, he is shown as 30 years old, with $8,000 in personal property. His wife Ellen, age 26, and sons John, 6, and Robert, 6 months, were the other members of the household. See Ninth Census of the United States, 1870 (U.S. National Archives Microcopy M593, no. 593, Lafayette County), 169. McDonald died in Howard City, Howard County (now Elk County), Kansas in 1874 (*Genealogy of the MacDonald Family*, 97).

12. "James" is James Alexander Black, Harvey Black's brother in Richland County, Wisconsin. "Retta" is Margaretta, his sister. See Introduction, note 17 for census information on the Black family in Wisconsin. It is unclear how the Wisconsin Blacks had been in communication with Crockett McDonald.

13. Major Harrison may be Major Henry Heth Harrison, on General Henry Heth's staff in November 1863. Harrison is shown as being granted 15 days leave on January 19, 1864, extended for 60 additional days on February 9. Though his service record does not specify the leave as sick leave, it probably was so (Compiled Service Records, General and Staff Officers, no. 120). Henry Heth Harrison was in the Third Corps, however, not the Second Corps, placing him outside of Black's aegis and making the identification a problematic one.

14. Black's cook may be James Cooley (Apperson diaries, no. 4, Virginia Polytechnic Institute and State University Libraries, January 6, 1863 and March 7, 1863). The 1860 Virginia census shows a James Cooley from John Apperson's neighborhood, 7 Mile Ford in Smyth County. Cooley is a 26-year-old brickmason, with no real estate or personal property value shown. Others in the household were Frances, 26; William H., 11; Mary E., 6; John, 4; and Albert Cooley, 2. Mary Cox, 66, also lived in the household. All are listed as mulattos (1860 Virginia census, no. 1377, Smyth County, 960).

15. The identity of Jim Price can only be speculated upon. He may be James C. Price, listed as an 18-year-old tanner in Christiansburg in the 1860 Montgomery County census. He lived in the household of George Price, 48, also a tanner, with $2,000 in real estate and $600 in personal property. Also in the household were Harriet Price, 52; John G., a 21-year-old engine runner; Henry C., 16; George A., 13; Emily V., 10; Lucy T., 7; and Harriet E. Price, 5. John McLaughlin, a 56-year-old currier, and Mary Price, 75, also lived there (1860 Virginia Census, no. 1363, Montgomery County, 565).

16. This is probably Ann Robison (or Robinson), who may have been the 38-year-old mother of David Tobias Robinson. See Chapter 2, note 7.

17. Dr. George W. Heagy was one of the surgeons in the Second Corps Field Hospital. His service record shows him as passing an examination for assistant surgeon on March 1, 1863, and being ordered to the Medical Director of the Second Army Corps for assignment to duty (Compiled Service Records, General and Staff Officers, no. 123). See also Letters Sent, Medical Director's Office, Army of Northern Virginia, 1862-63, Ch. VI, 641:104, U.S. National Archives. Hereafter cited as Letters Sent, Medical Director's Office, 1862-63, U.S. National Archives. Apperson provided a character sketch of Heagy (whose name he spelled "Hagy") in his diary entry of January 24, 1863. He wrote: "Dr. Hagy is unwell yet, and it seems indeed that he will not get out again soon. He is an odd one, I might say, and with all deference to his virtues and amiable qualities, there are few men who present so many characteristics of a dotage man. Simple as a child in his wishes and whimsical as some old spinster in the most flourishing times of our country. His skill as a surgeon is good, and gained by dint of much study and application, will be better appreciated in a country practice than here in the army" (Apperson diaries, no. 4, Virginia Polytechnic Institute and State University Libraries).

18. Lee reviewed the cavalry corps on November 5. He had been complaining of rheumatism in the days preceding the review, and wrote to his wife that day: "I had not been on horse back for five days previously & feared I would not get through. But to my surprize I got along very well." See Clifford Dowdey, editor, *The Wartime Papers of R. E. Lee* (Boston: Little, Brown and Company for the Virginia Civil War Commission, 1961), 619. Hereafter cited as Dowdey, *Wartime Papers of R. E. Lee*. For another account of the cavalry review, see Neese, *Three Years in the Confederate Horse Artillery*, 233-34. A contemporary newspaper account was published in the Richmond *Whig* of November 13, 1863 ("A Grand Cavalry Review," 1).

19. Richard Ewell married Lizinka Campbell Brown on May 24, 1863. She was an early sweetheart of his who had recently become a widow. At the time of this letter, they had been married five months.

20. Thomas E. Ballard was at this time a Commissary in the Army of Northern Virginia (Compiled Service Records, General and Staff Officers, no. 14). Edward Johnson singled him out in his report on Gettysburg,

dated September 30, 1863: "The troops are much indebted to Majs. T. E. Ballard and G. H. Kyle, of the commissary department, for supplies during the trying period covered by this report" (*Official Records*, 27, pt. 2:505).

21. "Josie T" cannot be identified. Presumably she had a brother in the Fourth Virginia Infantry. There is a reference to Jessie Taylor in Black's account book (Black medical account book, Virginia Polytechnic Institute and State University Libraries, 47), but there were no Taylors in the Fourth Virginia.

22. Dr. Stone may be Dr. James Love Stone. Although no service record for Stone could be located, his military career is summarized in another source. He enlisted in Confederate service in May 1861 as a private in Montague's infantry brigade, was discharged in May 1862, and later re-enlisted as a private under the command of Gen. Echols (*Confederate Military History*, 3:1190-91). James L. Stone is shown as a 26-year-old physician in Meherrin Depot, Prince Edward County, in the 1860 Virginia census. No real estate or personal property are listed under his name. Stone lived in the household of Robert Martin, a 40-year-old farmer with $2,000 in real estate and $8,488 in personal property, and Sarah C. Martin, 40. Two others lived in the household: Irby Hudson, a 74-year-old farmer with $9,000 in personal property, and Ann B. Hudson, 68 (1860 Virginia Census, no. 1371, Prince Edward County, 877).

23. Dr. David Wade served as surgeon of the 27th Battallion Virginia Cavalry (Partisan Rangers) and the 54th Virginia Infantry, tendering his resignation from Confederate service on December 12, 1863 (Compiled Service Records, General and Staff Officers, no. 255). The 1860 census for Christiansburg shows him as a 40-year-old physician with $20,000 in real estate and $12,000 in personal property. In the same household were Eliza W., 28; Mary Lucy, 10; Isabella, 5; Susan T., 3; and David Wade, 2 (1860 Virginia Census, no. 1363, Montgomery County, 569-70). Wade owned 9 slaves, according to the 1860 slave schedules (1860 Virginia Slave Schedules, no. 1394, Montgomery County, 109).

24. Reverend A. P. Neal served as chaplain of the Second Corps Field Hospital, perhaps unofficially. The evidence for Neal's service as chaplain for the hospital comes from two sources, one of Harvey Black's official letters and a diary entry of John Apperson. Black wrote from Orange Court House on January 22, 1864, to Col. A. J. Deyald, stating that he had sent an application to the Secretary of War asking for the appointment of A. P. Neal as hospital chaplain, but that he had not received a response to this petition. He wrote that Neal "has been discharging his duties since he made the application and it is but just to him that he should know as soon as practicable whether or not he is to receive the appointment. Mr. Neal is a minister in the M. E. Church and was on Botetourt Circuit last year . . ." (Letters Received by the Confederate Adjutant and Inspector General's Office, no. 133, 58-N-1864). About the same time, John Apperson wrote of Neal (whose name he misspelled as "Neil"): "I attended Church today

(Presbyterian). Rev. A. P. Neil preached from Romans 8th Chapter, 28 verse. Gen. Lee was one of the congregation. Mr. N. is Chaplain to our hosp't. A very worthy young man, but not a very edifying or brilliant minister yet. He will doubtless improve very much. . . . Mr. Neil is Methodist in his persuasion" (Apperson diaries, no. 5, January 31, 1864, Virginia Polytechnic Institute and State University Libraries). No service record for either A. P. "Neal" or "Neil" could be found in the Compiled Service Records, General and Staff Officers.

25. When Retta Black "came from the west" cannot be determined. Peterstown is in Monroe County, West Virginia.

26. Mr. Miller may be the Rev. Charles Miller (see Chapter 3, note 51). Mr. Lewis cannot be identified. The Compiled Service Records, General and Staff Officers includes no "Lewis" who was a chaplain.

27. Kent Black's "Cousin John" is probably a reference to John Black.

28. Both may have suffered from a skin disease such as scabies, to judge by the treatment Black suggested. See note 31 below.

29. This is a reference to William H. Palmer, who had recuperated at his home in Blacksburg after his injury at Chancellorsville.

30. Dr. Talcott Eliason served as surgeon of the First Virginia Cavalry Regiment in 1862 and was later chief surgeon of J. E. B. Stuart's cavalry division (Compiled Service Records, General and Staff Officers, no. 85). Stuart wrote about Eliason after Second Manassas: "My division surgeon, Talcott Eliason, besides being an adept in his profession, exhibited on this, as on former occasions, the attributes of a cavalry commander" (*Official Records*, 12, pt. 2:738). Eliason appears in the Fauquier County, Virginia census for 1860 as a 33-year-old doctor living in Upperville with his wife Sallie, 31, and daughter Mary, 5. Eliason is shown as having no real estate and $1,230 in personal property (1860 Virginia census, no. 1344, Fauquier County, 7).

31. Fowler's solution (liquor potassae arsenitis), named after English physician Thomas Fowler, was an arsenic solution used as a treatment for skin diseases such as scabies, caused by mites. For a description of its use, see the eleventh edition of George B. Wood, M.D., and Franklin Bache, M.D., *The Dispensatory of the United States of America* (Philadelphia: J. B. Lippincott & Co., 1858), 956-57.

32. The engagements at Rappahannock Bridge and Kelly's Ford on November 7, 1863 were a disaster and an embarrassment for the Army of Northern Virginia. Lee's troops were camped south of the Rappahannock River awaiting Meade. Lee fortified a bridgehead at Rappahannock Bridge and posted Jubal Early's Division there. He also posted Rodes's troops four miles down at Kelly's Ford. Harry Thompson Hays's Louisiana Brigade was placed on the northern bank of the river near Kelly's Ford to guard against a surprise attack, maintaining communication and an escape route through a pontoon bridge. The Fifth and Sixth Union Corps

successfully attacked the bridgehead; the Third Corps crossed at Kelly's Ford. That same night, Union forces attacked the bridgehead again, catching the Confederates off guard. Hays's brigade north of the river was routed, and Union troops captured large numbers of men from two North Carolina regiments at Kelly's Ford. The casualty statistics tell the story: total Confederate casualties were 2,023; the Federals lost 419. The Southerners retreated to between Culpepper Courthouse and Brandy Station (*Official Records*, 29, pt. 1:553-635).

33. Black must have been referring to an article that would appear in the November 10 issue of the Richmond *Enquirer*, even though his letter is dated November 9. He may have mistakenly dated his letter or may have somehow received advanced word of the article in question. The *Enquirer* wrote that two whole brigades of the Army of Northern Virginia were captured on the previous Saturday. "We learned this *not* as a rumor, but as a fact, from such a source, that we cannot question its accuracy. We could not learn whose brigades they were, not even whether they were cavalry or infantry. But it matters not who the brigadiers are, not whether their commands are infantry or cavalry, the honor of the army, the interest of the cause, the safety of the country all unite to demand their dismissal from the army upon which their negligence has brought such irreparable disgrace" ("The Rumors of Yesterday," Richmond *Enquirer*, November 10, 1863, 1). The issue of the *Enquirer* immediately preceding the November 10 one was on November 6, one day before the event in question.

34. Dr. G. W. Magruder was an assistant surgeon in the Second Corps Field Hospital (Compiled Service Records, General and Staff Officers, no. 162). George Magruder, apparently the same person, is shown in the 1860 Shenandoah County census as a 25-year-old physician living in the household of William Magruder, a 56-year-old physician in Woodstock. The elder Magruder is shown as having $9,025 in real estate and $18,000 in personal property. George Magruder has no property shown in his name. Others in the household were Philip W. Magruder, a 22-year-old attorney; John W., 16; Henry C., 16; and Mary E. Magruder, 19. Ann Jones, 63; Caroline V. Lee, 24; and Elizabeth S. Inge, 29, were other members of the household (1860 Virginia Census, no. 1377, Shenandoah County, 857). Apperson's diary entry for April 7, 1863 notes that "Dr. Magruder has been assigned to duty at this Hospital" (Apperson diaries, no. 4, Virginia Polytechnic Institute and State University Libraries).

35. Dr. Thomas B. Wilkerson, a North Carolinian, was another of the assistant surgeons in the Second Corps Field Hospital (Compiled Service Records, General and Staff Officers, no. 267). John Apperson compared him to the other surgeons in his acquaintance in his diary entry for January 24, 1863: "Dr. Wilkerson is a different man in most respects. Diffidence is his most prominent character. He has a large copious brain and it is well stored with medical fact which is useful at all times, not only to himself but to all around him. I have been tempted to call him lazy but perhaps

without justification" (Apperson diaries, no. 4, Virginia Polytechnic Institute and State University Libraries). There are three Thomas Wilkersons listed in Ronald Vern Jackson, ed., *North Carolina 1860 Census Index* (Bountiful, Utah: Accelerated Indexing Systems, 1987). None of them were physicians.

36. "Henry" may be Henry Johnson. According to John Apperson, Johnson was the brother-in-law of James Cooley ("Jim"), whom Black hired as a cook. Johnson began employment at the Second Corps Field Hospital on January 6, 1863 (Apperson diaries, no. 4, January 6, 1863, Virginia Polytechnic Institute and State University Libraries).

37. No application of this kind is part of Black's Compiled Service Record.

38. Major Kent is Joseph F. Kent, who enlisted as Captain of Company A of the Fourth Virginia in April 1861 at Wytheville. He was promoted to Major the next month. Resigning on January 31, 1862, he became commander of the Wythe County Home Guards (Compiled Service Records, Virginia, no. 408; *Official Records*, 29, pt. 2:666, 787, 822). Kent appears in the 1860 census as 40 years old, with no occupation shown. He lived in Wytheville and had $25,000 in real estate and $58,000 in personal property. Others listed in the household are Francis P., a 38-year-old female; Bettie, 12; John, 11; Jane, 7; Emily, 5; and Alexander, 11 months (1860 Virginia census, no, 1385, Wythe County, 724).

39. The Virginia legislature had just concluded a session on November 2 and would begin another on December 7. The Richmond *Enquirer* listed the acts passed by the legislative session in its November 6 issue, including several dealing with the production and distribution of salt and one suppressing the further issue of notes of currency by cities, towns, and counties in the Commonwealth (Richmond *Enquirer*, November 6, 1863, 1). Although Black may have referred to a specific act passed by the legislature, he may have also been referring to a lack of legislation to combat monetary ills such as rampant inflation and speculation.

40. The Federal demonstrations at Ely's Ford on the Rapidan River were a prelude to the Mine Run campaign, which would begin the next day and last until December 2. Lee's troops, south of the Rapidan, received orders to prepare for action on November 26. Lee sent the Second Corps north to meet the advancing Army of the Potomac, which it did, at Locust Grove, on November 27. After the battle, Confederate troops dug trenches and fended off Union advances for several days. Meade's army retreated across the Rapidan on December 2, ending the campaign and the winter fighting. Total casualties for the campaign were 1,653 Union and 601 Confederate.

Five: "I Tell You I am Tired of Such Work":
The Home Front, November 29-December 22, 1863

1. "Old brother Spickard" is John C. Spickard; see Chapter 1, note 62.

2. The identity of "Uncle Joe" and "Aunt Mary" is not known for certain. They are mentioned either singly or together by both Harvey and Mollie Black several times. One reference is to Aunt Mary's child, a "little fellow," having scarlet fever. Given the nature of the references, it is almost certain that they lived in Montgomery County. Limiting the search to married couples named Joseph and Mary with male children in the 1860 Montgomery County census, two possibilities emerge. One of these is Joseph J. M. Wilson, a 35-year-old overseer with $1,300 in personal property. Others in the household were Mary J. B., 32; James H., 4; and John W. Wilson, 3. They lived in the Lovely Mount area (1860 Virginia Census, no. 1363, Montgomery County, 652). Another possibility is Joseph Roop, a 49-year-old farmer with $4,000 in real estate and $400 in personal property. In the same household were Mary, 48; Bluford, a 26-year-old farmer with $100 in personal property; Malinda, 24; Fleming S., a 19-year-old farmer with $350 in personal property; Jacob, a 16-year-old farmer; Octavia, 14; Harvey, 12; and Juliet, 7. The Roops lived in the Childress Store area of the county (1860 Virginia Census, no. 1363, Montgomery County, 641-42).

3. This incident may have taken place during a raid by Union Brigadier General William Averell, commanding the First Separate Brigade, to Lewisburg, West Virginia and beyond in the early part of November. Averell set out from Beverly, West Virginia on November 1. He had been ordered to go to Lewisburg to attack and capture a Confederate force there. He was then to move into Virginia to destroy the Virginia and Tennessee Railroad bridge over the New River in Dublin. After engagements at Droop Mountain, West Virginia, and near Covington, Virginia, Averell came back to his camp at New Creek, West Virginia, on November 17 without attempting the second part of his mission (*Official Records*, 29, pt. 1:498-550). Pollie Gilmore, the old lady, and Oscar have not been identified. It is possible that "Pollie" Gilmore is Polly Gilmore, who appears in the 1860 Rockbridge County census for the 5th District. William C. Gilmore, a 48-year-old farmer with $17,500 in real estate and $8,000 in personal property is the head of household. Others in the household are Polly, 57; Samuel, 24; Harvey, 22; Gher Meredith, 16; Martha, 13; Mary V., 10; and Thomas Gilmore, 62, the last of these individuals with $500 in personal property (1860 Virginia Census, no. 1378, Rockbridge County, 178).

4. On Aunt Mary, see note 2 above.

5. Bill Payne may be William Paine, shown as a 17-year-old laborer in the 1860 Montgomery County census. Paine lived in the McDonald's Mill area in the household of John F. Bennett, a 33-year-old farmer with $1,500 in personal property. Others in the household were Elizabeth, 26; James

M., 2; and Robert N. Bennett, 1 (1860 Virginia Census, no. 1363, Montgomery County, 749).

6. Rumors of Ewell's death may have been circulating because illness kept him from commanding the Second Corps during the Mine Run Campaign (*Official Records*, 29, pt. 1:827). Ewell had never fully recovered from the amputation of his leg after Groveton in August 1862 and was incapacitated in part because of that lingering problem.

7. E. Anderson may be Eldred R. Anderson, shown in the Montgomery County census of 1860 as a 39-year-old merchant living in Christiansburg. Although it would seem unlikely for a merchant to preach, he may have been a lay preacher of some sort. This possibility is made more likely by the fact that his son-in-law was a Methodist minister. His daughter, Fannie Edwards, 20, had recently married William J. Edwards, age 26, a Methodist clergyman with $500 in personal property; both lived in the Anderson household. Others in the household were Mary J., age 40, and Elizabeth V. Anderson, 18 (1860 Virginia Census, no. 1363, Montgomery County, 565).

8. The term "f.t." probably stands for Fowler's Treatment, another name for Fowler's Solution. See Chapter 4, note 31.

9. Paine (or Payne) had apparently received word of the beginnings of the Mine Run Campaign; see Chapter 4, note 40.

10. Mr. Lybrook is John Lybrook, shown as a 40-year-old Blacksburg merchant in the 1860 census. In the same household were Mary Lybook, 24; Virginia E., 2; and George, 1. Lybrook had $5,200 in real estate and $12,000 in personal property (1860 Virginia Census, no. 1363, Montgomery County, 713). Cull Spickard is Collom Spickard, who lived in the household of Z. Wilson (see Chapter 3, note 22). Captain Jonathan B. Evans, who lived in the Lybrook household and was also a merchant (see Chapter 3, note 61), was killed on November 27, 1863, at the Battle of Payne's Farm (Compiled Service Records, Virginia, no. 405). On the death of Evans, see the report of Maj. William Terry, dated December 4, 1863 (*Official Records*, 29, pt. 1:851).

11. This is probably a reference to Harvey Black's letter of November 25.

12. Hamilton Wade was wounded in the shoulder at Payne's Farm on November 27 and returned to Montgomery County soon thereafter to recuperate; see note 50 below (Compiled Service Records, Virginia, 413; Robertson, *Fourth Virginia*, 29, 78).

13. Brigadier General John Echols commanded the First Brigade of the Army of Southwestern Virginia. His brigade engaged the forces of William Averell at the Battle of Droop Mountain, near Lewisburg, West Virginia, on November 6, 1863. Many of his troops dispersed in retreat at the battle; the brigade itself retreated to Lewisburg. For Echols' report on the action, see *Official Records*, 29, pt. 1:528-532. John McCausland (whose

name Mollie Black misspelled) was Colonel and regimental commander of the 36th Virginia Infantry at this time.

14. Mr. Earheart is probably George Earheart. See Chapter 3, note 43.

15. The Blacks were Methodists, members of the Blacksburg church now known as the United Methodist Church. An undated and unpaginated church Register dating from the Civil War years contains a "Record of probationers." Names included in the record are Ellen Bodell, Virginia Bodell, Belle Bodell, Lillie Sophronia Bodell, and Mary Ann Harvey. The church clearly had both black and white members and probationers. In the same volume are listed 12 black members of the church, in an entry for September 6, 1863 (Blacksburg Station, Montgomery County, Virginia, Baltimore Conference Church Register, Special Collections Department, Virginia Polytechnic Institute and State University Libraries).

16. "Nan T." is probably Nancy Thompson, the daughter of Archibald Thompson, and a close neighbor of the Blacks. Nancy Thompson is shown in the Blacksburg census as 17 years old. For other members of her household, see Chapter 2, note 45.

17. "Ida A." is probably Ida Argabright, another neighbor of the Black family. She is shown in the Blacksburg 1860 census as a 17-year-old living in the household of her parents, Wesley and Sarah Argabright. Wesley Argabright, 43, was a blacksmith with $1,000 in real estate and $350 in personal property; Sarah was 42 years old. Others in the household included William, 15; Malinda, 13; Henry, 11; Susan, 8; and Margaret Argabright, 2 (1860 Virginia Census, no. 1363, Montgomery County, 706).

18. "Phrone Surface" is Sophronia Surface, shown in the 1860 Blacksburg census as a 15-year-old living in the household of her parents, Henry Surface, a 41-year-old blacksmith with $450 in personal property, and Emily Surface, also 41. Siblings in the household included Emily, 17; George R., 13; Leoni J., 11; Samuel, 9; Edward A., 6; William N., 4; and Joseph P. Surface, 2 (1860 Virginia Census, no. 1363, Montgomery County, 712).

19. "Miss Bodelle from New Market" may be one of several people shown in the 1860 Shenandoah County census named Bodell rather than Bodelle. There is a Bodell family with one young daughter, Minerva, 16 years old (1860 Virginia Census, no. 1377, Shenandoah County, 122). Ann Bodell, 14, and Sarah Bodell, 12, also lived in New Market (1860 Virginia Census, no. 1377, Shenandoah County, 124). None of these names match the Bodells in the record of probationers mentioned above (note 15), however.

20. Mr. Shief is George Sheaf; see Chapter 2, note 47.

21. Mr. Carden is George Carden; see Chapter 2, note 8.

22. Charles L. Taylor is shown in the 1860 census for Craig County as a 41-year-old farmer living in the Sinking Creek Valley area. He had

$8,000 in real estate and $3,500 in personal property. Others in the household included Maria, also 41; Samuel, 16, a farm laborer; Albert 15, a farm laborer; Josephine, 9; Augustus, 7; and John Taylor, a 25-year-old farm laborer (1860 Virginia Census, no. 1341, Craig County, 763).

23. The "Misses Peterman" may have been sisters who were schoolteachers in Blacksburg. According to Mary Apperson, the Blacksburg Female Academy was run by five Peterman sisters: Ellen, Sue, Ollis, Ann, and Jonnie (Mary Apperson notebook, Virginia Polytechnic Institute and State University Libraries, 73). None of these names appear in the 1860 census for Montgomery County. Assuming the "Daniel" is Daniel Peterman, he may have lived outside the state. Only one Daniel Peterman is listed as a head of household in Jackson, *Virginia 1860 Federal Census.* He was a 42-year-old farmer who lived with his wife Periden and 9 children in Floyd Court House, Floyd County (1860 Virginia Census, no. 1345, Floyd County, 534). The daughters' names do not match the names of the Peterman sisters, however.

24. Achilles W. Luster enlisted in Company E of the Fourth Virginia on March 12, 1862, and was elected Corporal a month later at the regimental reorganization. He was detailed as an Ordnance Sergeant on September 28, 1863, and would be detailed as a provost guard on April 2, 1864. Nothing in his service record indicates why he may have "missed the fight" at Payne's Farm (Compiled Service Records, Virginia, no. 408; Robertson, *Fourth Virginia*, 61). The 1860 census for Montgomery County shows Achilles W. Luster as 32. No occupation, real estate, or personal property are listed in his name. In the same household lived Mary Luster, 26 (1860 Virginia Census, no. 1363, Montgomery County, 772).

25. "Nan" may be Nancy Thompson. See note 16 above.

26. William Averell's brigade departed from New Creek, West Virginia on December 5, with orders to proceed to Salem, Virginia, and to destroy Virginia and Tennessee railroad facilities there. On December 12th it began raining, and it continued raining for three days. Averell entered Salem on the morning of the 16th with an advance party of 350 cavalry and a section of artillery. His men tore up track and burned several bridges in the vicinity. They also burned the depot at Salem, with two warehouses containing grains, clothing, shoes, and various other items. They left Salem, heading back the way they came, the same day. Confronted with cold and heavy rain, they were forced to cross and recross a swollen Craig's Creek to reach New Castle, Virginia on the 18th. Much of Averell's ammunition had been destroyed by the repeated fordings of the creek. Although Mollie Black and others in the area may have thought that Averell would move toward the New River Bridge at Dublin after Salem—and thus pass near or through Blacksburg—they were wrong. General Samuel Jones, commanding the Department of Southwest Virginia, also believed that Averell would move to Dublin, as he indicated in his report on these events (*Official Records*, 29, pt. 1:943-45).

27. Jones sent all of the forces available to him, including the regiments of McCausland and William Jackson and Echols's brigade, in an attempt to catch the raiders, trying to prevent their escape by blocking their path north. By December 18th Averell was 12 miles north of New Castle; by the 19th he was at Covington, where his forces met 300 mounted rebels, probably a home guard unit. Colonel William L. Jackson's Nineteenth Virginia Cavalry was able to capture some of the men who failed to cross Jackson's River, though most of Averell's men got away.

28. Mollie Black's assessment of the damage at Salem was in accord with that officially expressed by General Jones, who wrote that the "loss of Government stores at Salem was small. The damage done the railroad was repaired in three or four days. The railroad was rather improved than injured by the raid, as the few small bridges burned were in such condition that they were scarcely safe, and would have required rebuilding very soon" (*Official Records*, 29, pt. 1:945).

29. "Uncle Will" may refer to William Wade or William Peck. Neither Tom or Thomas Evans appears in the 1860 Montgomery County census.

30. The Blacks sold their house to George Earheart in January 1864. A deed for a property "beginning at the southeast corner of the house in which the said Black now resides, formerly occupied by James Surface where the streets intersect opposite Wm H. Peck's store house, thence with the street leading to the town spring," dated January 9, 1864, appears in the Montgomery County Deed Book R (1860-68), 270-71. See also the Montgomery County Record of Plotts, Book F, 410. Both are in the Montgomery County Courthouse in Christiansburg, Virginia. The house, later known as Dutch Inn, was on the corner of present-day Main and Lee Streets. The Black family would move across the street and one block away, on the corner of present-day Main and Washington Streets. See Donna Dunay, ed., *Town Architecture: Blacksburg, Understanding a Virginia Town* (Blacksburg, Virginia: Town of Blacksburg, the College of Architecture and Urban Studies, and the Extension Division, Virginia Polytechnic Institute and State University, 1986), 112, 117, 140. Hereafter cited as Dunay, *Town Architecture*. On their move, see Chapter 6, note 6.

31. Lac Miller is probably Joseph Miller, the 48-year-old father of John T. Miller. Joseph Miller is shown in the 1860 Montgomery County census as a farmer with $2,950 in real estate and $350 in personal property. John T. Miller is shown as a 22-year-old farmer in the same household. Others in the household were John's mother Elizabeth, 47; and siblings George W., 20; Edward J., 18; Harriet V., 16; Giles P., 14; Joseph C., 12; Frances E., 6; William C., 4; and Jonathan T., 2 (1860 Virginia Census, no. 1363, Montgomery County, 745-46). John T. Miller enlisted in Company E of the Fourth Regiment on March 12, 1862. Captured at Payne's Farm, he was held at Old Capitol Prison until he was exhanged on March 17, 1864. He would be captured again at Spotsylvania in May 1864. Held at Point

Lookout Prison in Maryland, he would be exchanged February 20, 1865 (Compiled Service Records, Virginia, 409; Robertson, *Fourth Virginia*, 64).

32. "I. Hess Hymen" must be Samuel B. Hymon, who, along with John E. Peck and John T. Miller was captured at the Battle of Paynes's Farm, November 27, 1863. Hymon transferred to Company E of the Fourth Virginia from the 28th Virginia in September 1861; he was elected First Sergeant in the reorganization of April 22, 1862. Captured at Payne's Farm, he was held in Old Capitol Prison in Washington, D.C., and exchanged on March 28, 1864 (Compiled Service Records, Virginia, no. 407; Robertson, *Fourth Virginia*, 57). Hymon is shown in the 1860 Montgomery County census as a 20-year-old teacher living in the Matamoras area. He lived in the household of John R. C. Stephens, a 39-year-old farmer with $10,400 in real estate and $3,850 in personal property. In the same household were Rosannah, 30; Mary, 10; John H., 8; D. Josh, 6; and Cynthia Stephens, 4. Elizabeth Jones, 18, and Orlando Bailey, a 24-year-old laborer, also lived in the household (1860 Virginia Census, no. 1363, Montgomery County, 691).

33. Ed Peck was captured at Payne's Farm and held at Old Capitol Prison; he would be exchanged on March 7, 1864. Later captured at Spotsylvania in May 1864, he was held at Elmira Prison in New York until March 1865 (Compiled Service Records, Virginia, no. 410).

34. "Old Mr. Davis" is probably John Davis, age 78, a miller, in the Montgomery County census with no real estate and $400 in personal property. Elisabeth Davis, 37, also lived in the household (1860 Virginia Census, no. 1363, Montgomery County, 703).

35. Henry M. Dobbins, a 46-year-old farmer with $1,200 in real estate and $540 in personal property, lived in the Montgomery Springs area in the same household as Elizabeth Dobbins, 55 (1860 Virginia Census, no. 1363, Montgomery County, 729).

36. Major Kent is Joseph C. Kent. See Chapter 4, note 38.

37. There are two possibilities for John Keister. The first, a 35-year-old farmer with $1,500 in real estate and $835 in personal property, lived in the McDonald's Mills area with his wife Ellen, 33, and children Charles W., 4, and Lucy J., 3. In the same household were Henry Daniel, 12, and Sarah Daniel, 5, free blacks (1860 Virginia Census, no. 1363, Montgomery County, 750). Keister owned one slave (1860 Virginia Slave Schedules, no. 1394, Montgomery County, 120). The second possibility is John H. Keister, a 20-year-old farmer in the Matamoras area, who lived in the household of David, 50, and Elizabeth Keister, 48. The household also included B. Franklin Keister, 17; James R., 14; William J., 12; Louisa J., 21; Cynthia M., 16; Olivia, 5; and Elizabeth Olinger, 67 (1860 Virginia Census, no. 1363, Montgomery County, 688).

38. "Mitchel" is probably Mitchel Linkous, shown in the 1860 census for Blacksburg as a 63-year-old farmer with no real estate and $150 in

personal property. In the same household were Jane, 40; Mary A., 18; James, 17; William, 14; Edmonia, 11; Harrison, 9; Elizabeth, 7; and Sarah, 10 months (1860 Virginia Census, no. 1363, Montgomery County, 718).

39. Mr. Robinson is probably Matthew Robinson. See Chapter 2, note 7.

40. Mrs. Green King cannot be identified. No Green King appears in the 1860 Montgomery County census.

41. Aunt Judy cannot be identified. She may have been a favored slave of a neighbor, known familarly as "Aunt" Judy. "Nannie" may be Nannie T. Preston rather than Nancy Thompson, apparently known as "Nan." For information on Nannie T. Preston, see note 49 below.

42. Jim Henderson is probably James R. Henderson, 14 years old in the 1860 Blacksburg census. Henderson lived in the household of James M., 50; and Amanda M. Henderson, 38. The elder James Henderson was a hotel keeper with $3,150 in real estate and $8,000 in personal property. Catherine, 11, and John, 6, also lived in the household, as did three boarders: Leander Smith, a 45-year-old brickmason with $1,000 in personal property; Thomas R. Smith, a 40-year-old merchant with $1,000 in real estate and $8,000 in personal property; and Annie M. Lord, a 23-year-old teacher born in Maine (1860 Virginia Census, no. 1363, Montgomery County, 628).

43. It is unclear who "Mr. Alexander" is. In the 1860 census for Montgomery County, only one person named Alexander is listed — James Alexander in Christiansburg. He was an 18-year-old farmer with no real estate and $50 in personal property. Alexander lived in household of Crockett Roop, 37, a farmer with $1,800 in real estate and $375 in personal property. Other members of the Roop family in the household included Paratha, 24; Washington, 6; Isabella, 4; Laura A., 2; and Reid C. P., 1 (1860 Virginia Census, no. 1363, Montgomery County, 628).

44. Giles D. Thomas is shown in the 1860 Blacksburg census as a 28-year-old with no occupation listed, though he had $23,500 in real estate and $32,700 in personal property. In the same household were his wife, Mathilda C., age 21; and their two sons, James W., 3; and Henry E., 8 months (1860 Virginia Census, no. 1363, Montgomery County, 713). Thomas owned 6 slaves, according to the Montgomery County slave schedules (1860 Virginia Slave Schedules, no. 1394, Montgomery County, 118). Giles Thomas enlisted in Company E of the Fourth Virginia on October 17, 1864 (Compiled Service Records, Virginia, 412; Robertson, *Fourth Virginia*, 76). According to another source, Giles Thomas had enlisted in Company E of the 14th Regiment, McCausland's Brigade, in 1862 (*Hardesty's Encyclopedia*, 403).

45. Col. Linkous is Benjamin R. Linkous, at that time a lieutenant colonel in the 36th Virginia Infantry.

46. Jim Linkous may be the James Linkous mentioned above (note 37), a 17-year-old living in the household of Mitchel Linkous at the time of the 1860 census.

47. "Uncle Will" may be William Peck or William Wade.

48. Bird Linkous is probably Burgess R. Linkous, shown in the 1860 Montgomery County census as a 32-year-old trader living in the Matamoras area. In the same household lived Henry Linkous, a 69-year-old farmer with $12,500 in real estate and $3,000 in personal property; Fanny, 58; Edwin J. A., a 24-year-old farmer with $800 in personal property; Jaetta, 22; and Robert McG. Linkous, an 18-year-old farmer. Elizabeth Stover, a 22-year-old teacher, and Andrew Mares, a 17-year-old free black laborer, were also in the household (1860 Virginia Census, no. 1363, Montgomery County, 679).

49. Nannie T. Preston is shown in the 1860 Montgomery County census as the 17-year-old daughter of William B[allard] Preston, a 53-year-old farmer worth $132,000 in real estate and $251,330 in personal property. In the same household were Lucy S., 42; Waller, 19; Patton, 14; Lucy, 12; Jane, 9; and Keziah Preston, 6. The 83-year-old mother of William Ballard Preston, Ann T. Preston, also lived in the household (1860 Virginia Census, no. 1363, Montgomery County, 704). By this time, William Ballard Preston was no longer living; he died at Smithfield, his ancestral home, on November 16, 1862. Preston had been one of the area's most notable statesmen. He had represented Montgomery County in the Virginia General Assembly, was elected to Congress as a Whig, and had served as U.S. Secretary of the Navy. A member of the Virginia Constitutional Convention of 1861, he opposed secession and was one of three Virginians who met with Abraham Lincoln on April 12, 1861 in an unsuccessful effort to avert war. He served in the Confederate Congress as a senator until his death in 1862. For biographical information on Preston and members of his family, see Dorman, *The Prestons of Smithfield and Greenfield*, 260-265.

50. "Wade" is Hamilton Wade. His arm was sore from the wound he received at Payne's Farm.

51. Tom Jones may be Thomas W. Jones, a 45-year-old farmer with $1,000 in personal property. He lived in the McDonald's Mill area with his wife Catherine, also 45, and 6 children: Samuel M., 16, a farmer; Thomas P., 14; Mary, 12; John W., 10; James E., 8; and Giles M., 3 (1860 Virginia Census, no. 1363, Montgomery County, 758).

52. "Col. Wade" may be one of two individuals, both captains at this time: Hamilton Wade (see note 50 above) or James Wade, an assistant commissary of subsistence at Salem. For James Wade's report on these events, see *Official Records*, 29, pt. 1:969.

53. Jim Brown is most likely James C. Brown, a 31-year-old farmer with $7,500 in real estate and $3,350 in personal property. In the household lived Ann E. Brown, 29; Mollie, 6; John, 4; Howe, 2; Lucretia, 2

months; and Peter Carver, a 53-year-old laborer (1860 Virginia census, no. 1363, Montgomery County, 747). Brown owned 3 slaves, according to the 1860 slave schedules (1860 Virginia Slave Schedules, no. 1364, Montgomery County, 120).

54. The "150 men" is probably a reference to the Home Guard.

Six: "This War With All its Troubles
Will Leave Some Pleasant Reminiscences":
January 29-May 3, 1864

1. Apperson diaries, no. 5, January 25, 1864, Virginia Polytechnic Institute and State University Libraries.

2. Apperson diaries, no. 5, January 29, 1864, Virginia Polytechnic Institute and State University Libraries.

3. The shortage of food for the civilian and military population had reached crisis proportions by January 1864. Addressing the crisis, Lee issued his General Orders No. 7 on January 22. It stated that the temporary reduction in rations was beyond the control of the authorities, and it ended with a peroration: "Soldiers! You tread with no unequal step the road by which your fathers marched through suffering, privations, and blood, to independence. Continue to emulate in the future, as you have in the past, their valor in arms, their patient endurance of hardships, their high resolve to be free, which no trial could shake, no bribe seduce, no danger appal, and be assured that the just God who crowned their efforts with success will, in His own good time, send down His blessing upon yours" (Dowdey, *Wartime Papers of R. E. Lee*, 659).

4. Black had been granted 20 days leave of absence at Orange Court House on December 28, 1863 (Compiled Service Records, General and Staff Officers, no. 24). "My quartermaster" may refer to Captain Charles W. Hardy. John Apperson's memoirs note that a "Capt. Hardy" was quartermaster of the Second Corps Field Hospital during the 1863-64 winter while it was at Orange Court House ("Autobiography of John Samuel Apperson, M.D.," 96). The service record for Charles W. Hardy shows him serving as Captain and Assistant Quartermaster in the Second Corps on December 21, 1863, serving with the "Reserve Ambulance Train." On that same date, Hardy was granted a three-day extension of leave. No indication of any offense in overstaying his leave is noted, however. Hardy was appointed from Virginia as a Captain and Assistant Quartermaster on June 29, 1861 (Compiled Service Records, General and Staff Officers, no. 118). The 1860 Virginia census for Henry County shows Charles W. Hardy as a 24-year-old farmer with $1,600 in real estate and $5,900 in personal property, living in Carter's Store. Mary Hardy, 20, was in the same household (1860 Virginia census, no. 1354, Henry County, 106).

5. Mrs. Camper must be either Catherine Camper or Martha J. Camper, both of whom appear in the 1860 census for Blacksburg. Catherine Camper, 40, was married to Andrew Camper, also 40 years old and a weaver with $150 in personal property. They had seven children: Mary P., 16; Floyd S., 11; Lucretia E., 9; Georgienne, 7; Nancy C., 6; Sarah V., 4; and John H., 1 (1860 Virginia Census, no. 1363, Montgomery County, 711). Martha J. Camper is shown as being 35 years old in the 1860 census and married to 33-year-old Isaiah Camper, a plasterer with $250 in real estate and $50 in personal property. They had two children: William P., 3, and James T., 1 (1860 Virginia Census, no. 1363, Montgomery County, 710). Both Andrew Camper and Isaiah Camper are listed in Black's account book (Black medical account book, Virginia Polytechnic Institute and State University Libraries, 518, 418).

6. See Chapter 5, note 30 for information on the Black family's move.

7. On Joe and Aunt Mary, see Chapter 5, note 2.

8. John Apperson recalled in his autobiography that the Second Corps Field Hospital's location at Orange during Winter 1863-64 was "in a vacant lot on Main Street—a spot near a garden, just in front of the brick residence of Mr. James Chapman" ("Autobiography of John Samuel Apperson, M.D.," 96). His memory may have failed him about Chapman's first name. John M. Chapman is shown in the 1860 Orange County census as a 47-year-old lawyer who lived with his 36-year-old wife Susan and their six daughters: Mary, 17; Emma, 16; Susan, 14; Sally, 12; Rebecca, 4; and Jane, 2. Chapman had $29,000 in real estate and $4,600 in personal property (1860 Virginia Census, Orange County, no. 1369, 675). A photograph of the Chapman home is shown in Miller, *Antebellum Orange*, 15.

9. Mrs. Newton may be Elizabeth Newton, shown in the 1860 Orange County census as a 74-year-old farmer with $2,000 in real estate and $8,000 in personal property. Also in the household were Joseph, 11; and Elizabeth F. Newton, 5; and William Hunley, a 45-year-old overseer (1860 Virginia Census, no. 1369, Orange County, 627-28). Dr. Edwin Newton may be the doctor who insisted on Black seeing Mrs. Newton. He may have been her son.

10. Osborne may be E. H. Osborne, who appears in the 1860 Dinnwiddie County census as a 50-year-old Petersburg tobacco manufacturer with $6,500 in real estate and $41,500 in personal property (1860 Virginia Census, Dinnwiddie County, no. 1342, 143).

11. On February 6-7, troops from the 2nd Corps of Meade's army, including the cavalrymen of Brigadier General Judson Kilpatrick, crossed the Rapidan at Morton's Ford, overwhelming a Confederate guard party. In the engagement that followed, Ewell was able to rebuff the attack and drive the troops across the river. By the 8th, all had returned to normal. Union and Confederate reports on the engagement at Morton's Ford show

that it cost 255 Union and 60 Confederate casualties (*Official Records,* 33:118, 143).

12. W. G. Bean quotes this anecdote about Lacy from Black's letter ("Stonewall Jackson's Jolly Chaplain," 95). At the time his article was written, the Black letters were in the possession of Harvey Black's grand-daughter, Mary Apperson.

13. "Bob" is probably Robert Peck, who would be absent on sick fur-lough until April 1, 1864, when he was detailed to the Quartermaster's Department (Compiled Service Records, Virginia, no. 410).

14. Landonia Kipps, listed in the 1860 Montgomery County census as the 38-year-old wife of Noah Kipps, a 47-year-old carpenter with $2,200 in personal property, lived in the Matamoras section of Montgomery County. In the same household were their son John H. Kipps, a 19-year-old farmer, and their daughter Mary F., 17. Olia E. Custard, a 7-year-old female, also lived in the household (1860 Virginia Census, no. 1363, Montgomery County, 681). John H. Kipps enlisted in Company L of the Fourth Virginia on July 16, 1861, at Blacksburg. He was promoted to 3rd Sergeant on April 23, 1862. Taken prisoner at Gettysburg on July 3, 1863, he was sent to Fort Delaware, Point Lookout. He would be exchanged September 18, 1864 (Compiled Service Records, Virginia, no. 408; Robertson, *Fourth Virginia,* 59).

15. Mrs. Williamson is probably Marry Williamson; see Chapter 4, note 5.

16. Dr. Joseph E. Claggett served as surgeon in charge of Receiving and Forwarding Hospital, Army of Northern Virginia, from Nov. 25, 1862 to Jan. 13, 1865 (Compiled Service Records, General and Staff Officers, no. 55). In a letter to Surgeon General Moore of June 14, 1863, Lafayette Guild referred to Claggett as an "efficient and laborious officer" in charge of the Receiving Hospital (Letters Sent, Medical Director's Office, 1862-63, U.S. National Archives, 165). Black misspelled his name as "Clagget." Accord-ing to Dr. Edwin Newton, Claggett lived in Baltimore after the war, dying around 1908 (Newton, "My Recollections and Reminiscences," 483). Clag-gett does not appear in Jackson, *Virginia 1860 Federal Census.* Ronald Vern Jackson, ed., *Maryland 1860, Except for the City of Baltimore, Federal Census Index* (Salt Lake City, Utah: Accelerated Indexing Systems International, 1988) lists one Joseph Claggett. The census shows him not as a doctor, however, but a farm manager (1860 Maryland census, no. 478, Montgom-ery County, 153).

17. Mrs. Payne is possibly Mary Payne, shown in the 1860 Orange County census as the 52-year-old wife of Charles G. Payne, a 50-year-old farmer with $10,020 in real estate and $10,580 in personal property. In the same household were four children: Sarah F., 18; Benj. E.,16; Robert G., 12; and Louisa E., 4 (1860 Virginia Census, no. 1369, Orange County, 617). Another possibility is Mary G. Payne, the 20-year-old wife of John L.

Payne, a 25-year-old editor with no real estate and $2,000 in personal property. In the same household were J. F. Moppin, a 25-year-old printer; Walter S. Jones, 22; and Marion Thrift, a 61-year-old female (1860 Virginia Census, no. 1369, Orange County, 674).

18. John S. Hansbrough was Rector of St. Thomas' Episcopal Church in Orange Court House from 1870 to 1908. Originally from Petersburg, Virginia, he became a refugee at Orange during the Civil War, and conducted services at St. Thomas' during winter 1863-64, when the Army of Northern Virginia was encamped near the town. See *Bi-Centennial St. Thomas' Parish and Centennial St. Thomas' Church, Oct. 20-21, 1973: Historical Notes, Printed by Order of the Vestry* (n.p., n.d.), 44. Hansbrough (whose name Black misspelled) appears in the 1860 census for Garysville, Prince George County, as a 28-year-old minister with $2,000 in personal property. Others in the household were M. E., a 26-year-old female; E. C., a 49-year-old female; W. L., an 18-year-old female; A. C., a 15-year-old female; G. G., a 2-year-old female; and C. W. Hansbrough, an 8 month-old male. R. Thweate, a 35-year-old mulatto carpenter, was also a member of the household (1860 Virginia census, no. 1372, Prince George County, 337).

19. Dr. Edward G. Higgenbotham served as Surgeon in charge of the Receiving Hospital, Third Corps, Army of Northern Virginia, in 1863 and 1864 (Compiled Service Records, General and Staff Officers, no. 126) In the 1860 Virginia census, Higginbotham is shown as a 35-year-old physician living in the 2nd Ward of the city of Richmond. He is shown as having no real estate and $8,900 in personal property. Julia A. Higgenbotham, 28, a druggist; Amelia Higgenbotham, 6; and Julia H. Higgenbotham, 7 months; are also in the household. Sarah, 58; Lucy, 26; Sally, 21; and Ella Thompson, 18, lived in the household, as did Elizabeth Doyle, a 17-year-old nurse (1860 Virginia Census, no. 1352, Henrico County, 235).

20. It is unclear who Mrs. Higgenbotham — the former Miss Haxall of Richmond — is. Assuming that Higgenbotham's wife is Julia (see note 20 above), the likely person would be a Julia Haxall. Since Higgenbotham and Julia were already married by the time of the 1860 census, it is possible that a Julia Haxall might appear in the 1850 census for Henrico County, but no such name appears. See *Richmond City and Henrico County, Virginia 1850 United States Census* (Richmond: Virginia Genealogical Society 1977). It may be that Higgenbotham's first wife was named Julia, and that he had recently remarried. Attempts to trace his marriage in Henrico County records failed as well, however.

21. Mrs. Higgenbotham appears to have had a slanted eye.

22. Black's expression of class resentment was a common one, though it is hard to say just how accurate it may have been. It was aimed at those members of the upper classes who were able to avoid serving in the Confederacy by providing substitutes and at merchants who profited from the

skyrocketing inflation of the war and shortages of necessities by hoarding commodies like food, cotton, and shoes and selling them at exorbitant profits.

23. Mr. Webster is probably Charles H. Webster, who enlisted as a private in Company H of the 33rd Virginia Regiment at Winchester on March 2, 1862. There are no records after May 10, 1863, in his service record (Compiled Service Records, Virginia, no. 798).

24. Brigadier General (not Colonel) Samuel Jones had been in command of the Department and Army of Southwest Virginia since November 25, 1863. He faced heavy criticism during his command, chiefly for his inability to stop Federal raiders who sought to cripple the Virginia and Tennessee Railroad and thereby cut a significant communication and supply line for the Confederacy. Lee relieved Jones of his command on February 11, 1864 and appointed Major General John C. Breckinridge, a Kentuckian, to the position on February 25.

25. Sally Williamson is the daughter of Marry Williamson. See Chapter 4, note 5.

26. Mrs. Carden is Mary A. Carden; see Chapter 2, note 8.

27. "Bob" is probably Bob Peck.

28. Robert D. Gardner, who had received a severe facial wound at Fredericksburg in December 1862 and who had never fully recovered from the wound, would be retired from service on April 9 (Compiled Service Records, Virginia, no. 406; Robertson, *Fourth Virginia*, 51).

29. Governor Zebulon B. Vance of North Carolina, a strong supporter of states rights within the Confederacy who was at odds with the Jefferson Davis government over some of its centralist tendencies, was nevertheless a supporter of the Confederate war effort. He visited the Army of Northern Virginia in March 1864 and made a number of speeches that Lee himself "enjoyed greatly." See Douglas Southall Freeman, *R. E. Lee: A Biography* (New York: Charles Scribner's Sons, 1935), 3:223.

30. "John" is John Kent, identified in the April 6 letter as "your brother John." John Kent was the third child of Germanicus and Arabella Kent and thus the older brother of Mollie Black (*Germanicus A. Kent*, 6). He was born in Huntsville, Alabama, in 1833 and appears in the 1860 Missouri census as John E. Kent, 25, a store clerk with no real estate or personal property in Fulton Post Office, 18th District, Callaway County. He lived in the household of W. W. Tuttle, a merchant with $6,000 in real estate and $10,000 in personal property. Others in the household included Susan, 28; Elwood, 5; James, 3; and Edwin K. Tuttle, 1. In addition to Kent, two other store clerks were in the household: William Dritzan, 25, with $500 in personal property, and William F. Grant, 22 (1860 Missouri Census, Callaway County, no. 610, 974). Kent is apparently the John Kent who enlisted in Company K of the 1st Northeast Missouri Cavalry (Confederate) as a corporal on August 3, 1862. See Compiled Service Records of Confederate

Soldiers Who Served in Organizations from the State of Missouri (U.S. National Archives Microcopy M322), no. 12. His service record gives no indication that he was a prisoner of war at any point.

31. "Ed" is probably Ed Black. He may have been in Blacksburg at this time; his service record shows him as being absent with leave in November and December 1863, though he would later return to service with the 36th Virginia Infantry (Compiled Service Records, Virginia, no. 821). The likelihood that Ed is Ed Black is increased by a reference to him later in this same letter : "How has Ed Black gotten."

32. Longstreet and two of his divisions were detached to serve with the Army of Tennessee after Gettysburg. Longstreet was ordered to return from his command in East Tennessee to Virginia and to rejoin the Army of Northern Virginia in early April 1864. Ulysses S. Grant was promoted to rank of lieutenant general in early March 1864 and placed in overall command of Union armies. He made his headquarters with Meade's Army of the Potomac.

33. This is probably a reference to Henderson's service in the 12th Congressional District Mounted Guard, a military unit formed to support conscription officers (Compiled Service Records, Virginia, no. 211). According to his service record, Henderson served in this capacity from September 1863 to April 1864.

34. On Ed Black, see note 32 above.

35. "Mr. Bell" is probably William Anderson Bell, who enlisted in Company E of the Fourth Virginia Regiment on April 16, 1861 and who was detailed as an ambulance driver for the regiment. Wounded in a fight with another ambulance driver from the 2nd Virginia Regiment, he was captured at Warrenton, Virginia, in October 1862. Bell was confined at Point Lookout, Maryland, until he was exchanged on March 3, 1864. His release could be the cause of celebration in Blacksburg to which Black referred. Bell, however, would be recaptured at Ninevah eight months later, on November 12, 1864, and would be exchanged on February 18, 1865 (Compiled Service Records, Virginia, 402; Robertson, *Fourth Virginia*, 39). The 1860 census for Blacksburg shows Bell as a 22-year-old wagoner living in the household of James M. Evans, a 41-year-old carpenter with $3,000 in real estate and $1,000 in personal property. Sylvester Bell, 16, apparently a brother, also lived in the Evans household (1860 Virginia Census, no. 1363, Montgomery County, 707).

36. No individuals with the surnames Rice or Norvell appear in the Montgomery County 1860 census. Lizzie may have been taking music lessons of some kind; see the undated letter from ca. November 4-8, 1864, for a reference to such lessons.

37. Mr. Bell may be the William Anderson Bell mentioned above (note 33). His service record makes it unclear whether he would have been back

with the Fourth Virginia by this time (Compiled Service Records, Virginia, no. 402).

38. Minnie Humphrey could not be identified.

39. There is no Maither Aiken in the 1860 census for Montgomery County, nor does anyone with that name appear in Jackson, *Virginia 1860 Federal Census*.

40. On John E. Kent, see note 31 above.

41. This anecdote cannot be illuminated at all.

42. The word "miscegenation," meaning the practice of interracial marriage, can be dated from the 1864 United States presidential election, when the Democratic Party coined the term from the Latin words "miscere" (to mix) and "genus" (race). Democrats contended that Lincoln's Republican Party advocated racial mixture.

43. Bob Peck was assigned to the Quartermaster's Department; see note 14 above.

44. The use of the term "attacked" here may refer to Black's cough, which, as he notes several paragraphs above this, had nearly left him.

45. Ambrose Burnside returned east in Spring 1864 to take command of his old IX Corps at the Battle of the Wilderness, on May 5-7. With his forces reinforcing the Army of the Potomac, Union forces would total approximately 115,000, compared to 64,000 on the Confederate side. Soldiers in the Army of Northern Virginia began to see signs of movement across the Rapidan by Union forces on May 2 and 3 — smoke, dust clouds, and marching columns. The battle would begin early on May 5 near Chancellorsville, as Black suggested, in the "mean" and heavily-wooded country known as the Wilderness. Exact figures for casualties are lacking, but Union casualties would be around 18,000, Confederate casualties, 8,000-10,000. Despite the heavier Union casualties, Grant gained a tactical advantage as he was now able to move his army south unhindered by Confederate forces.

46. Major D. B. Bridgford served as provost-marshall of the Second Corps of the Army of Northern Virginia (*Official Records*, 21:635; 40, pt. 3:765; 51, pt. 2:864). No service record for Bridgford could be found in the Compiled Service Records of Confederate General and Staff Officers.

47. Black's allusion is to Confederate successes in Arkansas and North Carolina. Major General Sterling Price helped repulse Union Major General Frederick Steele's Camden Expedition in Arkansas and Louisiana lasting from March 23 to May 3, 1864. In late April and early May it appeared that eastern North Carolina, held by Union forces since 1862, would fall back into Confederate hands when Brigadier General Robert F. Hoke captured Union-held Plymouth, leading to the federal evacuation of Washington, North Carolina, on April 28. Hoke was ready to move against New Bern when he was called back to Petersburg, Virginia.

48. Mollie Black's cousin was William John Mastin, the son of James Hervey Mastin. According to genealogical files in the Apperson family papers, the Mastins lived in Alabama, and William Mastin was born in 1847 (Mastin family genealogical file, Apperson family papers, Virginia Polytechnic Institute and State University Libraries). The 1860 Alabama census shows William J. Mastin as the 12-year-old son of James H. Mastin, 45. The elder Mastin had been born in Virginia and had $20,000 in real estate property and $35,000 in personal property. The Mastins lived in Huntsville, Madison County. Others in the household were Mary J., 34; Mary J., 10; Alexander E., 8; and Frank Mastin, 6 (1860 Alabama Census, no. 15, Madison County, 215). William Mastin was a private in Company A of Russell's Fourth Alabama Cavalry, enlisting at Madison, Alabama, which bordered Huntsville. He is shown as surviving the war and surrendering at Gainesville, Alabama, on May 4, 1865. See Compiled Service Records of Confederate Soldiers Who Served in Organizations from the State of Alabama (U.S. National Archives Microcopy M311), no. 17. This cavalry regiment was in Martin's Cavalry Corps, Army of Tennessee, from April through November 1864. See Stewart Sifakis, *Compendium of the Confederate Armies: Alabama* (New York: Facts on File, 1992), 33. Simon Bolivar Buckner, in Bragg's Army of Tennessee at this time, was moved to command East Tennessee when Longstreet was called back to Virginia in April 1864.

49. Dr. J. Lewis Woodville was appointed as a surgeon in the Confederate Army on July 1, 1861, and was ordered to Montgomery White Sulphur Springs Hospital later that same year. When the hospital was formally established in 1862, he was made surgeon in charge. He was tried from April 16 to April 25, 1864, on a variety of charges but was found not guilty (Compiled Service Records, General and Staff Officers, no. 273; Bodell, *Montgomery White Sulphur Springs*, 14). In the 1860 census for Monroe County, Virginia (now West Virginia), Woodville is shown as a 38-year-old physician with $21,000 in real estate and $21,500 in personal property living in the Peterstown area. In the same household lived May A., 29; Emma G., 5; James L., 4; and Cary B. Woodville (1860 Virginia Census, no. 1363, Monroe County, 997).

50. "Geo. B." is probably George B. Bane, mentioned below (see Chapter 7, note 33). Bane is shown in the 1860 Montgomery County census as a 53-year-old farmer with $12,000 in real estate and $4,500 in personal property. Others in the household included Keziah, 46; Mary P. R., 22; Harriet E., 14; Virginia A., 12; and Margaret P. Bane, 10 (1860 Virginia Census, no. 1363, Montgomery County, 696). Bane owned 3 slaves (1860 Virginia Slave Schedules, no. 1394, Montgomery County, 116). The nature of Black's "truce" is unknown.

51. This is probably a reference to Celinda M. H. Henderson, the wife of Giles J. Henderson; see Chapter 1, note 18.

52. Several disjointed sentences have been omitted after this passage for the sake of the flow of the text.

**Seven: "Good Fortune Attends Me All the Time,
and I See No Reason Why it Will Not Continue":
October 8-December 3, 1864**

1. In the gap between Black's letters of May 1864 and this group of letters, much had happened. Jubal Early had been placed in command of the Second Corps to replace the ailing Richard Ewell in May 1864 after the Wilderness. Early's force had been renamed the Army of the Valley, an independent command that contained 10,000 infantry from the Second Corps (Jackson's old troops), now detached from the Army of Northern Virginia, and another 4,000 poorly-disciplined cavalry. Though Early received reinforcements, he was always at a severe numerical disadvantage against Philip Sheridan's Army of the Shenandoah.

2. At the time this letter was written, Sheridan's forces were withdrawing from Harrisonburg, beginning on October 6. Early's cavalry and infantry followed. Jed Hotchkiss's journal of the 1864 Shenandoah Valley campaign, printed as part of the *Official Records*, notes that Early's infantry encamped near Harrisonburg on the night of October 6 and stayed for several days (*Official Records*, 43, pt. 1:578).

3. On October 5, Brigadier General Thomas Lafayette Rosser arrived in the Valley with his Laurel Brigade to reinforce and take over the command of Fitzhugh Lee's cavalry division; Lee was wounded at Third Winchester. Great things were expected of Rosser, who was immediately given the epithet "Savior of the Valley."

4. Lieutenant John Rodgers Meigs, Sheridan's topographical engineer and the son of Union Quartermaster General Montgomery Meigs, was killed near Dayton, Virginia, on October 3, 1864. His killing, allegedly by Confederate bushwhackers, prompted Sheridan to order the burning of all houses within a five-mile radius of Dayton. He countermanded the order after a few houses were burned. Apperson's diary includes no comments about Meigs being killed.

5. As Sheridan retreated northward from Harrisonburg on October 6-8, his cavalry followed a scorched-earth policy, systematically destroying crops, livestock, barns, and farms — all in an effort to make the Shenandoah Valley barren (*Official Records*, 43, pt. 1:29). The damage done can be seen in Sheridan's reports to Grant, who issued the orders to devastate the region. Sheridan asserted that he had "destroyed over 2,000 barns filled with wheat, hay, and farming implements; over seventy mills filled with flour and wheat; [had] driven in front of the army over 4[000] head of stock, and [had] killed and issued to the troops not less than 3,000 sheep" (*Official Records*, 43, pt. 1:30). Apperson's diary on October 8 noted that the "enemy has burned everything edible in the country. Many almost heartrending

tales are told of their outrages. They seem particularly fond of oppressing poor helpless women" (Apperson diaries, no. 6, Virginia Polytechnic Institute and State University Libraries).

6. Edward Black, Harvey Black's cousin and a member of Company F of the 36th Virginia Infantry, was captured at the Battle of Third Winchester (or Opequan Creek) on September 19, 1864. Sent to Fort Delaware, he was released June 17, 1865 (Compiled Service Records, Virginia, no. 821). The newspaper article mentioned by Harvey Black appears in the October 7, 1864, issue of the Richmond *Whig*. The article, "Confederate Officers Captured at the Battle of Opequan Creek, Sept. 19," mentions "Second Lieutenant E. Black, 36th Virginia."

7. There are two mentions of a "Mr. Alexander" in the letters. The first mention is by Mollie Black, possibly referring to James Alexander of Christiansburg (see Chapter 5, note 43, for census information on him). Harvey Black may be referring to the same individual, although it is unlikely; this "Mr. Alexander" appears to be in the Shenandoah Valley.

8. Mrs. Carson cannot be identified. There is only one Carson in the 1860 Shenandoah County census—a Thomas Carson in Strasburg, age 66, with no wife listed (1860 Virginia Census, Shenandoah County, no. 1377, 628).

9. Mrs. Magruder is possibly the wife of Dr. George W. Magruder, one of the surgeons in the Second Corps Field Hospital. The 1860 census reference to Magruder, who lived in Woodstock in 1860, does not include a wife. It is, of course, possible that Magruder had married since the census information was recorded. See Chapter 4, note 34 for information on Magruder.

10. Dr. Love is William Samuel Love, surgeon in charge of a Confederate hospital in Winchester (Compiled Service Records of Confederate General and Staff Officers, no. 159). See also *Medical and Surgical History of the Civil War*, 7:347, for a mention of Love performing an operation in Winchester after the Battle of Third Winchester on September 19, 1864. Another Union letter mentions a Confederate hospital in Winchester "under charge of Dr. Love and two assistant surgeons, C. S. Army," on August 14, 1864 (*Official Records*, 43, pt. 1:621). There are three William Loves who appear as heads of household in Jackson, *Virginia 1860 Federal Census*. None proved to be a physician.

11. Miss Russell is Matilda N. Russell, shown as being 21 years old in the 1860 census for Winchester, Virginia. She lived in the household of Eliza A. Russell, her mother, a 43-year-old housekeeper with $1,100 in real estate and $1,700 in personal property. Others in the household were Jame B., an 18-year-old clerk; Isaac H., 16; Mary, 9; Lucey W., 7; and Sally S., 5 (1860 Virginia Census, no. 1347, Frederick County, 391). Black notes that Miss Russell was giving her attention to Lieutenant McDonald; another instance of Matilda Russell's care for wounded Confederate soldiers is the

topic of an article her sister Lucy wrote about her, "A Night on the Battle-field." In the story, "Tillie" Russell, "dark-eyed and pretty," nurses a severely wounded Southern soldier all night on an unidentified battlefield in the 1864 Shenandoah Valley Campaign. See Louisa M. Green, Katherine Glass Greene, and Philip Williams, eds., *True Stories of Old Winchester and the Valley* (Winchester, Virginia: Civic League of Winchester, n.d.), 12-14. For the connection between Matilda Russell and Lieutenant McDonald, see note 12 below. The brother who was on duty with Black would have been Jame, who was around 22 years old at this time, or Isaac, who was around 20.

12. Lieutenant McDonald, later identified as Lieutenant Taylor McDonald, was actually Floyd Joseph McDonald. Black seems to have confused Charles Taylor McDonald with his younger brother, Floyd. Both brothers were soldiers in the First Tennessee Cavalry Regiment; Floyd J. McDonald died in October 1864 and Charles (Taylor) took an oath of allegiance to the Union the same month. The 1860 census for Rhea County, Tennessee, shows their father, Bryant R. McDonald, as a 63-old farmer with $5,750 in real estate and $10,000 in personal property. Others in the household were his wife Elizabeth, 52; Mary E., 25; Floied J., 21; and George A. McDonald, 15. Charles T. McDonald, 27; his wife Caroline McDonald, 25; and Caroline E. McDonald, 3 months, also lived in the household (1860 Tennessee Census, no. 1268, Rhea County, Tennessee, 10th District, Smiths and Roads Post Office, 525). Bryant (or Bryan) McDonald was the brother-in-law of Floyd McDonald (see note 23 below), who married Harvey Black's sister Jane (*Genealogy of the MacDonald Family*, 64). See note 24 below for further information on Floyd McDonald. Both Floyd Joseph and Charles Taylor McDonald enlisted in Company D of the First (Carter's) Tennessee Cavalry Regiment at Knoxville on August 5, 1861. Floyd J. McDonald was promoted to Second Lieutenant in May 1862 and to First Lieutenant in June 1863. His service record shows him as dying in November 1864 from wounds received in action at Darkesville, West Virginia. Though the date of his wound isn't given, there were skirmishes at Darkesville involving Confederate cavalry on September 2 and 10, 1864 (*Official Records*, 43, pt. 2:65-66). Charles McDonald was captured at Kingston, Tennessee, in November 1863 and was sent to Rock Island Barracks, Illinois, where he took an oath of allegiance to the United States on October 27, 1864. Both service records are in Compiled Service Records of Confederate Soldiers Who Served in Organizations from Tennessee (U.S. National Archives Microcopy M368), no. 3. Floyd J. McDonald's service record is incorrect in placing his death date in November 1864. The *Genealogy of the MacDonald Family* gives his date of death as October 21, 1864 (64). A list of soldiers buried in the Stonewall Cemetery in Winchester places his death on October 20, adding that he died at the home of Mrs. Eliza A. Russell. See Lucy Fitzhugh Kurtz and Benny Ritter, *A Roster of Confederate Soldiers Buried in the Stonewall Cemetery, Winchester, Virginia* (Winchester, Virginia: Farmers and Merchants National Bank, 1962), 38.

To add to the confusion over McDonald's identity, the roster of those buried in the Stonewall Cemetery identifies him as "J. L." McDonald. According to V. C. Allen, Floyd McDonald was engaged in the mercantile business at Smith's Cross Roads (present-day Dayton), Tennessee, before the war. He writes of McDonald that he was "a brave, gallant soldier, a noble young man." See V. C. Allen, *Rhea and Meigs Counties in the Confederate War*, published with *Records of Rhea* (Dayton, Tennessee: Rhea County Historical Society, 1976), 28. See note 11 above for information on Eliza Russell. Although Black probably did not know it, another of his relatives had died nearby in October 1864. Adam Black, a grandson of William Black of Ohio, was a private in the 8th Ohio Cavalry Regiment. He died at Front Royal, Virginia, on October 13, 1864, and was buried in Winchester. See Chapter 3, note 31.

13. As Sheridan's forces were withdrawing from Harrisonburg, Confederate cavalry under Rosser attacked their rear guard. Rosser pursued them successfully for 2 days but was counterattacked at the Battle of Tom's Brook on October 9. After a fierce two-hour battle, the Confederate cavalry folded. Ultimately, Custer's cavalry routed Rosser's men. According to the report of Union Major General Alfred T. A. Torbert, Rosser retreated for twenty miles, losing artillery, supply wagons, ambulances, as well as 350 men who were captured (*Official Records*, 43, pt. 1:431).

14. Major Andrew L. Pitzer was an aide-de-camp on General Early's staff. He was appointed on April 23, 1863, and was reported as serving with the Army of the Valley District, Second Corps, on October 31, 1864 (Compiled Service Records, General and Staff Officers, no. 198).

15. Dr. Munsie could not be identified. Nobody named Munsie who was a surgeon appears in the Compiled Service Records, General and Staff Officers or in the Index to Compiled Service Records, Soldiers Who Served in Organizations from the State of Virginia, nor are there any Munsies in Jackson, *Virginia 1860 Federal Census*. Although the index lists three Munseys, none of them proved to be physicians.

16. McGuire's letter must be the same one mentioned by General Early in his report of October 9. Like Black's letter of the same date, Early's report was written at New Market: "The enemy's loss at Winchester was very heavy. Doctor McGuire has received a letter from a member of his family who states that 5,800 of the enemy's wounded were brought to the hospital at Winchester, and that the total wounded was between 6,000 and 7,000..." (*Official Records*, 43, pt. 1:556). Actual Union casualties at Third Winchester numbered 5,018 (697 killed, 3,983 wounded, and 338 missing); Confederate casualties were 3,921 (276 killed, 1,827 wounded, and 1,818 missing).

17. Although this letter cannot be precisely dated, it is likely that it was written early in November 1864, probably between November 4 and 8. References to "perfect quiet" in the army and preparation for moving

into winter quarters suggest that active campaigning had come to an end, and this would place the letter after the Battle of Cedar Creek in mid-October. Black notes that "Taylor" McDonald (actually Floyd J. McDonald) had died two weeks earlier; his actual date of death is October 20. Finally, Black indicates that he had received two letters from Mollie dated the 28th [of October?] and November 1.

18. James A. Templeton appears in the Blacksburg 1860 census as a physician. Dr. Templeton was 32 years old at the time the census was taken, had $3,000 in real estate and $500 in personal property. In the same household were Templeton's wife Margaret, age 30; and three children: Mary, 11; Howard, 7; and Emily, 4 (1860 Virginia Census, no. 1363, Montgomery County, 710). Templeton served as an assistant surgeon at Montgomery White Sulphur Springs Hospital beginning in January 1863; previously he had been in the 22nd Virginia Infantry Regiment (Register of Appointments, Medical Director's Office, Richmond, Virginia, 1861-63, Record Group 109, Ch. VI, 143:68, U.S. National Archives; Compiled Service Records of Confederate General and Staff Officers, no. 244).

19. The Union Sixth Corps had been detached from the Army of the Potomac to serve with Sheridan's Army of the Shenandoah. It was engaged at the Battle of Cedar Creek on October 19. Thus the rumor of the Sixth Corps moving down the valley to Harper's Ferry—where Sheridan's forces were headquartered—would have been reasonable early in November 1864.

20. Gilmore is possibly John C. Gilmore, shown in the 1860 Blacksburg census as a 28-year-old teacher living at a hotel operated by John M. Jordan. Gilmore is shown as having $7,200 in personal property (1860 Virginia Census, no. 1363, Montgomery County, 713). Although there are three Gilmores in the Montgomery County census, John Gilmore seems the most likely choice of the three. Black refers to him as a talker, a characteristic more associated with a teacher than with a laborer or a farmer, the occupations of the other two Gilmores (1860 Virginia Census, no. 1363, Montgomery County, 590, 117). Secondly, Black's prewar medical ledger includes references to John Gilmore (Black medical account book, Virginia Polytechnic Institute and State University Libraries, 341, 440) and not to the other two.

21. "Mr. Lacy" is presumably Beverly Tucker Lacy (see Chapter 3, note 71). Jed Hotchkiss's journal entry for December 5 contains a brief reference to Lacy, noting that "Mr. Lacy spent some time with us" (*Official Records*, 43, pt. 1:586). For Lacy's reputation as a story-teller, see Bean, "Stonewall Jackson's Jolly Chaplain," 96.

22. McCarson cannot be identified. Nobody named McCarson appears in the Compiled Service Records, General and Staff Officers, nor is there a McCarson in the Index to Compiled Service Records, Soldiers Who Served in Organizations from the State of Virginia.

23. On Taylor McDonald, see note 12 above.

24. "Floyd" is probably Floyd McDonald, Harvey Black's brother-in-law, the husband of Black's sister Jane. The 1860 Montgomery County census shows him as a 41-year-old farmer with $7,000 in real estate and $4,860 in personal property. Others in the household were Jane, 33; Jonas C., 7; Ellen, 5; and James McDonald, 45, with $1,000 in personal property (Virginia Census, no. 1363, Montgomery County, 694). Floyd McDonald owned six slaves (1860 Virginia Slave Schedules, no. 1394, Montgomery County, 116). For a biographical sketch of Floyd McDonald, see *Hardesty's Encyclopedia*, 409-10. Floyd McDonald was the uncle of Charles Taylor McDonald and Floyd Joseph McDonald (see note 12).

25. For speculation on the identity of Aunt Mary and her child, see Chapter 5, note 2.

26. Ellen, Susan, and Mollie Spickard were the daughters of John C. and Nancy Spickard, according to the 1860 Blacksburg census. At the time the census was taken, they were 19, 20, and 21 years old, respectively (see Chapter 1, note 62).

27. Early's views against getting married during war were widely known, as was his opposition to wives being brought into camp.

28. Dr. John A. Straith was appointed assistant surgeon of the 2nd Virginia Infantry on May 23, 1861. From September 1, 1863, until the end of the war he served as chief surgeon of the artillery corps, Second Corps of the Army of Northern Virginia (Compiled Service Records, General and Staff Officers, no. 238; *Official Records*, 29, pt. 1:419). John Apperson commented on Straith's character in his diary entry for October 25, 1862. He wrote that Straith was "sensible and minute in his conversation, well-read and has good understanding of manners, and is quite precise in their use. His writings are prolix, aye, profuse with every point explained until from explanation itself it becomes confused. No error escapes him, and his own works are done in strict accordance with his conscience. He will make his mark in the world and do humanity a vast amount of good" (Apperson diaries, no. 3, Virginia Polytechnic Institute and State University Libraries). Straith could not be located in Jackson, *Virginia 1860 Federal Census*.

29. Major John D. Rogers was quartermaster of Robert Rodes' division in Early's Army of the Valley District. Rogers' service record shows him as being on duty with the Valley Army on October 31, 1864, and again on December 29, 1864; on the latter date he received a furlough at Fishersville (Compiled Service Records, General and Staff Officers, no. 215).

30. "Bob" is probably Robert Peck.

31. A letter from Surgeon General Samuel P. Moore to Gen. Sam Cooper, Adjutant and Inspector, dated November 30, 1864, requests that a medical board comprised of surgeons H. Black, W. S. Mitchell, J. A. Straith, J. C. Hill, and W. T. Arrington be set up to examine medical officers in

General Early's command (Letters Received by the Confederate Adjutant and Inspector General's Office, no. 145, letter 3450-S).

32. "Poor Daniel" is probably Daniel Hoge (see Chapter 4, note 7) who was known to be a member of the underground Unionist and peace organization, the Heroes of America (HOA). Originating in North Carolina, the Heroes of America first came into Southwest Virginia in 1863, according to an investigation by Confederate authorities. By fall 1864, when the investigation took place, it was thought that the organization had 800 members in Montgomery County (*Official Records*, Series IV, 3:803). Two detectives posing as sympathizers to the HOA cause visited Hoge at his home on September 20, 1864, and according to their report, got Hoge to boast that he had been "opposed to the war from its commencement, and had been fighting against it ever since" (*Official Records*, Series IV, 3:809).

33. For information on George B. Bane, see Chapter 6, note 51.

34. Rosser's New Creek raid took place on November 28, 1864. It was a remarkable success, given earlier reversals for the cavalry. Rosser left Timberville, Virginia, on November 26, with the Laurel Brigade and the brigade of Brigadier General William H. Payne. Their objective was the rich storehouses of foodstuffs, ammunition, and other supplies at New Creek Depot, on the Baltimore and Ohio line, in present-day Keyser, West Virginia. It was defended by Fort Kelley, with Colonel George R. Latham of the Fifth West Virginia Cavalry in charge of defending the New Creek supplies. Payne had Captain F. Fitzhugh of the Fifth Virginia Cavalry put 20 of his men in Union uniforms to approach the pickets of the fort; they were able to capture all of the enemy pickets. The regiments then entered Fort Kelley with minimal resistance; Colonel Latham escaped. Rosser's men were able to take meat, flour, sugar, coffee, ammunition, as well as clothing. They burned a number of buildings and damaged railroad facilities at Piedmont, five miles west. Rosser drove nearly 500 cattle and a few sheep back to Virginia. He took 700 prisoners, though many of them escaped on the trip back. Confederate losses were only two killed and one or two wounded, according to Rosser (*Official Records*, 43, pt. 1:670). See also the reports of Robert E. Lee (*Official Records*, 43, pt. 1:667-68) and the disgraced Colonel Latham (*Official Records*, 43, pt. 1:660-61).

35. Both Union and Confederate scouts sometimes dressed in the uniforms of the enemy in order to pass unnoticed. The idea that this was like a "Yankee trick" may relate to Sheridan's more formal corps of "Jessie Scouts"—mounted scouts outfitted in Confederate uniforms.

36. Colonel George Latham, who had been elected to Congress to represent his West Virginia district and who was still in uniform until he could take office, was later court-martialed for neglect of duty in the New Creek affair and was dismissed from the army, though his dismissal would be reversed in March 1865. He took his seat in Congress the same month.

37. None of the reports on the New Creek affair refer to Major Massie. He may be Lieutenant Colonel Thomas B. Massie, in command of the 12th Virginia Cavalry, one of the regiments in Rosser's brigade, as of October 23-25, 1864 (*Official Records*, 43, pt. 1:903). Massie's service record makes no mention of the incident (Compiled Service Records, Virginia, no. 119).

38. Captain Smith is probably the Rev. James Power Smith, Captain and Assistant Adjutant-General on Early's staff. Smith had been on the staff of the Second Corps since Stonewall Jackson's command. See Compiled Service Records of Confederate General and Staff Officers, no. 229; "Last of Stonewall Jackson's Staff," *Confederate Veteran* 32, no. 3 (March 1924): 85.

39. Custer and Rosser had been West Point classmates and friends. During the Shenandoah Valley campaign the two were pitted against each other at several engagements, usually to Rosser's discredit. The incident in question may have taken place after Rosser withdrew from New Creek. On November 29 and 30, Custer's cavalry forces followed Rosser without engaging him; Moorefield, West Virginia was one of the places they nearly crossed paths. Although the *Official Records* say nothing about this event, see Francis Haselberger, "General Rosser's Raid on the New Creek Depot," *West Virginia History* 26, no. 2 (January 1965): 105-07.

Appendix A: Free and Slave Inhabitants in Blacksburg, Virginia, 1860

1. For the history of Blacksburg, see the historical analysis by Dan Pezzoni in Dunay, *Town Architecture*, 92-154. For the Appalachian homefront during the Civil War, see Noe, *Southwest Virginia's Railroad*, 109-138.

2. Howe, *Listen to the Mockingbird*, 43-44. John Howe was not a resident of Blacksburg, though he enlisted there. His fate would be an inglorious one. Wounded and captured at Gettysburg, he would spend 18 months in a Union prison before being released in January 1865. For further information on Howe, see Chapter 1, note 32.

3. Those residents of Blacksburg known to have been in Confederate service are Joseph Barton, William Bell, Edward Black, Harvey Black, John Black, Robert H. Calbert, Charles Carden, William D. Croy, Jonathan B. Evans, Robert L. Francisco, John C. Galloway, Robert M. Harris, John E. "Ed" Peck, Robert W. "Bob" Peck, Charles A. Ronald, George W. Sheaf, Giles D.Thomas, James Thompson, and John Thompson. It is possible, perhaps likely, that others not listed here served at some time in the Confederacy. Those listed include men who served in the Fourth Virginia Infantry and those known to have served in other regiments. The figure of 75 eligible to serve is an estimate based on the number of white males between the ages of 12 and 44 in the 1860 census for Blacksburg. Those who had been 12 in 1860 would have been 16 or 17 by 1865.

4. Joseph Barton died of illness in a hospital in Winchester in April 1863. Robert H. Calbert was killed at Gettysburg in July 1863. Jonathan B. Evans was killed at Locust Hill in November 1863. There is some overlap among those wounded and those made prisoners of war, with two individuals suffering both fates. Ed Black, Charles Carden, Ed Peck, Bob Peck, and Charles Ronald were wounded; William Bell, Ed Black, and Ed Peck were imprisoned. William Davidson Croy deserted to the Union.

5. The list of free and slave inhabitants in Blacksburg in 1860 collocates information from two sources: the U.S. Census Bureau, Population Schedules (Free) of the Eighth United States Census, 1860 (National Archives Microcopy 653, no. 1363, 705-13) and the U.S. Census Bureau, Population Schedules (Slave) of the Eighth United States Census, 1860 (National Archives Microcopy 653, no. 1394, 118-19).

6. In addition to Harvey Black, James Templeton and Thomas T. Jackson are listed as physicians.

7. The two hotels were kept by James Henderson and John Jordan.

Bibliography

Manuscript and Archival Sources

Apperson family papers. Virginia Polytechnic Institute and State University Libraries.

Apperson, John S. "Autobiography of John Samuel Apperson, M.D." Manuscript in the possession of Mrs. Barbara Rennie of Richmond, Virginia; partial photocopy covering the Civil War years in the possession of Glenn L. McMullen of Ames, Iowa.

Black, Dr. Harvey. Medical Ledgers. Duke University Library.

Black family papers. Virginia Polytechnic Institute and State University Libraries.

Blacksburg Station, Montgomery County, Virginia, Baltimore Conference, Church Register. Whisner Memorial Church records. Virginia Polytechnic Institute and State University Libraries.

Caperton family papers. Virginia Polytechnic Institute and State University Libraries.

Charlton family papers. Virginia Polytechnic Institute and State University Libraries.

Compiled Service Records of Volunteer Soldiers Who Served in the Mexican War. Record Group 94. U.S. National Archives.

Kent family papers. Virginia Polytechnic Institute and State University Libraries.

Miller, Rev. Charles A. Family papers. Virginia Polytechnic Institute and State University Libraries.

Montgomery County Deed Book R—1860-68. Montgomery County Courthouse. Christiansburg, Virginia.

Montgomery County Record of Plotts, Book F. Montgomery County Courthouse. Christiansburg, Virginia.

Montgomery County Register of Births, 1853-68. Montgomery County Courthouse. Christiansburg, Virginia.

Newlee family papers. Virginia Polytechnic Institute and State University Libraries.

Robinson, David Tobias. "Company 'E' 4th Va. Inftry" [photocopy]. Virginia Polytechnic Institute and State University Libraries.

Sydnor, Charles W. Papers. Southern Historical Collection, University of North Carolina, Chapel Hill.

United Daughters of the Confederacy, Dr. Harvy Black Chapter. Records. Virginia Polytechnic Institute and State University Libraries.

War Department Collection of Confederate Records. Hospital Rolls, Virginia and Miscellaneous. Record Group 109, Box 27. U.S. National Archives.

———. Letters Sent, Medical Director's Office, Army of Northern Virginia, 1862-63. Record Group 109, Ch. VI, vol. 641. U.S. National Archives.

———. Letters Sent, Medical Director's Office, Army of Northern Virginia, 1863-5. Record Group 109, Ch. VI, vol. 642. U.S. National Archives.

———. "Muster Roll of Steward, Wardmaster, Cooks, Nurses, Matrons, and Detached Soldiers, Sick, in the Hospital of 2nd Corps, A N Va, Guiney's Station, April 1 - 31 May 1863." Record Group 109, Box 20. Hospital Rolls, Virginia and Miscellaneous. U.S. National Archives.

———. North Carolina, South Carolina, Tennessee, Texas, Virginia Confederate Field and Staff. Record Group 109, Ch. VI, vol. 104. U.S. National Archives.

———. Register of Appointments, Medical Director's Office, Richmond, Virginia, 1861-63, Record Group 109, Ch. VI, vol. 143. U.S. National Archives.

Microfilm Sets

Compiled Service Records of Confederate General and Staff Officers, and Nonregimental Enlisted Men. U.S. National Archives Microcopy M331.

Compiled Service Records of Confederate Soldiers Who Served in Organizations from the State of Alabama. U.S. National Archives Microcopy M311.

Compiled Service Records of Confederate Soldiers Who Served in Organizations from the State of Missouri. U.S. National Archives Microcopy M322.

Compiled Service Records of Confederate Soldiers Who Served in Organizations from the State of Virginia. U.S. National Archives Microcopy M324.

Compiled Service Records of Volunteer Union Soldiers Who Served in Organizations from the State of Kentucky. U.S. National Archives Microcopy M397.

Confederate Papers Relating to Citizens or Business Firms. U.S. National Archives Microcopy M346.

Index to Compiled Service Records of Volunteer Soldiers Who Served in the Mexican War. U.S. National Archives Microcopy M616.

Index to Compiled Service Records of Volunteer Union Soldiers Who Served in Organizations from the State of Kansas. U.S. National Archives Microcopy M542.

Index to Compiled Service Records of Volunteer Union Soldiers Who Served in Organizations from the State of Ohio. U.S. National Archives Microcopy M552.

Index to Compiled Service Records of Volunteer Union Soldiers Who Served in Organizations from the State of Wisconsin. U.S. National Archives Microcopy M559.

Letters Received by the Confederate Adjutant and Inspector General's Office. U.S. National Archives Microcopy M474.

Letters Received by the Confederate Secretary of War, 1861-65. U.S. National Archives Microcopy M437.

Records of the Nitre and Mining Bureau. U.S. National Archives Microcopy M258.

Unfiled Papers and Slips Belonging in Confederate Compiled Service Records. U.S. National Archives Microcopy M347.

Union Provost Marshall's File of One-Name Papers re Citizens. U.S. National Archives Microcopy M345.

United States Census Bureau. Ninth Census of the United States, 1870. U.S. National Archives Microcopy M593.

——. Population Schedules (Free) of the Eighth United States Census, 1860. U.S. National Archives Microcopy M653.

——. Population Schedules (Slave) of the Eighth United States Census, 1860. U.S. National Archives Microcopy M653.

Published Sources

Adams, George W. "Caring for the Men: Hospitals, Medicines, Doctors, and Do-Gooders." In *The Image of War, 1861-1865*. Vol. 4: *Fighting for Time*. Garden City, New York: Doubleday, 1983.

———. "Confederate Medicine." *Journal of Southern History* 6 (1940): 151-156.

Alison, Joseph Dill. "I Have Been Through My First Battle and Have Had Enough of War to Last Me." *Civil War Times Illustrated* 5 (February 1967): 40-46.

———. "With a Confederate Surgeon at Vicksburg." *American History Illustrated* 3 (July 1968): 31-33.

Allen, V. C. *Rhea and Meigs Counties in the Confederate War*. Published with *Records of Rhea*. Dayton, Tennessee: Rhea County Historical Society, 1976.

Annual Report of the Southwestern Lunatic Asylum at Marion, Virginia, to the General Assembly of Virginia, for the Fiscal Year Ending Sept. 30, 1887. Richmond: Wm. Ellis Jones, Book and Job Printer, 1887.

Annual Report of the Virginia Eastern Lunatic Asylum for the Fiscal Year Ending September 30, 1877. Richmond: R. F. Walker, Superintendent of Public Printing, 1877.

[Apperson, John S.] "Sketch of His Life." In *Annual Report of the Southwestern Lunatic Asylum at Marion, Virginia, for the Fiscal Year Ending September 30, 1888*. Richmond: J. H. O'Bannon, Superintendent of Public Printing, 1888, 35-41.

The Appomattox Roster: A List of the Paroles of the Army of Northern Virginia issued at Appomattox Court House on April 9, 1865. New York: Antiquarian Press, 1962.

Atkinson, George Wesley, ed. *Prominent Men of West Virginia*. Wheeling, West Virginia: W. L. Callin, 1890.

Atkinson, William B., M. D., ed. *The Physicians and Surgeons of the United States*. Philadelphia: Charles Robson, 1878.

Atlas of Richland Co. Wisconsin, Drawn From Actual Surveys and the County Records. Madison, Wisconsin: Harrison & Warner, 1874.

Baruch, Simon. "A Surgeon's Story of Battle and Capture." *Confederate Veteran* 22 (January 1914): 545-548.

Bean, W. G. *The Liberty Hall Volunteers: Stonewall's College Boys*. Charlottesville: University Press of Virginia, 1964.

——. "Stonewall Jackson's Jolly Chaplain, Beverly Tucker Lacy." *West Virginia History* 29, no. 2 (January 1968): 77-96.

Beaudot, William J. K. "A Virginian in the Iron Brigade: The Civil War Experiences of Lewis Amiss Kent of Blacksburg, Virginia." *Blue & Gray* 7, no. 4 (April 1990): 26-30.

Bi-Centennial St. Thomas' Parish and Centennial St. Thomas' Church, Oct. 20-21, 1973: Historical Notes, Printed by Order of the Vestry. N.p., n.d.

Black, Harvey. "The Duties of the Society and the State Regarding Irregular Practitioners and Adulterated Medicines." In *Transactions of the Fourth Annual Session of the Medical Society of Virginia, Held in Norfolk November 11th, 12th, 13th and 14th, 1873.* Richmond: Fergusson & Rady, Printers, 1874, 41-53.

Blaisdell, F. William. "Medical Advances During the Civil War." *Archives of Surgery* 123 (1988): 1045-1050.

Blanton, Wyndham B. *Medicine in Virginia in the Nineteenth Century.* Richmond: Garrett & Massie, 1933.

Bodell, Dorothy H. *Montgomery White Sulphur Springs: A History of the Resort, Hospital, Cemeteries, Markers, and Monument.* Blacksburg, Virginia: Pocahontas Press, 1993.

Bollet, Alfred Jay. "Scurvy, Sprue, and Starvation: Major Nutritional Deficiency Syndromes During the Civil War." *Medical Times* 117 (November 1989): 69-74; 118 (June 1990): 39-44.

——. "To Care for Him that has Borne the Battle: A Medical History of the Civil War." *Medical Times* 117 (April 1989): 121-126; (May 1989): 101-108; (October 1989): 74-80.

Bowers, John. *Stonewall Jackson: Portrait of a Soldier.* New York: William Morrow, 1989.

Brooks, Stewart M. *Civil War Medicine.* Springfield, Illinois: Charles C. Thomas, 1966.

Burnett, Edmund Cody, ed. "Letters of a Confederate Surgeon: Dr. Abner McGarity, 1862-1865." *Georgia Historical Quarterly* 29 (1945): 76-114, 159-190, and 222-253; 30 (1946): 35-70.

"Capt. H. D. Wade." *Confederate Veteran* 16, no. 8 (August 1908): 412-413.

Church, Charles A. *Past and Present of the City of Rockford and Winnebago County, Illinois.* Chicago: S. J. Clarke Publishing Co., 1905.

Clark, Champ. *Gettysburg: The Confederate High Tide.* Alexandria, Virginia: Time-Life Books, 1985.

Coco, Gregory A. *A Vast Sea of Misery: A History and Guide to the Union and Confederate Field Hospitals at Gettysburg, July 1 to November 20, 1863.* Gettysburg, Pennsylvania: Thomas Publications, 1988.

"Confederate Officers Captured at the Battle of Opequan Creek, Sept. 19." Richmond *Whig.* October 7, 1864.

Cunningham, Horace H. "The Confederate Medical Officer in the Field." *New York Academy of Medicine Bulletin* 34 (1958): 461-88.

——. *Doctors in Gray: The Confederate Medical Service.* Revised edition. Baton Rouge: Louisiana State University Press, 1960.

——. *Field Medical Services at the Battles of Manassas.* Athens: University of Georgia Press, 1968.

Davis, Burke. *They Called Him Stonewall: A Life of Lt. General T. J. Jackson, C.S.A.* New York: Rinehart, 1954.

Dorman, John Frederick. *The Prestons of Smithfield and Greenfield in Virginia: Descendants of John and Elizabeth (Patton) Preston through Five Generations.* Louisville, Kentucky: Filson Club, 1982.

Dowdey, Clifford, ed. *The Wartime Papers of R. E. Lee.* Boston: Little, Brown and Company for the Virginia Civil War Commission, 1961.

Dunay, Donna, ed. *Town Architecture: Blacksburg, Understanding a Virginia Town.* Blacksburg, Virginia: Town of Blacksburg, the College of Architecture and Urban Studies, and the Extension Division, Virginia Polytechnic Institute and State University, 1986.

Evans, Clement A., ed. *Confederate Military History: A Library of Confederate States History. Expanded Edition.* 12 vols. Atlanta: Confederate Publishing Co., 1899.

Farwell, Byron. *Stonewall: A Biography of General Thomas J. Jackson.* New York: Norton, 1992.

Freeman, Douglas Southall. *Lee's Lieutenants: A Study in Command.* 3 vols. New York: Scribner's, 1942-44.

——. *R. E. Lee: A Biography.* 4 vols. New York: Charles Scribner's Sons, 1934-35.

Freemon, Frank R. "Administration of the Medical Department of the Confederate States Army, 1861 to 1865." *Southern Medical Journal* 80 (1987): 630-637.

——. *Microbes and Minie Balls: An Annotated Bibliography of Civil War Medicine.* Rutherford, New Jersey: Fairleigh Dickinson University Press, 1993.

Germanicus A. Kent, Founder of Rockford, Illinois, 1834. N.p., n.d.

"A Grand Cavalry Review." Richmond *Whig.* November 13, 1863.

Green, Louisa M., Katherine Glass Greene, and Philip Williams, eds. *True Stories of Old Winchester and the Valley.* Winchester, Virginia: Civic League of Winchester, n.d.

Greene, A. Wilson. *J. Horace Lacy: The Most Dangerous Rebel of the County.* Richmond: Owens Publishing Company, 1988.

Hall, Courtney R. "Confederate Medicine." *Medical Life* 42 (1935): 443-508.

——. "The Lessons of the War Between the States." *International Review of Medicine* 171 (1958): 408-430.

——. "The Rise of Professional Surgery in the United States, 1800-1865." *Bulletin of the History of Medicine* 26 (1952): 231-262.

Hardesty's Historical and Geographical Encyclopedia, Illustrated . . . Special [Montgomery County] *Virginia Edition.* New York: H. H. Hardesty & Co., 1884.

Harmon, Nolan B., ed. *The Encyclopedia of World Methodism.* Nashville: United Methodist Publishing House, 1974.

Harris, Brayton, and Kathleen Kelley. "Invisible Enemies." *Civil War: The Magazine of the Civil War Society* 9 (May-June 1991): 26-29.

——. "Myths and Miracles: Medicine in the Civil War." *Civil War: The Magazine of the Civil War Society* 9 (May-June 1991): 18-22.

Haselberger, Francis. "General Rosser's Raid on the New Creek Depot." *West Virginia History* 36, no. 2 (January 1965): 105-07.

"He Served His Country Well." *Confederate Veteran* 4, no. 3 (March 1896): 69.

History of Clark County, Ohio. Chicago: W. H. Beers, 1881.

History of Crawford and Richland Counties, Wisconsin, Together with Sketches of their Towns and Villages, Educational, Civil, Military and Political History; Portraits of Prominent Persons, and Biographies of Representative Citizens. Springfield, Illinois: Union Publishing Company, 1884.

History of Virginia. Vol. 5, *Virginia Biography.* Chicago and New York: The American Historical Society, 1924.

Hoge, J. "The Hoge Otey House." *Mountainside* 1, no. 3 (1981): 28-30.

Hoge, Nellie Jane. "The Tragedy of Devil's Den." *Confederate Veteran* 33, no. 1 (January 1925): 20.

"Honorary Fellow Harvey Black." In *Transactions of the Nineteenth Annual Session of the Medical Society of Virginia Held at Norfolk, Virginia, October 23, 24, 25 and 26, 1888.* Richmond: J. W. Fergusson & Son, 1888, 261.

Houck, Peter W., ed. *Confederate Surgeon: The Personal Recollections of E. A. Craighill.* Lynchburg, Virginia: H. E. Howard, 1989.

Howe, Daniel Dunbar. *Listen to the Mockingbird: The Life and Times of a Pioneer Virginia Family.* Boyce, Virginia: Carr Publishing Company, 1961.

Hunt, John Warren. *Wisconsin Gazetteer.* Madison, Wisconsin: Beriah Brown, 1853.

Jackson, Ronald Vern, ed. *Alabama 1860 Census Index.* Bountiful, Utah: Accelerated Indexing Systems, 1981.

———. *Georgia 1860 Census Index.* North Salt Lake, Utah: Accelerated Indexing Systems International, 1986.

———. *Maryland 1860, Except for the City of Baltimore, Federal Census Index.* Salt Lake City, Utah: Accelerated Indexing Systems International, 1988.

———. *North Carolina 1860 Census Index.* Bountiful, Utah: Accelerated Indexing Systems, 1987.

———. *Virginia 1860 Federal Census, Excluding Present Day West Virginia.* North Salt Lake, Utah: Accelerated Indexing Systems International, 1984.

Johnson, Patricia Givens. *The United States Army Invades the New River Valley, May 1864.* Christiansburg, Virginia: Walpa Publications, 1986.

Jones, Gordon W. "The Medical History of the Fredericksburg Campaign: Course and Significance." *Journal of the History of Medicine and Allied Sciences* 18 (1963): 241-256.

———. "Sanitation in the Civil War." *Civil War Times Illustrated* 5 (November 1966): 12-18.

Kinnear, Lyle Duncan. *The First 100 Years: A History of Virginia Polytechnic Institute and State University.* Blacksburg, Virginia: Virginia Polytechnic Institute Educational Foundation, 1972.

Krick, Robert K. *Lee's Colonels: A Biographical Register of the Field Officers of the Army of Northern Virginia.* 3rd ed. Dayton, Ohio: Morningside, 1991.

———. *Stonewall Jackson at Cedar Mountain.* Chapel Hill: University of North Carolina Press, 1990.

Kurtz, Lucy Fitzhugh and Benny Ritter. *A Roster of Confederate Soldiers Buried in the Stonewall Cemetery, Winchester, Virginia.* Winchester, Virginia: Farmers and Merchants National Bank, 1962.

[Lacy, Beverly Tucker]. "Religion in the Army." *Central Presbyterian,* April 30, 1863, 2.

"Last of Stonewall Jackson's Staff." *Confederate Veteran* 32, no. 3 (March 1924): 85.

Lewis, Samuel E., M.D. "General T. J. Jackson (Stonewall) and His Medical Director, Hunter McGuire, M.D., at Winchester, May, 1862: An Important Incident of the Shenandoah Valley Campaign." *Southern Historical Society Papers 30* (January-December 1902): 226-236.

Marshall, Mary Louise. "Medicine in the Confederacy." *Bulletin of the Medical Library Association* 30 (1942): 279-299.

Marvel, William. *The Battles of Saltville: Southwest Virginia in the Civil War.* Lynchburg, Virginia: H. E. Howard, 1992.

Mathers, Augustus Henry. "The Civil War Letters of Henry Mathers, Assistant Surgeon, Fourth Florida Regiment, C.S.A." *Florida Historical Quarterly* 36 (1957): 94-124.

[McDonald, F. V.] *Genealogy of the MacDonald Family: Edition B, Comprising all Names Obtained up to February, 1876.* New Haven: Tuttle, Morehouse & Taylor, 1876.

McGuire, Hunter. "Death of Stonewall Jackson." *Southern Historical Society Papers* 14 (January-December 1886): 154-63.

——. *Last Wound of the Late General Stonewall Jackson: The Amputation of the Arm and His Last Moments and Death.* Lynchburg, Virginia: Warwick House Publishing, 1991. Reprint of McGuire's article in the May 1866 issue of the *Richmond Medical Journal.*

——. "Operative Treatment in Cases of Enlarged Prostate." *Virginia Medical Monthly* 15, no. 7 (October 1888): 445-56.

——. "Progress of Medicine in the South." *Southern Historical Society Papers* 17 (January-December 1889): 1-12.

——. "Prostatic Enlargement." In *Transactions of the Nineteenth Annual Session of the Medical Society of Virginia Held at Norfolk, Virginia, October 23, 24, 25 and 26, 1888.* Richmond: J. W. Fergusson & Son, 1888, 199-207.

——. "Wounding and Death of Jackson." In *The Confederate Cause and Conduct in the War Between the States* by Hunter McGuire and George L. Christian. Richmond: L. H. Jenkins, n.d., 219-29.

McMullen, Glenn L. "Tending the Wounded: Two Virginians in the Confederate Medical Corps." *Virginia Cavalcade* 40, no. 4 (Spring 1991): 172-83.

Miller, Ann L. *Antebellum Orange: The Pre-Civil War Homes, Public Buildings and Historic Sites of Orange County, Virginia.* Orange, Virginia: Orange County Historical Society, 1988.

Miller, Francis Trevelyan., ed. *The Photographic History of the Civil War.* 10 vols. New York: The Review of Reviews Co., 1911.

Mitchell, Enoch L., ed. "Letters of a Confederate Surgeon in the Army of Tennessee to His Wife." *Tennessee Historical Quarterly* 4 (1945): 341-353; 5 (1946): 60-81, 142-181.

Monteiro, Aristides. *War Reminiscences by the Surgeon of Mosby's Command.* Richmond: C. N. Williams, 1890.

Moore, Edward A. *The Story of a Cannoneer Under Stonewall Jackson.* Freeport, New York: Books for Libraries Press, 1971.

Morrison, J. G. "Wounding of Lieut. Gen. T. J. Jackson." *Confederate Veteran* 13, no. 5 (May 1905): 229-232.

"Names of Presidents and Vice-Presidents of the Medical Society of Virginia, From its Organization, Nov. 2d, 1870, through 1889." In *Transactions of the Twentieth Annual Session of the Medical Society of Virginia Held at Roanoke, Virginia, September 3rd, 4th and 5th, 1889.* Richmond: J. W. Fergusson & Son, 1889, 342.

Neese, George M. *Three Years in the Confederate Horse Artillery.* New York and Washington: Neale Publishing Company, 1911.

Nevin, Alfred., ed. *Encyclopedia of the Presbyterian Church in the United States of America.* Philadelphia: Presbyterian Encyclopedia Publishing Co., 1884.

Newton, Edwin. "My Recollections and Reminiscences." *Southern Practitioner* 30 (October 1908): 474-489.

———. "Reminiscences of the Medical Department, Confederate States Army and Field and Hospital Service, Army of Northern Virginia." *Southern Practitioner* 25 (January 1903): 36-43; 26 (March 1904): 168-174.

Noe, Kenneth W. *Southwest Virginia's Railroad: Modernization and the Sectional Crisis.* Urbana: University of Illinois Press, 1994.

Noll, Arthur Howard, ed. *Doctor Quintard: Chaplain CSA and Second Bishop of Tennessee, Being His Story of the War.* Sewanee, Tennessee: University Press of Sewanee, 1905.

Official Roster of the Soldiers of the State of Ohio in the War of the Rebellion, 1861-1866. Akron: The Werner Printing and Manufacturing Co., 1891.

Palmer, W. H. "Another Account of It." *Confederate Veteran* 13, no. 5 (May 1905): 232-33.

Parrish, T. Michael, and Robert M. Willingham, Jr., eds. *Confederate Imprints: A Bibliography of Southern Publications from Secession to Surrender.* Austin, Texas: Jenkins Publishing Co., n.d.

Porcher, Francis Peyre. "Confederate Surgeons." *Southern Historical Society Papers* 17 (January-December 1889): 12-21.

Porter, Nannie Francisco. *Blacks and Other Families.* N.p., n.d.

Regulations for the Medical Department of the C.S. Army. Richmond: Ritchie & Dunnavent, Printers, 1862.

Reidenbaugh, Lowell. *33rd Virginia Infantry.* Lynchburg, Virginia: H. E. Howard, 1987.

Reynolds, Cathleen Carlson. "A Pragmatic Loyalty: Unionism in Southwestern Virginia, 1861-1865." Master's thesis, University of Alabama at Birmingham, 1987.

Richmond City and Henrico County, Virginia 1850 United States Census. Richmond: Virginia Genealogical Society, 1977.

Richmond *Enquirer.* November 6, 1863.

Riley, Harris D., Jr. "Medical Furloughs in the Confederate States Army." *Journal of Confederate History* 2 (1989): 115-131.

——. "Medicine in the Confederacy." *Military Medicine* 118 (1956): 53-64 and 144-153.

Robertson, James I., Jr. *The Fourth Virginia Infantry.* Lynchburg, Virginia: H. E. Howard, 1982.

——. *Soldiers Blue and Gray.* Columbia: University of South Carolina Press, 1988.

——. *The Stonewall Brigade.* Baton Rouge: Louisiana State University Press, 1963.

Rockford Weekly Gazette: General History and Description of Rockford and Winnebago County, Form its Earliest Settlement to the Present Time, Written Exclusively for the Rockford Gazette. N.p., [1989].

"The Rumors of Yesterday." Richmond *Enquirer.* November 10, 1863.

Scaife, William R. *Confederate Surgeon: Civil War Record of Dr. William L. Scaife.* Atlanta: William R. Scaife, 1985.

Schildt, John W. *Hunter Holmes McGuire: Doctor in Gray.* Chewsville, Maryland: John W. Schildt, 1986.

Scott, J. L. *36th Virginia Infantry.* Lynchburg, Virginia: H. E. Howard, 1987.

Shaffner, Louis. "A Civil War Surgeon's Diary." *North Carolina Medical Journal* 27 (1966): 409-415.

Shanks, Henry T. "Disloyalty to the Confederacy in Southwestern Virginia, 1861-1865." *North Carolina Historical Review* 21, no. 2 (April 1944): 118-135.

Shaw, Maurice F. *Stonewall Jackson's Surgeon Hunter Holmes McGuire: A Biography.* Lynchburg, Virginia: H. E. Howard, 1993.

Sifakis, Stewart. *Compendium of the Confederate Armies: Alabama.* New York: Facts on File, 1992.

——. *Compendium of the Confederate Armies: Tennessee.* New York: Facts on File, 1992.

——. *Compendium of the Confederate Armies: Virginia.* New York: Facts on File, 1992.

Smith, James Power. *With Stonewall Jackson in the Army of Northern Virginia.* In *Southern Historical Society Papers* 43 (September 1920): 1-110.

Smyth, Ellison A. *A History of the Blacksburg Presbyterian Church.* Blacksburg, Virginia: n.p., 1982.

Stanbery, Jim, ed. "A Confederate Surgeon's View of Fort Donelson: The Diary of John Kennerly Farris." *Civil War Regiments: A Journal of the American Civil War* 1 (1991): 7-19.

Stark, Richard Boies. "Surgeons and Surgical Care of the Confederate States Army." *Virginia Medical Monthly* 87 (1960): 230-241.

Steiner, Paul E. *Disease in the Civil War: Natural Biological Warfare in 1861-1865.* Springfield, Illinois: Charles C. Thomas, 1968.

Students at the University of Virginia: A Semi-Centennial Catalogue, with Brief Biographical Sketches. Baltimore: Charles Harvey & Son, [1878?].

Swem, Earl G., and John W. Williams. *A Register of the General Assembly of Virginia, 1776-1918, and of the Constitutional Conventions.* Richmond: Davis Bottom, Superintendent of Public Printing, 1918.

Taylor, William H. *De Quibus: Discourses and Essays*. Richmond: Bell Publishers, 1908.

Tribble, Anna Laura Henderson. *The Family Tree of Henderson*. Blacksburg, Virginia: n.p., 1981.

Tyler, James Hoge. *The Family of Hoge*. James Fulton Hoge, ed. N.p.: 1927.

Tyler, Lyon G., ed. *Men of Mark in Virginia, Ideals of American Life: A Collection of Biographies of the Leading Men in the State*. 5 vols. Washington, D.C.: Men of Mark Publishing Company, 1906-09.

United States. Surgeon General's Office. *The Medical and Surgical History of the Civil War*. 15 vols. Wilmington, North Carolina: Broadfoot Publishing Company, 1990-92. Reprint of *The Medical and Surgical History of the War of the Rebellion (1861-65)*. Washington, D.C.: Government Printing Office, 1870-78.

United States. War Department. *The War of the Rebellion: A Compilation of the Official Records of the Union and Confederate Armies*. 128 vols. Washington, D.C.: Government Printing Office, 1880-1901.

Vandiver, Frank E. *Mighty Stonewall*. New York: McGraw-Hill, 1957.

Virginia Agricultural and Mechanical College: Its History and its Organization. N.p.: [1874?].

Walker, Gary. *Hunter's Fiery Raid through Virginia Valleys*. Roanoke, Virginia: A & W Enterprise, 1989.

——. *The War in Southwest Virginia, 1861-65*. Roanoke, Virginia: A & W Enterprise, 1985.

Wallace, Lee A. Jr. *5th Virginia Infantry*. Lynchburg, Virginia: H. E. Howard, 1988.

——. *A Guide to Virginia Military Organizations, 1861-1865*. 2nd ed. Lynchburg, Virginia: H. E. Howard, 1986.

Weaver, George H., M.D. "Surgeons as Prisoners of War: Agreement Providing for their Unconditional Release during the American Civil War." *Bulletin of the Society of Medical History of Chicago* 4, no. 3 (January 1933): 249-61.

Weiland, Florence Black. *Fifty New England Colonists and Five Virginia Families*. Boothbay Harbor, Maine: Boothbay Register, 1965.

Welch, Spencer Glasgow. *A Confederate Surgeon's Letters to His Wife*. New York: Neale Publishing Co., 1911.

Wisconsin Volunteers: War of the Rebellion, 1861-1865. Madison, Wisconsin: Published by the State, Democrat Printing Company, 1914.

Wood, George B., M.D., and Franklin Bache, M.D. *The Dispensatory of the United States of America.* Philadelphia: J. B. Lippincott & Co., 1858.

Zellem, Ronald T. "Wounded by Bayonet, Ball, and Bacteria: Medicine and Neurosurgery in the American Civil War." *Neurosurgery* 17 (1985): 850-860.

Zwelling, Shomer S. *Quest for a Cure: The Public Hospital in Williamsburg, Virginia, 1773-1885.* Williamsburg: Colonial Williamsburg Foundation, 1985.

– C –